A Detective's Analysis of Harry Potter and the Mysteries Within

By

Mary C. Baumann

authorHOUSE™

1663 LIBERTY DRIVE, SUITE 200
BLOOMINGTON, INDIANA 47403
(800) 839-8640
WWW.AUTHORHOUSE.COM

© 2004 Mary C. Baumann.
All Rights Reserved.

First published by AuthorHouse 07/22/04

ISBN: 1-4184-4550-9 (sc)
ISBN: 1-4184-4551-7 (dj)

Library of Congress Control Number: 2004094014

Printed in the United States of America
Bloomington, Indiana

This book is printed on acid-free paper.

Copyrights and trademarks

In Loving Memory of my Nana
Ellen Lucille Newell Brown
April 13, 1922-April 26, 2003

Introduction

J.K. Rowling has provided readers with a fascinating series. Many people, like myself, may never have read these books without a challenge from a relative or a good friend. I am one of the many who was extremely critical of the books before reading them and have since become one of J. K. Rowling's biggest fans and most ardent defenders. I used to call them "children's books" and told my sister and college roommate to "grow up" and "get a life." My sister eventually threw Book 1 at me and told me to read it before I made another criticism. Thanks Lisa! I finished it in one night and decided to reserve judgment until I had read Books 2 and 3. Needless to say, I loved them. I found the series to be extremely deep. I would even go so far as to call her a modern day Shakespeare. I was truly impressed! Before Harry Potter, I never enjoyed reading. This is primarily due to the fact that I like to analyze books. Most modern authors do not have the skill and depth of J. K. Rowling. Typically I am bored halfway through and don't finish books let alone pick them up for a second analytical reading. That has not been true with the Harry Potter Series. In contrast, I have detected clues I missed on my first reading. Then, I thought there might be others who enjoy analyzing the Harry Potter series as I have done. Possibly they need a hand in developing their theories or they just want to see if someone else thinks the same way they do.

In this book, we are going to analyze the mysteries of Harry Potter. As detectives, we will examine character development, literary techniques, and word use. Each of these techniques is a crucial aspect of J.K. Rowling's work, as they provide insight into the story being told and foreshadowing in to future mysteries. This book will discuss all the characters because some may seem minor at face value, but provide a great deal of insight into the greater mystery. For example, Sirius Black was mentioned in the first chapter of Book 1, but his significance was not discovered until much later.

The use of clues as a literary technique is brilliant! This series is filled with clues so readers can read the books over and over again and continually catch tidbits as if they had just magically appeared. Rowling has many different levels of hints and clues to interest a detective. The first clue the Detectives like to refer to is the Bludger. This type of clue will knock you off your broom if you are not paying attention. It is so obvious, if you don't catch it; you deserve to fall 50 feet from your broom. An example of a Bludger clue is when Moody tells Harry what he hates most is a Death Eater who walked free, while looking at the corner of the map containing

Snape's office. If you did not catch that Snape was a Death Eater, then the Bludger knocked you off your broom. The next type of clue is the Snitch. This is a fairly difficult kind of clue to catch, but the well-trained Detective can manage, just like the well trained or highly skilled Seeker catches the Snitch. A Snitch example is when Umbridge sent the Dementors after Harry. Note: many Snitch clues can be pointed out, but not necessarily proven until later books. The Head Detective believes she is on the right track with these based on the fact her predictions have proven to be true when both Books 4 and 5 were finally published.

Rowling's mastery of words is apparent in her choice of names for her characters. The names are often obvious clues, as to the character's importance to the story. The classification varies with each one. Rowling often uses historical, Shakespearean, Mythological, Latin, French, or clever combinations in her development of the plot. These names offer insight into the role that person will play.

Disclaimer: If you are looking for someone to paraphrase the books for you, this book is not for you. Read the series! I am not here to do it for you, nor will I waste my time or yours' paraphrasing the books. If you haven't read J.K. Rowling's original work, this book is of no use to you. In addition, I have included many theories as to secrets that have not yet been revealed about the characters and how the series will end. These theories are all based on clues Rowling has left her readers in Books 1-5. If you want to be surprised, again this book is not for you. Otherwise, if you wish to delve into the depths of Harry Potter, enter now into the chamber of many secrets!

Table of Contents

Chapter 1

Harry's early years or his life with the Dursleys will help mold him into the man who will defeat Voldemort. On the surface, Aunt Petunia and Uncle Vernon seem cruel and uncaring, but this could be their way of keeping Harry both safe and humble. Humility will prove to be one of many keys to Harry's success. As Dumbledore stated, "[Fame] would be enough to turn any boy's head[1]." This is true, but in Harry's case, humility was already instilled before he knew he was famous or had a destiny. Each of the Dursleys are examined, including the relationship with Harry, the foreshadowing surrounding their characters, and then attempts to uncover the mystery within.

The Dursleys

Aunt Petunia, Uncle Vernon, and Dudley Dursley are said to be Harry's only living relatives. They are muggles. Harry has lived with them ever since he was a year old following the deaths of his parents, James and Lily Potter. Aunt Petunia was Lily's sister, but the Potters are never mentioned under the Dursley's roof. The Dursleys live in Surrey at Number 4 Privet Drive. It is interesting to note privet is an English word for a shrub or hedge, which is often used as a hiding place for animals and small children. In addition, Privet sounds a great deal like privy or private.

So, what do they want to keep private? Well, one thing is obvious. They want everyone to believe they live a normal life and want nothing to do with magic. They would die if anyone discovered they were related in any way, no matter how distantly, to the wizarding world. The main rule in the Dursley's household is "Don't ask questions!" For the first ten years of Harry's life with them, they kept him in the cupboard under the stairs. Was this also a form of protection? Harry was clearly kept out of sight and unknown to most people with whom they interacted.

Aunt Petunia Dursley

Petunias and lilies are flowers, and flowers often symbolize certain characteristics. In both of these cases, the Detectives believe them to be clues to the characters. Petunias represent anger and resentment. Well, that explains a great deal. Clearly, Aunt Petunia resented her sister, Lily, possibly for going to Hogwarts without her. She, then, was extremely angry with her for getting killed. This is a very common stage of grief. The Detectives do not believe the anger and resentment is due to the fact Lily died and left her to raise Harry. This is merely a cover for a deeper secret. A lily represents purity and fragility. They only bloom for a short time. The most common variety is the Easter lily. Well, again, this is very true. Lily died quite young. It is clear Lily and Petunia Evans were biological sisters, but the Detectives wonder, were they twins? They had their first and only child the same year, less than a month apart. Lily was very pretty and had thick, shoulder length, dark red hair and almond-shaped green eyes. Petunia has blond hair and large pale eyes. She was tall, thin, and has a long neck. Petunia is obsessed with cleaning. One trip into her kitchen would cure the Malfoys of their misconception that all Muggles are filthy.

One point the Dursleys and Dumbledore have kept from Harry is that Petunia kept in touch with Lily before her death. This is clear in Chapter 1, Book 1. Vernon asks, "Petunia, dear—you haven't heard from your sister lately, have you[2]?" Asking this question clearly implies that they do talk from time to time. If they did not talk, there would be no need to ask. Did they perhaps see each other as well? Was this pretense that she did not have a sister, Lily's idea due to the danger that existed for defenseless Muggles? Next, Dumbledore left a note. To whom was the note addressed? We have never been told. Was it just addressed to Petunia? Or was it addressed to both of them? Or were there two notes? Aunt Petunia was the one who found Harry on the front steps. The Detectives believe she was the one who made the decision to keep him. If Uncle Vernon had his way, Harry would have gone to an orphanage. (Well, Harry would never have ended up there. McGonagall and Dumbledore would have raised him themselves before they would have let that happen.) The Detectives do have a question. Lily and James Potter were killed Monday night, but the scene outside the Dursley's house does not take place until Tuesday night at midnight, so technically Harry doesn't start his life with the Dursleys until Wednesday morning. So, where did Harry go during all that time? In theory, Hagrid would have picked the baby up right away. Otherwise, Sirius would have gotten him when he was checking on Wormtail, which is why he got to the scene of the crime so quickly. Thus, there is a gap of more than a 24-hours when Harry's location is questionable. Hagrid told McGonagall where Dumbledore would be in the early hours of Tuesday morning. This means Hagrid was at Hogwarts that morning. It also means Harry was at Hogwarts and Hagrid managed to effectively send McGonagall away. Why? Well, it was clear in Chapter 1, Book 1 McGonagall did not want to leave Harry with the Dursleys. Perhaps, Dumbledore told Hagrid to get rid of her so that she could not interfere. If she were waiting for Dumbledore and Harry all day, she would not risk leaving for fear of missing them. (More on this issue in the section on Harry Potter.) Hagrid must have hid the bike in the forest, until evening. This must be when Dumbledore put all the protection spells on Harry and wrote the letter to Petunia. Perhaps, Dumbledore even met with Petunia during the brief time period that Vernon left and McGonagall arrived. The Detectives believe she is a descendent of Dumbledore, (see the section on Harry Potter) so Dumbledore will be able to reason with her.

It is clear Petunia knows a great deal more than she indicates. So, what exactly does Petunia know and when is she going to tell us? Maybe in the next book, Harry will corner her after finding out that she was in contact with Dumbledore. The Head Detective would, but then again she would do many things that Harry doesn't think to do. Petunia's rule "do not ask questions" is primarily due to her fear that she will slip up and answer the question. Petunia is part of a well-organized and intricate plan to keep Harry alive. When Lily sacrificed herself to save Harry, she gave him a lingering protection. Dumbledore used this protection to put a charm on Harry. Lily's blood still lives in her sister, her nephew, and her son, so their home has become a safe house of sorts. Voldemort cannot touch him within their walls as long as Harry can call it home. Petunia knows all of this. This actually serves more than one purpose if the Detectives stop to consider it. Despite the fact they house the number one target, this charm keeps them all safe for as long as Harry lives there. So, it behooves Harry and the Dursleys, for Harry not to move out until he kills Voldemort.

The Detectives also believe Petunia is in regular contact with Dumbledore. They do not buy even for a minute that she got the letter and that was the end of it. No way! No one would agree to that. Nope! You get your butt over here, Dumbledore, and explain to me what is happening. In addition, Petunia knows about owl post and how to use it. The evidence of this is her suggestion they that write back and say Harry will not attend Hogwarts. Another example is her accusation that Harry is getting his news from all of the owls. This is a case in point that she communicates with wizards. The real question is with what frequency do they talk? The Detectives believe they communicate, at least once a year, shortly before Harry comes home from Hogwarts, so Dumbledore can catch Petunia up on recent events. He missed their little chat after year 4, which is why she was taken by surprise by the news of Voldemort's return. Who can blame him? He was a bit busy finding a new headquarters, reorganizing the Order of the Phoenix, and protecting two very important assets—Harry and the prophecy.

So, what does Petunia know? She will only leave Harry with Mrs. Figg. Why? She knows Dumbledore trusts Arabella and there is some protection for Harry in place when he is with her. She flat out refuses to leave Harry with anyone else. The next instance is when she recognizes Sirius Black on the news. She would have met Sirius at the Potter's wedding. One would assume the bride's sister would attend the wedding. Also, that she would meet the best man, who just happens to be extremely good looking. Perhaps, Lily was hoping Petunia and Sirius would get together instead of her marrying Vernon, who doesn't sound good looking at all. She also seems to think he might be after Harry, since she keeps looking out her window as if he might be hiding in her bushes. So, Petunia either "knows" Sirius betrayed the Potters or she thinks he might kidnap Harry because he is his godfather and wants to raise him. Again, clearly Dumbledore has filled Petunia in on the details surrounding Lily's death. Then, in Book 5, Aunt Petunia shocks the readers and Harry completely by answering Vernon's question about Dementors. She knows exactly what they are and says it as though it were common knowledge. Now that is scary! Her reaction to herself is really quite interesting. Once she realizes what she said, she "clapped her hand over her mouth as though she had let slip a disgusting swear word[3]." She slipped. "Aunt Petunia looked quite appalled with herself[4]." She is wondering if she has blown her cover completely. She then comes up with the cover that she heard "'that awful boy—telling *her* about them—years ago' she said jerkily… Aunt Petunia ignored him. She seemed horribly flustered[5]." One assumes Aunt Petunia was talking about Harry's parents here, but nonetheless the

Detectives believe it was obvious she was lying. Jerkily and flustered are not descriptions typically used to describe Petunia Dursley. She does not want to reveal how she knows about the Dementors. The Detectives are quite sure one would not remember a scrap of information from someone else's conversation from sixteen years ago and then repeat it as if it were common knowledge. No, this suggests she has had several discussions about Dementors. Given her nephew has had a few encounters with them, one can see where the subject might have come up in a discussion between Aunt Petunia and Dumbledore. When the Howler arrived, the Detectives were intrigued. They first thought of Lily. Then reason quickly caught up with them. Lily is dead and cannot send a Howler. Dumbledore sent the Howler, "REMEMBER MY LAST, PETUNIA[6]." Dumbledore says it is a reminder of the pact she had sealed. Is it? Or is it a reminder of something else? Did he tell her Voldemort was getting stronger and he might come after Harry, her, or worse, Dudley? Well, regardless Petunia did not let Vernon throw Harry out and told Harry that he was not allowed to leave the house. Amazingly, that is what all of his letters instructed him to do. You would think the boy would have caught the hint. Voldemort says he can't touch you there. All these people tell you to stay in the house. Hmmm, maybe something has been done to this house. This is not rocket science, more like a Bludger.

There is one other point on which the Head Detective will have to disagree with Harry and that is his comment that Aunt Petunia does not love him. Dumbledore chose to ignore this comment completely. The Detectives, however, believe Aunt Petunia does indeed love Harry, but does not show it. One does not take a child in and raise him as her own from the age of one until adulthood without loving him even a little. It is not possible. She is protecting this child with her very blood. This means that she has the full knowledge that she has made herself a target by doing so. Dumbledore says Lily's blood lives in both Harry and Petunia, which means if you kill Petunia, the bond is broken. Dumbledore is no doubt keeping a close eye on this situation. Given Petunia is a housewife, she is at home most of the time. Nonetheless, you do not become a target for a person whom you do not love. You would not give your life for someone you did not love. Another indication of this is how Aunt Petunia looks at Harry after he tells her that Voldemort is back. "Harry fully appreciated that Aunt Petunia was his mother's sister. He could not have said why this hit him so powerfully at this moment…Aunt Petunia had never in her life looked at him like that before[7]." Learning someone is in danger of being killed has an interesting effect on people. It often frightens them into showing how they really feel. Aunt Petunia is looking at Harry, knowing he is the number one target and fears for his life. If Vernon and Dudley were not around, she would probably have held him at this moment and really blown her cover. The unprecedented understanding that passes from Aunt Petunia to Harry at this point is a bludger. There is something else here that interests the Detectives, Aunt Petunia seems to know what it means for Voldemort to be back. Has she met Voldemort? Perhaps she was present when Lily and James fought him and escaped before Harry's birth. Regardless, Aunt Petunia will play a part in the battle. She is already involved and cannot back out now. The Detectives believe Aunt Petunia may perform magic if Harry is attacked while he is with her, she may be able to help defend him. The Detectives are not sure how, but if a non-magic performing character is going to perform magic, we are banking on Petunia doing it to save Harry.

Uncle Vernon Dursley

Uncle Vernon is a bad-tempered, large man with very little neck and a large mustache. He has a sister, Marge. Vernon works for a company called Grunnings, which makes drills. His thoughts, about magic parallels the Malfoy family's thoughts about muggles. The Detectives question whether Vernon wanted to keep Harry in the first place and believe the answer is no. Petunia made the decision to keep Harry. An interesting scene occurred the morning after Lily and James were killed. Diggle, a member of the Order of the Phoenix, was outside Vernon's office and Vernon knocked him down. Was this a coincidence? Check the guidelines again; there are no coincidences. Diggle proceeded to hug Vernon and actually calls Vernon "dear sir[8]." Why did he hug Vernon? Did he put a protection spell on him? The Detectives believe this is exactly what Diggle did. And to call Vernon "dear sir?" Who would call Vernon a dear man, except someone who knew he was about to raise a special baby? Perhaps Petunia's protection was voluntary, but it is likely Diggle did something extra to Vernon when he hugged him. This would make Harry safe with him too. The Detectives believe Vernon is clueless to Petunia's involvement with Harry's protection. It would only upset Vernon, so why tell him? He thinks she only took Harry in because he had nowhere else to go. Vernon knows nothing of the protection. After all, he wanted to send Harry to another baby-sitter in Book 1, but it was Petunia who found excuses as to why he could not go and eventually concluded he would have to come with them.

In Book 5, after the Dementor attack, Vernon tried to throw Harry out of the house. Again, it was Petunia who intervened and said Harry had to stay. Vernon wants no part of the battle. He wants a quiet life, free from magic. Unfortunately for him, the number one magical target lives under his roof and his wife has sworn to protect him with her very blood. Vernon loves his wife and son, so he will not create any waves.

Dudley Dursley

Dudley is Harry's cousin and they are the same age. They appear to be complete opposites. Dudley has blond hair and is extremely overweight. In the fifth book, he has become a junior heavyweight-boxing champion. Dudley and his friends bullied Harry for the first eleven years of his life. Dudley is quite the spoiled brat and he and Harry have never gotten along. Dudley is his mother's little prince and goes to his father's alma mater, Smeltings. Draco Malfoy and Dudley are a great deal alike, so it is advantageous they are in different worlds. By all accounts, Harry and Dudley act like brothers because they continually pick on each other. On Dudley's eleventh birthday they went to the London Zoo. Harry talked to a boa constrictor. When Dudley pushed Harry, he did magic and caused the glass to vanish, setting the boa constrictor free. This is Harry's first use of Parseltongue. Also, this snake owes his freedom to Harry. If it is anything like Dobby, then it will want to do anything it can to help Harry. Is this a Snitch? The Detectives expect to see this snake again. (See the section on the Final Battle for more details on the Boa Constrictor.) When Hagrid came to tell Harry about wizarding world, he took out his anger with Vernon and Petunia on Dudley, giving him a pig's tail. Then, when the Weasleys came to pick Harry up for the World Cup, Dudley ate a toffee, which made his tongue a foot long. Unsurprisingly, Dudley is a bit afraid of wizards.

At the beginning of the fifth book, Dudley and Harry were fighting as usual when Dementors attacked them. Harry saved both of their lives. This event really frightened Dudley. Dementors have the power to make their victims remember the worst memories of their lives. It is noteworthy, most of the people at Hogwarts did not fall down when they encountered the Dementors. Lupin told Harry it had nothing to do with weakness, it was just his worst memories would make anyone fall off their broom. So, the Detectives must ask, what is it Dudley remembered that made him fall down? J.K. Rowling takes the time to point out to her readers twice that Dudley fell. If the detectives will kindly check the guidelines this means, it is an important point. Dudley is incapable of saying what he heard. Following Lupin's logic, it is something as horrible as the murder of Harry's parents. Could Petunia and Dudley have been attacked, when

Dudley was just a baby? Perhaps this is why he is such a pampered prince. This would also explain why Lily kept her distance from them. It was her way to protect them. Dudley believed Harry had done this to him, but learns it was the Dementors. Now Dudley owes his life to Harry. Dudley also learns that his cousin's life is in danger. The Detectives wonder if this will make a difference. After all, they are pretty much brothers and he doesn't want him dead any more than Petunia wanted Lily dead. It should also be noted that Dudley is Petunia's son, thus he shares the same blood as Petunia, Lily, and Harry and can also provide some protection. In addition, Dudley may have a new respect for Harry, but given his fear of wizards and lack of magical powers, the Detectives do not believe he will want to enter the battle. Dudley, like his mother, may become a key player only because he wants to keep Harry alive. His role will be bitter, unwilling, and resentful, but the Detectives have seen Draco does not know what to do when someone comes at him with his/her fist. They also believe Dudley and his friends would be a match for Crabbe and Goyle, especially if Dudley has powers that have yet to be seen.

Aunt Marge Dursley

Aunt Marge is Vernon's sister, but Harry is still required to address her as "aunt." She is a large, beefy woman with very little neck, just like Vernon. Marge lives in the country and raises bulldogs. When visiting Privet Drive, Aunt Marge brings her oldest and favorite dog, Ripper. How old is Ripper and is he an animagus? Ripper clearly hates Harry and even chased him up a tree. When she comes to visit she leaves the other dogs with Colonel Fubster. Who is this man? Is he a wizard or muggle? J.K. Rowling answered this question-- Colonel Fubster is a muggle neighbor of Aunt Marge[9]. Regardless, remember the Colonel, he was given a name and mentioned twice, thus, odds are he will come up again. Marge loves to criticize Harry. She makes no bones about the fact she would not have raised Harry had he been placed on her front steps. During one episode when Aunt Marge was insulting Lily and James, Harry lost control and not only shattered her wineglass, but caused her to inflate like a balloon. This was an absolute disaster and the Ministry of Magic had to send The Magical Reversal Squad to reverse the magic Harry had done. This episode was very interesting. Harry was able to do magic without a wand or a potion and without any intention of doing so. How did he do this? The Detectives suspect Harry has magical powers in his eyes. Yes, the continual reference to "Lily's eyes" is extremely important because Lily, like Dumbledore, had power in her eyes. Although, the Detectives are unsure whether Lily was able to tap into this power before her death. Perhaps Harry should have read the book he took out of the library before the second task, *Powers You Never Knew You Had and What to Do with Them Now You've Wised Up* [10].

Although it would make more sense for Aunt Petunia and Uncle Vernon to have Marge visit when Harry is away at school since they dislike each other and the visits are always disastrous, the Detectives expect to see Aunt Marge again. Based on the fact Aunt Marge visited the summer before Harry went to Hogwarts and is mentioned in Book 1, appeared in Book 3, and was mentioned again in Book 5, it is logical she will appear again in Book 7.

H

Chapter 2

The Hogwarts Professors

The professors at Hogwarts School of Witchcraft and Wizardry are a particularly interestingly set of characters who play a key role in molding Harry Potter to be man he needs to become. Due to the nature of a boarding school, the professors serve, in locus parentis, in raising Harry for all but two months of the year. These characters are extremely deep, but the true Harry Potter detective can discover some key information about these characters with the assistance of the clues J. K. Rowling leaves for her readers and the help of a twisted mind. The first important point to note is each professor has a questionable past, which has either been revealed in part or not at all to the readers. Dumbledore is a "forgiving man" in the words of Moody, which means Dumbledore would hire teachers others would never employ. Another point to note is a statement made by J.K. Rowling in an interview, the Hogwarts teachers do not stay at the school during school holidays, only Filch, the caretaker remains[1]. In addition, she says some of the Hogwarts Professors have spouses and they are key to the plot[2]. Hmmm, and we thought they were a bunch of spinsters, well, except for the one couple everyone has suspected of having an affair from the very beginning. Well, now we know. It isn't an illicit affair after all folks. They're married!

The Headmaster

Albus Percival Wulfric Brian Dumbledore

Albus Dumbledore is the Chief Warlock of the Wizengamot, Supreme Mugwump, the Chairman of the International Confederation of Wizards, Grand Sorcerer, recipient of the Order of the Merlin First Class, the Headmaster of Hogwarts, founder and leader of the Order of the Phoenix[3]. This is quite a resume. Dumbledore's name is a Bludger regarding his character. Albus is Latin for white, which typically represents purity and goodness. The Detectives believe this means Dumbledore is not only pure of heart, but also pureblood wizard. According to legend, Percival, one of King Arthur's knights, found the Holy Grail. This is a fitting name for a man mentoring the future of the wizarding world. St. Wulfric was born in Bristol. He led a worldly life before a personal conversion and retired a hermit. He was known for being a miracle worker and had the gift of prophecy. This may provide insight into Dumbledore's powers-- past and future[4]. Brian is a Celtic name, which means the strong one[5]. This again fits a man considered to be the most powerful wizard of the age. Dumbledore comes from the Old English for the word bumblebee and was chosen because J.K. Rowling likes to think of him walking around humming to himself[6]. It also should be noted, bumblebees, unlike wasps, typically do not attack unless they are provoked. If someone comes into their nest or attempts to do them harm, watch out! They are fierce insects. The stingers not only hurt, but are also deadly in some cases. Furthermore, in Mary Kay Cosmetics, the bumblebee is the "ultimate symbol of achievement[7]." "Aerodynamics engineers studied this amazing insect and concluded it simply *could not fly*. Its wings were too weak and its body too heavy for flight…everybody knew this—but they forgot to tell the bumblebee, and he went right on flying[8]." This is also appropriate for Dumbledore, who has flown to the top and has faith in others when no one else believes he should. The appearance of Dumbledore is described in great detail. His description creates an image of Merlin or Gandalf, from J.R.R. Tolkien's *Lord of the Rings*. Dumbledore is tall, thin, has extremely long silver hair and beard and a very long, crooked nose. Dumbledore has blue eyes that twinkle and wears a pair of half moon spectacles. He also has very long fingers, which the Detectives believe are a sign of great power.

The Headmaster of Hogwarts, Albus Dumbledore (age 150), like his staff, is an extremely deep man with a past that has not been revealed to the readers at this point[9]. He has been described as a whimsical man, who likes sweets, chamber music, and ten-pin bowling. Dumbledore also has a great affection for those who are muggle born. In contrast, Dumbledore is also widely considered to be the most powerful wizard in the world and the only one Voldemort ever feared. So, how is it this man who has the image of fun and light-heartedness is also the only one the most evil wizard ever feared? What did Dumbledore do to make people believe he is the greatest wizard of modern times? Possibly this has something to do with his defeat of the dark wizard, Grindelwald, in 1945. It appears the muggle and wizarding worlds are on parallel planes, given the defeat of Grindelwald and Hitler happened the same year. Furthermore, the Detectives believe there are several Snitch clues that Dumbledore is a descendent of Godric Gryffindor. Dumbledore was in Gryffindor House when he attended Hogwarts. His phoenix, Fawkes is scarlet and gold, which are the colors of Gryffindor

House. Also, Gryffindor was the most powerful wizard of his age, which is a characterization now applied to Dumbledore. Gryffindor united the other founders against Slytherin. Likewise, Dumbledore united the wizarding world against Voldemort during his last reign of terror. Remember there are no coincidences. Finally, Dumbledore's second middle name is Wulfric and Wulfric de Croxton was a descendant of Godric a Saxon[10]. Thus, it is clear Dumbledore is Gryffindor's descendant.

Dumbledore is indeed an extremely powerful wizard. A glimpse of Dumbledore's power is seen at the end of Book 4. He knocks down the door and stuns Crouch, Jr. with a single spell. Wow! Snape and McGonagall have their wands drawn, but there was no need for them to act. "At that moment, Harry fully understood for the first time why people said Dumbledore was the only wizard Voldemort had ever feared...more terrible than Harry could have ever imagined...there was cold fury...a sense of power radiated from Dumbledore as though he were giving off burning heat[11]." Also, detectives should note Dumbledore could see through the door to hit Crouch and not Harry. Perhaps those half moon spectacles are not because he is nearsighted, but a cleverer version of Moody's magical eye.

Dumbledore's whimsical personality is also his way of dealing with the burdens he bears. Thus, his whimsical personality is a front, which he has earned, due to the fact he has already made his name in society. This is common in older people, who have seen a great deal of suffering in their lives. Dumbledore knows many secrets, which he will reveal to both Harry and the readers in time. He seems to bear the weight of the wizarding world on his shoulders and comes across to the readers as the "all knowing" character. The Detectives would describe Dumbledore as the Yoda equivalent from Star Wars.

Another Bludger, Hagrid tells Harry on their first meeting the wizarding community wanted Dumbledore to take the job of Minster of Magic, but he turned it down saying he would never leave Hogwarts. So, Fudge got the job instead. Why is it Dumbledore would never leave Hogwarts? When did Fudge get the job? Well, that question was answered in Book 5, in the most unlikely of places. The Quibbler article about Fudge and the goblins contained the answer. Fudge got the job five years ago, which was the same year Harry started at Hogwarts. The Detectives believe the most important place for Dumbledore to be is, in fact, wherever Harry is at the time.

Another interesting tidbit about Dumbledore is the way he addresses people. Unlike any other character, Albus Dumbledore addresses every adult by his/her first name. Why? Although, Dumbledore is so familiar with his contemporaries, very few seem to seem to take this liberty with him in public. Not even the Minister of Magic. One would think the President of the United States would be more likely to address a university president by his first name instead of the reverse. Interesting. In private conversations, the readers have heard Minerva McGonagall address him by his first name. This is intriguing. Why does she address him one way in public and another way in private? It is almost as if they are leading a double life. We will discuss this in more detail in the section on Professor McGonagall. There have only been three other characters we have heard take this liberty with Dumbledore. Crouch, Sr. called him Albus after giving out the instructions for the first task. Was this Crouch breaking through the Imperius Curse, or was this Voldemort's mistake? Dumbledore seemed concerned about Crouch following this event and wanted him to spend the night at Hogwarts. Perhaps this is why. Interestingly enough, Mr. Crouch addresses him as Dumbledore from that point on and returns to his curt nature, so it is possible Voldemort may have realized he had made a mistake. Another person who has addressed Dumbledore, as Albus, is Moody in Dumbledore's pensive. This shows they have known each other a long time. Well, given their ages and the fact they were sitting together on the bench talking like schoolboys would be another Bludger. The final character to call Dumbledore, Albus, was Lucius Malfoy, after he has gotten Dumbledore suspended from Hogwarts. Both Lucius and Draco believe Dumbledore is gone for good and apparently are making plans for a new Headmaster—their first choice would be Snape. ***Shudder*** The Detectives believe the reason Malfoy called Dumbledore, Albus, was out of disrespect. It was Lucius Malfoy's way of saying, "I have conquered the great Dumbledore. I am now his equal." It should be noted, he was back to addressing him as Dumbledore once the Headmaster returned to Hogwarts and discovered the tricks Lucius had played. Not smart Lucius, not even Voldemort wants to tango or, be on a first name basis with the great Albus Dumbledore! In contrast to the way Dumbledore addresses the adults, he addresses all the students as Mr. or Miss, with two known exceptions, Tom Riddle and Harry Potter. One theory as to why this could be is Dumbledore regards them as his equals, even before they have finished school. Snitch, anyone?

Deputy Headmistress

Minerva McGonagall

Minerva was a character in Roman Mythology. She was the Goddess of war, invention, agriculture, handicrafts, and the protector of civilized life. She was considered the embodiment of wisdom, reason, and purity[12]. Athena was her counterpart in Greek Mythology and their symbol was the owl[13]. As the favorite daughter of Zeus or Jupiter, she was mostly considered "warlike only to defend the State and the home from outside enemies[14]." It should also be noted that Minerva's eyes "flashed," which is also a characteristic of Minerva McGonagall when she is exceptionally angry. Her name alone tells the Detectives this is a woman who should not be provoked. She will make a formidable enemy. The name, McGonagall, is Scottish. The Scots are fierce fighters, especially when they believe in someone or something, as demonstrated in the Scottish Revolution. Minerva McGonagall is no exception.

Minerva McGonagall is the first magical person whom the readers met in the Harry Potter Series, even before Harry. This is a vital key to both the story and the mystery. McGonagall is a tall, thin woman with black hair, which she keeps in a tight bun. She wears square spectacles over her beady eyes. She is a stern, brisk woman, who Harry determines at first sight is someone not to be crossed. McGonagall teaches Transfiguration and is the Head of Gryffindor House, which means we can expect her to be brave, daring, chivalrous, and have nerves of steel. She does not appear, at first sight to have a dark secret, but if the other professors are any example, she does indeed have one. Perhaps, it is hidden in the Chamber of Secrets. ***Wink*** Typically, when people appear to be too clean, they have a dirty past or secret. This rule holds true not only in Harry Potter's world, but in life, as well. McGonagall appears to be too rigid to be true. A little too much like Crouch to be honest. Both Crouch and the Dursleys have appeared to be "normal," which turned out to be a massive cover up for a secret they thought would be the end of their world if discovered. Well, does it not logically follow Minerva McGonagall might be doing the same thing? What a Snitch! Crouch and the Dursleys could be clues to tip the readers off as to the patterns of cover-ups people attempt. Possibly the only person who knows her secret is Dumbledore. McGonagall has been teaching at Hogwarts for 39 years. That is a long time. Why did she start in December? That is the middle of the school year. Clearly the Transfiguration professor did not die, given her predecessor was Albus Dumbledore. Based on years 2-5, the Detectives know if something happens to the Headmaster in midyear, someone acts or replaces them until the end of the year, but continues to teach their classes. Now this is strange. What happened in December of 1955?

Another key characteristic about McGonagall is her obsession with Quidditch. She cannot stand losing the cup, especially to Slytherin. She could easily be a Buckeye during football season. Don't you dare lose to

Michigan! Lose to anyone else, anyone except Michigan, or Slytherin, in this case! McGonagall was also the one who discovered Harry for the Gryffindor team. This suggests McGonagall is not only a fan, but she has some experience recruiting team members. The Detectives believe there is a strong possibility McGonagall played Quidditch as a chaser and was the team captain. The reason the Detectives do not believe McGonagall was a seeker is simple. McGonagall is too tall. Seekers are typically the smallest players. If Harry would explore the Trophy Room for us, which is always unlocked, we would find out. It would also tell us if she was Head Girl too. Alas, if Harry were as nosy as the Detectives, we would know a great deal more. Well, at least that mystery would be solved.

The Detectives have determined several facts about McGonagall. She is 70 years old, which coincidentally is the same age as Tom Riddle or Voldemort[15]. This is, of course, based on his age when he opened the Chamber of Secrets. Thus, they would have been in the same year at Hogwarts. Tom was Head Boy. The Detectives believe based on Minerva's intelligence and leadership she was Head Girl.

The sequence of events following Harry, Ron, and Ginny's return from the Chamber of Secrets is fascinating. McGonagall was in control of the conversation until the discussion turned to Voldemort and Tom Riddle. At this point, Dumbledore took over for her and she remained silent. This is uncharacteristic for McGonagall. When has she ever remained silent? Why did Dumbledore take over for her? She was at Hogwarts then as well. Also, Ginny is not punished for her role in opening the Chamber of Secrets due to the fact "older and wiser wizards have been charmed by Lord Voldemort." Really? Charmed? Most of the people are either bewitched or forced into the dark arts, but charmed? Now that really is different. Very interesting! In addition, Dumbledore gives McGonagall a ready-made excuse to leave the office following the discussion. Again, the Detectives ask why? So, Tom Riddle was charming. Who did he charm? The Detectives believe Dumbledore was referring to McGonagall. The Detectives believe it is possible Tom and Minerva were not only Head Boy and Girl, but also friends.

Another interesting point about Minerva McGonagall is that she is a mother, but her children are kept a secret. We will keep their names a secret for now, but think who else wears tartan? It is strange Minerva McGonagall began her teaching career in December 1955. What did she do all that time? She graduated in 1938 and did not start teaching until 1955. The gap is seventeen years, which allows for a child or twins to be born and graduate from school. Could Minerva have started teaching after her children reached adulthood? The Detectives also wonder if Minerva

McGonagall's husband and the father of her children is still alive? If not, does she ever fall in love again? The Detectives believe Minerva does indeed fall in love again. This time she bestows her heart on a much older and wiser wizard—Albus Dumbledore. The Detectives believe this explains the two different ways for addressing him, public and private. The marriage has clearly been kept quiet. Their love has been clear, since the very first chapter of Book 1. Until the interview where J.K. Rowling stated some of the professors had spouses, the Head Detective suspected an affair, but post interview, she settled on marriage. Further evidence, McGonagall is always seated next to Dumbledore at the staff table and has access to him at anytime she pleases. Also, on the night Colin Creevey is attacked, McGonagall discovers him in the middle of the night. Dumbledore just happens to be walking down the same hallway a few minutes later. This suggests a late night rendezvous between the two of them. Hmmm. Sneaking around together at night in their pajamas makes them sound like two teenagers. Well, it would fit well with Dumbledore's personality. Maybe this is a Snitch regarding McGonagall's personality!

McGonagall was not an original member of the Order. Why not? Was this because of her relationship to Tom Riddle? Was she not keen to fight her own family? We see this with Andromeda Tonks, not taking an active role in a war which would involve fighting her two sisters. What is McGonagall doing for the Order now? Why was she wearing a muggle dress and coat? Clearly her mission is in the muggle world. Is she meeting with Petunia? Is she meeting with Mrs. Figg? The Detectives are very interested in what McGonagall is doing for the Order. Perhaps it is McGonagall's involvement with the Order, which has led to her discussions with Mrs. Longbottom. Were they are old school friends or, even family, since they seem to be around the same age and talk with some frequency. Mrs. Longbottom sent Neville's Hogsmeade permission form directly to McGonagall in the third year, which was the first Bludger showing they had contact. In the fifth year, it was a little more discreet. Umbridge had arrived and it was crucial Neville remember the password to the Gryffindor tower. This is similar to when Durmstrang came to Hogwarts. McGonagall did not want them to have any ammunition against Neville. Likewise, she did not want Umbridge to have any. Perhaps McGonagall knows something about Umbridge, given she warned Harry too. Both Neville's Grandmother and McGonagall know it will be a near miracle for Neville to remember the passwords. Well, Neville has been given a plant, which he loves, by his great-uncle. So his grandmother tells McGonagall about the plant and she makes the Gryffindor password the name of the plant. Convenient and very nice! This just goes to show she really is an old softy. Another interesting tidbit about Professor McGonagall is the way she addresses the students. McGonagall, like Dumbledore, addresses the majority of the students as Mister and Miss., but there are a few exceptions. All of the Weasleys are addressed simply as Weasley, Percy is even called by his first name, Neville is addressed as Longbottom, and Harry is simply called Potter. So, why does she change her mannerism when addressing this select group of students? The Detectives know their parents were close to Dumbledore. Are they perhaps close to McGonagall as well? Is this McGonagall's way of being less formal with this group and feeling closer to them?

The Detectives believe Minerva McGonagall will be key to the to the downfall of Voldemort. If she was related to him, then she will definitely be helpful in the effort to humanize Voldemort. The role of Minerva McGonagall is expected to increase a great deal where both Voldemort and Harry are concerned.

Severus Snape

Severus Snape is an excellent example of a Snitch clue. His first name can be divided into two words, sever us meaning divide us. So, whom is he going to divide? Where do his loyalties lie? An additional clue is the two Roman Emperors named Severus. The first was Lucius Septimius Severus, who was the Emperor of Rome from 146-211 A.D.. He created a powerful military and ruled as a tyrant[16]. Wow, the Detectives are eternally gratefully Sirius gave James the opportunity to save this man's life. It sounds like things would have been very painful otherwise. The second was Alexander Severus, the Roman Emperor from 222-235 A.D.. His reign represented a return to a sense of sanity and "preferred to negotiate peace by buying off the enemy[17]." He was "murdered in a mutiny[18]." This suggests Severus Snape will attempt to save both Death Eaters and members of Order, but will, in the end, be murdered. The word snape is a shipbuilding term which means to make timber fit against an inclining surface. This is exactly what Snape does. He makes the pieces fit together which would not otherwise fit, well, at least for the Order.

Severus Snape (36) is one of the deepest characters in the series[19]. Snape could have easily have come from the pages of Shakespeare. He is the tragic hero. He has a fascinating internal battle and a past that was revealed to the readers in Book 4. In addition, he is the perfect example of a professor, most Headmasters would not have hired. Snape went to school with Harry's father, James Potter, and hated him. But James saved Severus' life, which apparently formed a bond between the two wizards. The readers know very little about this bond up to this point. Accordingly to Dumbledore, the one thing Snape could never forgive was being in James Potter's debt. Well, Snape's hatred for James Potter seems to have carried over to Harry, but so did his debt. Snape apparently believes even though he was unable to save James Potter's life, he can repay his debt if he keeps Harry alive.

Severus Snape is a nasty man. Snape is the Potions Master and the Head of Slytherin House. He goes out of his way to treat Harry poorly and Draco Malfoy is his favorite student. But is this only a front? In fact, he does everything he can to help Harry. The Detectives have determined although Snape is a nasty git, he is not unlike another teacher who fights the Dark Side by stealth. Of course we are speaking about Obi-wan Kenobi. The Detectives would not be a bit surprised if Snape intervenes and sacrifices his life in order to allow Harry to escape from Voldemort. An important thing for both the readers and Harry to remember about Snape, even if he appears to be insulting Harry, if he tells him something, gives him extra work, insults him for not knowing an answer, or asks him a question, take note; it is something Harry <u>needs</u> <u>to</u> <u>know</u>.

Another interesting point to note about Snape is his worst memory; James, tormenting him in front of the whole school, and Lily stepping in to save him. This is one of the few times we see Snape lose control. It should be noted Snape prides himself on being in control of his emotions at all times and there are very few people who can push Snape over the edge. Harry has that power! The memory of James is a sure way to do it, too. When Snape saw Sirius, Snape was beyond reason and lost control. In contrast, Lupin was able to make Snape livid, but he still seemed to be in control. So, there are three people who have the power to make Snape really angry and cause him to lose control of his emotions and thereby, lose control of the situation. They are Sirius, James, and Harry.

Another Bludger, Snape now has to trust Harry will not reveal two key secrets about him. Now that is a great deal of trust to put in someone who you despise and treat like dirt. The first secret deals with Snape being a spy for the Order and it benefits both Snape and Harry for Harry to keep his trap shut that Snape is their spy. As for the second secret, regarding Snape's humiliation at the hands of James and Sirius, in Snape's mind, there is nothing to stop Harry from running his mouth. Fortunately for Snape, what Harry saw disturbed him and he had no desire to share the information with anyone. In fact, the only people he discussed the scene with were Lupin and Sirius, who had been there at the time.

The readers have learned Snape has a dark secret. Knowing this, only Dumbledore would hire him. Severus Snape was a Death Eater, one of Lord Voldemort's supporters. According to Dumbledore's pensive, Snape was indeed a Death Eater, but left before Voldemort's downfall and became a spy for the Order of the Phoenix at great risk. So, why did Snape leave the Death Eaters and become a spy? Seems like a strange thing for someone, who has always been fascinated with the dark arts to do. According to Sirius, Snape knew more about the dark arts in year 1 than most people did when they graduated from Hogwarts. So, we must ask ourselves, why would someone who was clearly in his element, leave when Voldemort was growing more and more powerful to become a spy? J. K. Rowling has not told her readers outright yet, but she has left many clues. Thus, it is not rocket science, the combination of all of these clues amount to a Bludger. There is a bond formed between wizards when one wizard saves the life of another. We have been told the Potters knew Voldemort was after them. So, it logically follows, as a Death Eater, Snape learned Voldemort intended to kill the Potters and because of this bond he could not allow it to happen. This bond must be stronger than the bond Voldemort puts on his Death Eaters. To interfere with this plan would have been extremely dangerous. He would have had gone to Dumbledore and told him everything. This degree of betrayal of Voldemort would have been huge and extremely dangerous. If it had been discovered, Snape would have been tortured and then brutally killed. Snape is the Death Eater Voldemort refers to in his speech. "One, who I believe has left me forever…he will be killed, of course[20]." Well, there are Voldemort's intentions for Snape. He, like Harry, is a marked man. Unfortunately, the Detectives believe Snape has a habit, which will give him away. When Voldemort's name or the Dark Mark is mentioned Snape grasps his left forearm. This seems to be an involuntary reaction. This is similar to a WWII American spy, Virginia Hall. She had the distinctive habit of walking with a limp. When she was in disguise. Hall taught herself to walk without a limp because the

Gestapo "circulated a wanted poster with the warning, 'the woman with the limp is one of the most valuable Allied Agent, in France and we must find and destroy her[21].'" Snape should learn from Hall or he may find himself dueling Lord Voldemort.

The Detectives believe there is substantial evidence to prove Snape is a vampire. In the World Book Day Chat, J.K. Rowling answered a question, "Is there a link between Snape and vampires?" Her answer was, "Erm…I don't think so[22]." This answer is inconclusive at best. Furthermore, the question was not asked properly. A link is not the same as turning into a vampire and we know J.K. Rowling is very precise with words. There is a great deal of evidence to support this theory. The word Snape includes the word nape, which is a part of the neck, generally bitten by vampires. In addition, Snape looks like a vampire. He has greasy black hair, ashen skin, and always dresses in rippling black robes. In addition, he bares his "uneven yellowish teeth" when he is angry[23]. One should note a trademark characteristic of vampires is often uneven teeth. Snape lives in the dungeon, which is darker and colder than the rest of the castle. This atmosphere would be essential for vampire comfort. Furthermore, there are multiple statements regarding vampires and bats. Quirrell describes Snape as "an overgrown bat[24]." It is important this information comes from a man close to Voldemort, as the Detectives are sure Voldemort would have any incriminating information on all of his Death Eaters, in order to control them. It is the equivalent of "I know what's in your FBI file." Then, there is Harry's statement, "not unless, [Snape] can turn himself into a bat[25]." Seamus says, "I wonder what they will give us next year? Maybe a vampire" Dean suggested[26]." This is fitting given the Detectives believe Snape will eventually get the Defense Against the Dark Arts' job. The final and most incriminating piece of evidence is Lupin's retaliation. Snape taught the class about werewolves and assigned an essay on the subject. Lupin then taught the class about vampires and assigned an essay. Also, he deliberately brought the subject up when Harry and Ron were in Snape's office. Given the fact Snape and Lupin do not care very much for each other, it would be reasonable to assume this battle of essays said, "if I go down you are coming with me." It is also reasonable to conclude, if Snape can make the extremely complicated Wolfsbane potion, which the Detectives believe he invented, he would be able to make a potion so that he could go outside. The combination of all these clues adds up to a Bludger. Snape is a vampire!

Remus John Lupin

Remus comes from Roman Mythology. He had a twin brother, Romulus, both of whom were raised by wolves. Do you think there is a wolf connection here? There are many famous John's in history. King John signed the Magna Carta, which reduced the power of the monarchy and gave the British people more freedoms. Also there is the Apostle John, who was brother of James the Great, and wrote four books of the Bible, including Revelations. Again, this is appropriate because Remus and James were very close. Also, Lupus is Latin for wolf. Gee, that was a bludger! Lupin is also a plant in the pea family. They have leaves and variously colored flowers grouped in spikes. Also, the pea plant was originally used in studies regarding genetic variation. Again, this would fit given Lupin is a genetic mutation or half-breed. Remus Lupin is clearly a questionable appointment. He is a werewolf. J.K. Rowling says this is a metaphor for illness and disability[27]. Also, he went to school with James Potter, Sirius Black, Peter Pettigrew, and Severus Snape. He was only a friend to the first three and a foe of the final one. Lupin was hired to teach Defense Against the Dark Arts in the third year. This appointment was done despite many objections. Dumbledore not only appointed a werewolf, but a man whose best friend from school had escaped from Azkaban prison and is thought to be a mass murderer after Harry. Yet, Dumbledore says he trusts Lupin. Comforting, eh? Even when Sirius Black manages to get inside Hogwarts and Snape states it would be impossible to do so without inside help, Dumbledore holds firm that he does not believe anyone from inside Hogwarts would help Black get inside.

Lupin has a prematurely aged face and his eyes twinkle. He has a personality similar to Dumbledore. Also, the twinkling of the eyes is exactly like Dumbledore. While attending Hogwarts, Lupin was a prefect. While teaching at Hogwarts, Lupin agreed to give Harry anti-Dementor lessons, teaching him the Patronus Charm. This has enabled Harry to save countless lives since that time. Another interesting point is the relationship between Lupin and Peeves. Peeves treats Lupin like dirt. This is strange because Peeves typically shows some respect for the teachers. It is just as interesting Lupin does not speak crossly to Peeves, but tries to keep him out of trouble with Filch and in the end does a spell reminiscent of a teenager dealing with a pest. So, why does Peeves treat Lupin so poorly? The Detectives believe Peeves regards Lupin as a sell out. He is not causing trouble anymore, he became a teacher and isn't even harassing Snape!

Aside from these facts which were revealed about Lupin at the end of the third book, the Detectives believe Lupin holds many more secrets. Lupin was James Potter and Sirius Black's best friend. He would have been told things others would not have been privy to. James would have confided in Sirius and Remus. After James's death, Sirius would have confided in Remus, particularly, regarding Harry. Both Remus and Sirius believe themselves to be responsible for Harry after his father's death and we know they lived at the Order together. Remus Lupin, like Dumbledore, knows a great deal, which will be revealed in time.

Rubeus Hagrid

Rubeus is Latin for red and Hagrid is Old English for "you had a bad night[28]." Also, hagridden means "obsessed or harassed by fears or nightmares[29]." This is appropriate given Hagrid spent time in Azkaban, but what are Hagrid's fears? Given his name it is no surprise Hagrid is good guy, but has a depressing history. Rubeus Hagrid (65) is the first wizard Harry meets. He is an extremely large man. In fact, he is half-giant. This is huge! The wizard community as a whole fears the giants. They are known to be violent and those who remained after the giant wars joined the ranks of Voldemort. Thus, Hagrid's appointment to the Hogwarts' staff is clearly one of trust. Harry learns Hagrid is not a fully qualified wizard. Hagrid attended Hogwarts and was in Gryffindor, but he was expelled from Hogwarts in his third year[30]. Hagrid is one of the first characters we meet shortly after Dumbledore and McGonagall, which tells the Detectives this Keeper of keys holds a key to the mystery.

In the Chamber of Secrets, we learn Tom Riddle framed Hagrid and for the past 50 years people believed Hagrid had opened the Chamber of Secrets. Well, believed by everyone except Dumbledore. Yet Dumbledore allowed Hagrid to be the Gamekeeper. This seems strange! A girl at the school dies and the suspected killer is kept on as Gamekeeper. We also learn not only does Dumbledore keep Hagrid on as Gamekeeper, but also has him do other important tasks. He transported Harry as a baby, picked him up to get his school supplies, and retrieved the Sorcerer's Stone. Does Hagrid have some powers we do not know about? What are these powers? Clearly his wand was repaired. When Ron's wand broke, it did not work, in fact, it backfired. In contrast, Hagrid's wand works well. Hagrid would not have the skill to repair a wand, but the one man who believed in his innocence, would definitely have that skill—Dumbledore. Hagrid hides his repaired wand in his pink umbrella and clearly did not want Mr. Ollivander to have a look at it. Perhaps in addition to repairing Hagrid's wand, Dumbledore finished his education. Regardless, Hagrid is not a fully qualified wizard, yet he is entrusted with important errands. How does he protect himself and those with whom he is entrusted? It is clear why they say Dumbledore is a trusting man. Well, we learned Hagrid was innocent. So, Dumbledore appoints him as the Care of Magical Creatures teacher when Professor Kettleburn retires. Hagrid is clearly one of the most trusted people at Hogwarts. In the words of Dumbledore, "I would trust Hagrid with my life[31]." The Detectives believe this is not merely a statement, but a depressing note of foreshadowing. The time will come when Dumbledore will trust Hagrid with this life and Hagrid will not let him down. Hagrid will freely give his own life to save Dumbledore's. Hagrid has said on countless occasions, Dumbledore is a great man. In addition, the quickest way to make Hagrid blow his top is to insult Dumbledore. In fact, this is the only time we have ever seen any violence out of Hagrid. The first time was when Uncle Vernon insulted Dumbledore and Hagrid put a pig's tail on Dudley and the second time was when Karkaroff spit at Dumbledore's feet and accused him of treachery. Hagrid picked him up and threw him against a tree demanding he apologize to Dumbledore. The Detectives would hate to see someone really attack Dumbledore in front of Hagrid.

Sibyll Patricia Trelawney[32]

In mythology, a sybil is a woman with prophetic powers[33]. Sibyll Trelawney is tall, thin and has overly magnified eyes. She is the Divination teacher and her class is a bit of a joke. She continually predicts Harry's premature death. Hermione is insistent Trelawney is a fraud and McGonagall says she will not speak ill of her colleagues when discussing Trelawney. So, why has Dumbledore hired this flake? Well, the Detectives will note often times what Trelawney sees is correct, it is only her interpretation, which is wrong. For example, the large dog she kept seeing in Harry's tea leaves and crystal ball was not the Grim, but Sirius Black as an animagus. Thus, she does truly possess the inner eye, but she does not know how to use it. This is really sad. Also, in Book 4, she notices the strange angle of Mars and Neptune. Again, Trelawney knows this is strange and just not right, but she does not know what it means. During Harry's final exam, Trelawney makes the prediction the Dark Lord will rise again. Later, when Harry tells Dumbledore about this prediction, he says, "That brings her total of real predictions up to two." So, what was her other prediction? When did she make it? Is this the reason she is teaching at Hogwarts? That mystery was solved in Book 5. The prophecy was made 16 years ago; the year prior to Harry's birth. It stated the one with the power to vanquish the Dark Lord would be born as the seventh month dies to those who had defied him three times and the Dark Lord would mark him as his equal. So, has Dumbledore kept Trelawney at Hogwarts because it is not safe for her to leave? The Detectives believe Umbridge knew Trelawney had made real prophecies because of her position in the Ministry and her attempt to force Trelawney to see upon command. Thus, Umbridge was pleased to throw Trelawney from the castle when she failed to give her a prophecy. Voldemort wants the rest of this prophecy and she cannot remember it. If Trelawney left Hogwarts, Voldemort could capture and torture her just as he did Bertha Jorkins. Since Trelawney is a true seer, who has made two accurate predictions, Dumbledore may want someone on the side of good, not evil, to hear, if she makes, another prophecy. The Detectives look for Trelawney to predict the timing of the final battle and possibly the outcome.

Firenze

Firenze is the Italian name for Florence. This city is famous for being the center of learning during the Renaissance. During the Middle Ages, the masses were dark, secretive, and feared speaking out. Florence represented a rebirth and other cities in Italy and Europe followed its lead. Firenze is a young centaur who represents the same ideals of Florence in a Centaur society, which subscribes to the mentality of the masses during the Middle Ages. Firenze has a palomino body and white blond hair. He also has astonishingly blue eyes, like pale sapphires. The Detectives believe this description of his eyes is a sign Firenze is powerful. Very few characters have their eyes described, particularly non-human characters. Thus, it is highly probable Firenze is important to the story.

In the first year, Firenze saved Harry from Voldemort in the Forbidden Forest. In addition, unlike Ronan and Bane, Firenze does not simply tell Harry Mars is bright. Instead, Firenze asks Harry questions, which help him to solve the mystery. Firenze also allows Harry to ride to safety on his back. This is disgraceful for a centaur. Bane was furious and called Firenze a common mule. Ronan defended Firenze saying he is sure Firenze felt he had acted for the best. Firenze stated at this point, "I set myself against what is lurking in this forest, Bane, with humans alongside me if I must[34]." Firenze stated his intentions loud and clear at this point. He will fight Voldemort at all costs. It doesn't matter to him, whether he fights with centaurs or humans, he will fight! Thus, Firenze will be a key player in the upcoming battles.

When Firenze agrees to help Dumbledore and teach Divination it does not appear Ronan stepped in to help him. Firenze was banished from his herd, and they intended to kick him to death. Hagrid, however, rescued

Firenze. This story is right out of Greek Mythology with a happier ending. Firenze is Chiron, the kind, old centaur and Hagrid is Hercules. Hagrid or Hercules was more than a match for the centaurs attacking Firenze or Chiron, but in this case Firenze lived in spite of the centaurs. Firenze taught after his banishment and Chiron taught and trained many famous heroes before his final battle[35]. Thus, Firenze sends Hagrid a warning through Harry that his attempt is not working and it would be better for him to abandon it. The Detectives are not sure whether Firenze sent this warning because he believed Grawp was a hopeless case or because he believed the centaurs would wage a full-scale war on Hagrid when he was unprepared. Possibly both. Firenze tells Harry, Hagrid earned his respect long ago. Also, the Detectives should note Hagrid has just saved Firenze's life. Although Firenze is not a wizard, the Detectives wonder if a bond will not be formed between the two due to this event.

Firenze's class is interesting. The Detectives finally find out what the centaurs meant by "Mars is bright tonight[36]." We thought it had something to do with Armageddon. He tells the students, the position of Mars describes wizardkind as living through nothing more than a brief calm between two wars. Wow, so Harry saving the stone just put off the war for three years! Well, now that the war has begun and Dumbledore has returned to Hogwarts, as Headmaster, who will teach Divination? Maybe Firenze and Trelawney will share the position? Firenze cannot return to the Forest, unless Dumbledore was able to smooth things over when he rescued Umbridge. Possibly Firenze can teach Trelawney how to understand and control her gift. That would make her gift more useful to herself and others. Regardless, Firenze will be a great help in the ensuing battle and could possibly have the Centaurs join the fight for good.

Madam Poppy Pomfrey

A poppy is a plant, known for the poppy seeds used for medicines, commonly found in narcotics and other painkillers. Thus, this is an appropriate name for Poppy Pomfrey, who is the Hogwarts school nurse. Madam Pomfrey is clearly a highly intelligent and a powerful witch based on the qualifications to become a healer, "at least an E at the NEWT level in Potions, Herbology, Transfiguration, Charms, and Defense Against the Dark Arts[37]." She is extremely skilled! There has only been one incident, of which the Detectives are aware, when she was not able to heal someone and sent the individual to St. Mungo's.

Madam Pomfrey is not a member of Dumbledore's inner circle at Hogwarts, which includes only McGonagall, Hagrid, and Snape, but is trusted quite a bit. Also, the poor nurse has to deal with more than the average aches and pains. If the Dementors, dragons, petrified cats, ghosts, students, and countless accidents that take place at Hogwarts weren't enough, the dramatic scenes, which tend to take place in her hospital wing, are enough to give the poor woman heart failure. At the end of year 3, Snape and Fudge came storming into the hospital wing with Snape raging at Harry Potter, who had helped Sirius Black escape. Both Fudge and Pomfrey thought Snape had completely lost his mind. In year 4, Madam Pomfrey is present for the discussion regarding the return of Voldemort between Dumbledore and Fudge meaning she is one of the first to be made aware of this information. This suggests she is someone who Dumbledore trusts not to turn against him. Proving Pomfrey is not in Dumbledore's inner circle, she is sent away before Sirius reveals himself to Snape. In contrast, Mrs. Weasley is permitted to remain in the room. It should also be noted in the 5th year, some students do not seem to recover and yet, are not sent to St. Mungo's, like McGonagall. For example, Hermione, who is 15 years old, jinxed Marietta Edgecombe. The Detectives find it extremely hard to believe someone, as qualified as, Madam Pomfrey would not be able to cure Marietta. In fact, it is far more likely she thought Marietta deserved what she got since she was responsible for getting rid of Dumbledore. Also, Montague remained in the hospital wing for the remainder of the year, making very little improvement. Even though Madam Pomfrey called his parents to visit, she did not seem to be concerned enough to send him to St. Mungo's. Finally, Madam Pomfrey seemed to take her time curing the Slytherins from their many injuries during the Inquisitional Squad's reign of terror. The Detectives believe this is due to the fact the Slytherins are troublemakers. She is doing her part keeping them out of commission for as long as possible without arousing suspicion.

Argus Filch

Argus comes from Greek Mythology. He was a watchman with 100 eyes, so he could keep watch and sleep at the same time. He worked for Hera, Zeus's wife, who used Argus to imprison her enemies. Hermes killed Argus[38]. The fact he worked for Hera is definitely cause for concern given she was not exactly a noble goddess. The word filch means to steal. This is definitely a clue to Filch's character. The Detectives have been warned not to trust Filch and to keep their distance. Filch is the caretaker at Hogwarts. He is a Squib and has a cat, named Mrs. Norris. Filch is a really nasty git. He is always asking to bring back the old punishments in order to torture students. Filch's purpose in life seems to be to make the students' lives miserable. Filch especially dislikes Hagrid. Anytime Hagrid is in the castle, Filch has Mrs. Norris follow Hagrid. Also, Filch hates Peeves and wages a constant war with him.

In the first year, Filch helps Snape with his wound from Fluffy, but apparently keeps his silence. Why would he do this? It was clear Snape had gone near the three-headed dog and did not want to see Madam Pomfrey. So, why wouldn't Filch expose Snape? His loyalty seems to be to Snape, not Dumbledore. Interesting! In Year 4, when Filch finds the egg, he thinks it's his golden opportunity to get Peeves expelled from the castle. Then Snape turns up and tells him that his office has been broken into and he wants Filch to help him search for the intruder. Filch is willing to give up this dream opportunity to help Snape. This suggests to the Detectives a strong bond between Filch and Snape. How far will this bond stretch? Would Filch give his life for Snape? Interestingly enough, Filch was also the only staff member at Hogwarts willing to help Umbridge. He could not do enough for her. Granted she signed a decree saying he could whip students and promised to get rid of Peeves. (She did not fulfill the promise to get rid of Peeves.) Also, she seemed to hate students as much as he did. This does make the Detectives wonder if Filch is from a family of Dark wizards? If so, why does Dumbledore allow him to stay at Hogwarts? Another interesting clue regarding Filch is when he is sick in the second year he has a tartan scarf covering his mouth. So, who do the Detectives know who wears tartan and accessorizes in tartan? Minerva McGonagall is obsessed with tartan and it would make sense that she would give her children, gifts of tartan. Further evidence is Filch was irate when McGonagall defended Harry after Mrs. Norris was petrified. It appears the Detectives have found one of McGonagall's children. Unfortunately, Filch does not seem to have inherited his mother's personality or loyalty, but will he allow harm to come to her? It is interesting after McGonagall was attacked, Filch no longer played an active role assisting Umbridge. It is also said Filch is miserable at the end of Book 5. Ginny says this is because Umbridge is no longer the Headmistress. The Detectives disagree. They believe this is directly related to McGonagall's hospitalization. So, maybe Filch does care about his mother. The Detectives will be interested to see if he shows more loyalty to her in future books and is less willing to aid the dark side.

Quirrell

Quirrell sounds a great deal like quarrel and looks like the word squirrely. Either is appropriate for Professor Quirrell, the Defense against the Dark Arts teacher in year 1. He is quite a squirrely character. Quirrell allowed Voldemort to possess his body and attempted to steal the Sorcerer's Stone. Throughout the year he attempted to kill Harry because he kept getting in his way and was "too nosy to live[39]." Harry Potter fought Quirrell and Voldemort over the Sorcerer's Stone at the end of year 1. The end result was prolonged direct contact with Harry's skin killed Quirrell. This brings a whole new meaning to the phrase killing someone with your bare hands. Thus, this was Harry's second defeat of Voldemort and first time killing a person.

Gilderoy Lockhart

J.K. Rowling explained Gilderoy was the name of "a handsome Scottish highwayman[40]." It should be noted a highwayman is a thief. She also said she found the name "Lockhart on a war memorial to the First World War[41]." This is interesting because the name sounds like locked heart meaning closed heart. This is appropriate because Hitler preyed on the broken hearts of the German people in order to start WWII. Gilderoy Lockhart was the Defense Against the Dark Arts Professor in year 2. He was an extremely self-absorbed man who thought he was God's gift to mankind. It is also important to note he is an honorary member of an organization called the Dark Force Defense League. Lockhart is the author of several books describing *his* heroic deeds. Although, he claims he has done these deeds, he seems inept at magic. He cannot mend Harry's broken arm rather he removes the bones. Also, he cannot control a room full of pixies and instead leaves students to handle the situation. Yet he is continually bragging about his accomplishments. Detectives do not need much to figure out this man. We have all met people like him. The more people brag the less they have done and are capable of doing. For example, you never hear Dumbledore bragging. Yet he is considered the most powerful wizard of the age and the only one Voldemort ever feared. Why is that? It goes without saying he does not need to brag. Interestingly enough, Lockhart admits to Harry and Ron he is took credit for what other wizards had done and casts a memory charm on them. Thus, he is a thief just as his name suggests. When Lockhart attempted to wipe Harry and Ron's memories, with Ron's damaged wand, the spell backfires on him and his memory is damaged. The result is that he cannot remember anything, including his name or the fact he is a wizard. It could not happen to a nicer man.

Lockhart is not seen again until Book 5, when Harry, Ron, and Hermione run into him on their way to the Tea Room at St. Mungo's Hospital for Magical Maladies and Injuries. The Healer thinks they are there to visit him. Apparently, the only thing Lockhart can remember from before the memory charm is giving autographs. Well, this could be because his life was a complete scam. Nonetheless, Lockhart is a bit more honest in this state. He tells the three of them, "Gladys Gudgeon writes weekly...I just wish I knew why... I suspect it is simply my good looks[42]." Oh, how right he is. Well, we will just have to see if he gets his memory back. If so, Harry and Ron had better watch out. He might be out for vengeance.

Barty Crouch, Jr. Or the Impostor Moody

The Impostor Moody was the Defense Against the Dark Arts' Professor in Year 4. It was discovered after Voldemort's rebirth, the impostor Moody was in fact Crouch, Jr. Crouch is an interesting name. To crouch means to stoop. Crouch, Sr. stooped to the Death Eaters' level, according to Sirius. The impostor endears himself to both the readers and the characters by tormenting everyone Harry and the readers cannot stand. Snape is terribly uncomfortable around him. Of course, the non-Slytherin students and most readers think Snape is a jerk. So, whatever makes him uncomfortable is okay with them. Also, Karkaroff is petrified of Moody. It is easy to see why. Moody put him in Azkaban. Then, of course, best of all is when the impostor turns Draco Malfoy into a bouncing ferret. When Draco muttered the threat of his father, "oh yeah?" said Moody "well, I know your father of old, boy... You tell him Moody's keeping a close eye on his son... you tell him that from me... Now, your Head of House'll be Snape, will it[43]?" It is extremely important to note Mr. Malfoy made no effort to get Moody fired over this incident. He would have had a legitimate grievance against the man for his unorthodox punishment of his son. So, why was no action taken by dear old daddy when precious Draco was embarrassed so thoroughly? This is so uncharacteristic of Lucius Malfoy. Fear of Moody is, of course, the reason. All of the Death Eaters are afraid of Moody. After the impostor Moody left the office, Snape probably went off on Draco asking him what the hell he thought he was doing attacking Harry Potter right in front of Moody. His father probably said the same thing. Are you trying to bring him down on us all, Draco?

Crouch, Jr. is a villain who managed to find a soft spot near and dear to the Detectives. That must be why he got the Dementor's kiss. We liked a villain just a little too much. Speaking of the Dementor's kiss administered to Crouch, Jr., is it possible to get your soul back from the Dementors? What happens to the body afterward? Where exactly does the soul go? Can Voldemort intervene in this situation? Will they cut a deal with him to restore his most faithful servant?

Dolores Jane Umbridge

J.K. Rowling gives the readers a clue with Umbridge's name. This name sounds almost exactly like a word frequently used in Shakespeare, *umbrage,* meaning to take offense. Thus, the readers may correctly assume the character, Umbridge, will be offensive. This name can also be broken into two words *um* meaning doubt or uncertainty and *bridge* a structure to provide passage over a gap or barrier. Umbridge's character certainly creates doubt and uncertainty at Hogwarts. Also, her primary job is to fill in a gap and provide passage over a barrier—Dumbledore and those loyal to him. Both of these explanations of the name provide insight into the character of Umbridge. Dolores Umbridge is short with very little neck. Harry describes her as resembling a toad. Umbridge also has very short stubby fingers, which suggests she is a very poor witch. She is appointed the Defense Against the Dark Arts teacher in Year 5 by a last minute decree the ministry forced through giving them unprecedented control over Hogwarts. The ministry does not only seek to have a teacher working at the Hogwarts, but controlling the school. Shortly after her appointment as the Defense Against the Dark Arts teacher, she is also named the first Hogwarts High Inquisitor. This is right out of the Spanish Inquisition. Umbridge's goal after being given this position is to put every aspect of life at Hogwarts under her personal control. She is such a nasty piece of work, she makes Snape look like a lovable person. Dolores Umbridge was clearly in Slytherin House when she was at Hogwarts based on her favoritism of students in that house and her robes of green tweed.

Umbridge interrupted Dumbledore's speech at the opening banquet. There were several points made which Hermione failed to point out to Harry and Ron. Fear not, the Detectives caught these Snitches. Of course, as Hermione pointed out, the Ministry is interfering at Hogwarts. Well, if you did not expect this at the end of Book 4, you missed a Bludger and fell off your broom again. This was as obvious as Snape being a Death Eater and a spy and Hagrid being the envoy to the giant. There were, however other components in the speech which were equally important clues about Umbridge. For example, the bit about magic being "passed through generation" and "amassed by our ancestors[44]." Umbridge is clearly talking about purebloods here. Muggle-born people clearly had no ancestors there to collect this knowledge, so she is saying they should not benefit from the efforts, which have been made. Slytherin certainly would have agreed, as would Voldemort and the Death Eaters. Mudbloods beware!

Umbridge refuses to teach the students magic and her class consists of them reading a theory textbook. In addition, her goal seems to be to drive Harry to the point his temper explodes, so she has a reason to give him detention. Umbridge's detentions are unconventional to say the least. During Harry's detentions, he is forced to write lines, but the quill she gives him does not use ink instead it cuts his hand open and writes the message in his blood. The twisted old bat! This woman is clearly deranged, a trademark quality of a Death Eater, especially the female Death Eater. (The only one that we can compare her with is Bellatrix Lestrange and the Detectives certainly know she is deranged.) Back to Harry being forced to cut his hand open for weeks at a time. Is there a reason the Ministry of Magic or the Death Eaters wants samples of Harry's blood? Are they testing it? If so, what do they hope to learn?

There is a great deal of evidence that Umbridge is a poor witch. Umbridge refuses to teach the students magic for several reasons. One of these reasons is that she does not want them to use the magic against her. Another example of her lack of skill is she cannot find a counter jinx for a jinx placed on a student by a fifteen-year-old witch. Also, she cannot remove the swamp Fred and George placed in the corridor, but Professor Flitwick was able to remove it in 10 minutes. Frankly, if a fully qualified witch, who is almost at the top of the Ministry of Magic, cannot counter the spells of students, there is a serious problem.

Another aspect about Umbridge, which makes her completely untrustworthy is her relationship to the Malfoy family. She is a good friend of Lucius Malfoy. She trusts his opinion above all others. It is almost as if he is her boss, instead of Fudge. Maybe he is, in another organization. *Wink* In addition, she calls Draco Malfoy by his first name, suggesting a whole new range of familiarity with him. Again, clearly, she is a friend of his family.

The suspicion of a Death Eater connection grows deeper after Umbridge has caught Harry using her fire. She makes the statement "what Cornelius doesn't know won't hurt him… He never knew that I ordered dementors after Potter last summer[45]." There are two important points here. What else doesn't Fudge know? Well, many things undoubtedly, but let's limit them to Umbridge. How about the fact he is surrounded by Death Eaters and they could overtake him or eliminate him at anytime? Of course, there is still possibility he is a Death Eater, as well. But if he is playing the role of France, then he is arrogant enough to believe he is in control the situation and they will not hurt him because they need him. Dictators kill those who put them in power first. Hitler took over France right after Poland and the Czech Republic. You cannot appease evil. Just because you work with them does not mean they will keep you alive. As soon as you have served your purpose, you get hit by a car or your plane crashes. The second issue in the quote is, of course, the Dementors were ordered to attack Harry. Did the Detectives catch the Snitch? During the Harry's hearing, Dumbledore suggests someone at the Ministry ordered his attack. Umbridge makes a small movement and tries to make Dumbledore's suggestion seem ludicrous to the rest of the Wizengamot. Also, Harry had thought Voldemort had ordered the attack. Well, it appears Umbridge did it. Or did she? Was she just the point man? Was this really her idea? Sure, she is sick enough to do such a thing, but she could easily have been following orders.

Next, she thinks of an alternate way to force information out of an individual when Snape informs her no Veritaserum is available. She chose to use the Cruciatus curse. Hmmm, the Detectives have heard of this method being used before and it was not by the Ministry of Magic. It was by Voldemort and Bellatrix Lestrange. Voldemort used it on Bertha Jorkins and Bellatrix Lestrange used it on Frank and Alice Longbottom. It seems strange to the Detectives such a senior-ranking member of the Ministry of Magic would want to use an Unforgivable Curse on a child. In most governments this would end a promising career. Again, the only people we have seen or heard about using unforgivable curses on children are Voldemort and Bellatrix. Voldemort has used all three unforgivable curses on Harry. Bellatrix suggested using the Cruciatus curse on Ginny to get the prophecy from Harry and quickly stated she would do it to her male Death Eater companions. This suggests to the Detectives, she thought they might not have been too keen to torture a child, so she was providing assurance they would not be responsible for the task. Later she does use the curse on Neville, when the other Death Eaters simply wanted to stun him. Bellatrix informs Harry later, you have to enjoy causing pain in order to perform the curse properly. This gives us insight into Umbridge's personality, which the Detectives suspected all along. She's deranged! This incident is some of the strongest evidence supporting the theory Umbridge is a Death Eater. Yes, the Detectives acknowledge during the days of Voldemort, Crouch, Sr. authorized the Unforgivable Curse to be used on the Death Eaters when they were being rounded up. Be that as it may, she is not planning to use the curse on a Death Eater; she is planning to use the curse on a child. What a Bludger!

During Umbridge's inspections of the other professors, there is an intriguing interchange between Umbridge and Snape. She inquires about Dumbledore's refusal to appoint him to the Defense Against the Dark Arts' job. Snape tells her to ask Dumbledore and asks if it is relevant. Her response is "The Ministry wants a thorough understanding of teachers'-er-backgrounds...[46]." This comment is interesting. Again, is it common knowledge Snape was a Death Eater? So, for what is she really fishing? Snape looked around the room for Harry and made his potion vanish, giving no marks for the class and assigned a punishment essay. This does the trick. He passes his inspection. Did Umbridge simply want to know if he was still on their side? Is it the Ministry or the Death Eater's side? Along these same lines, before the dream was planted in Harry's head about Sirius being tortured, Umbridge eliminated all known members of the Order stationed at Hogwarts, who could have helped Harry and let him know Sirius was safe at Headquarters, Dumbledore, McGonagall, and Hagrid. In fact, Hagrid and McGonagall were eliminated the previous night. Umbridge could have just fired Hagrid, but she attacked him. She knew attacking Hagrid in the middle of the night was sure to bring Minerva McGonagall out of the castle, wand drawn, charging at them, leaving them free to attack her as well, either killing or hospitalizing her. This got McGonagall out of the way at the same time as Hagrid. Very Convenient!

Detectives are sorry to say they will have to disagree completely with the context of Sirius' comment, "the world isn't split into good people and Death Eaters[47]." Although, this comment is true in principle, as are many of Sirius' comments, the Detectives believe it was wrongly applied to Umbridge. There is very little doubt in the Detectives minds that she is a Death Eater. On the off chance Umbridge does not yet have the Dark Mark burned into her arm at this point, she certainly will by the end of the series.

Other Professors

There are other professors who play a minor role, but have been named, and therefore, are important to the story. It is also important to know why they were hired. What is in their pasts? The Detectives have learned if a character has been given a name and has been played a role throughout the series, then the character is important. For example, Mrs. Figg and Aunt Petunia appear to be minor characters and hardly worth noticing. But the true detective had better take notice; they hold many important keys to the plot. Thus, these professors will be outlined simply because they are named, not just the professor of this subject or that subject, like many of the Dursley's unimportant neighbors.

Professor Flitwick is the Charms' professor and the head of Ravenclaw house. Thus, we know he is extremely wise. He is a tiny little wizard. We also know Flitwick was a dueling champion when he was younger. In addition, we know the Ministry of Magic would like to outlaw dueling. Thus, dueling is not very popular in today's wizarding world. It seems again, Dumbledore has made a decision to hire someone, who was less than popular at the time. These circumstances have long since been forgotten due to Flitwick's charming personality.

Professor Sprout is the Herbology professor and the Head of Hufflepuff house. She is really a mystery to the readers. Her name is interesting. Unsurprisingly, she is named for a plant, but it is the selection of the name is both interesting and the clue to her character. To sprout means to come forth and grow. Thus, the Detectives believe she will be encouraging growth in another character. That character is Neville, since Herbology is his best subject. To sprout also means to emerge and develop rapidly. Thus, the Detectives believe Professor Sprout's character will be one that will develop late in the series, but very quickly. She will be a key player in the ensuing battle. Remember Hufflepuffs are supposed to be patient, just, loyal, and unafraid of toil. Sprout will be important. Watch out Voldemort! Upon your rebirth, your first victim was a Hufflepuff student. You made a powerful enemy and the Detectives believe you will pay for the murder of Cedric Diggory, the Hufflepuffs will aid your enemies.

Professor Wilhelmina Grubbly-Plank is the substitute teacher for Care of Magical Creatures. She is an elderly witch with a severe haircut and a prominent chin. Professor Grubbly-Plank also smokes a pipe. She thinks highly of Dumbledore and will not give any information regarding Hagrid. She is also the one who nurses Hedwig back to health after Umbridge attacked her.

Hooch is slang for "crude, alcoholic liquor[48]." This is an interesting name for Madam Hooch, who is the flying instructor and the Quidditch referee. Nonetheless, she has appeared in each book, thus must be important. She is also trusted with Harry. In Book 3, she is given the job of overseeing his team's Quidditch practices in order for him to remain safe from Sirius Black. Thus, she must be loyal to Dumbledore and a powerful witch.

Madam Pince is the librarian. She is a very stern woman and has appeared in every book, thus far. The Detectives know very little about her. The name sounds a great deal like pincers, which Spiders use to hold item. This is appropriate given she is entrusted with all the books in the Hogwarts library, including the Restricted Section, which mostly contains books regarding Dark Magic. Madam Pince is very cautious about who touches these books.

Professors Vector and Sinastra are only mentioned by name. Professor Vector is a witch, who teaches Arithmancy. This is fitting because a vector is a mathematical term meaning a quantity and is often represented as a line. In biology, it is an agent, which carries pathogen from one organism to another, like a mosquito spreading or transferring malaria[49]. This suggests Professor Vector may be used to spread information, but the question is, for whom? Professor Sinastra teaches Astronomy. Her name sounds like sinister, which causes alarm due to the fact she was walking near the north tower around the same time as the Bloody Baron. Are the two of them up to something? Both Professor Vector and Sinastra are a complete mystery to the readers, we only know the subjects they teach. However, they are mentioned in Books 3, 4, and 5, so beware.

Chapter 3

Portraits at Hogwarts

The Hogwarts portraits play a key role in the Harry Potter series. Since they can talk and move from picture frame to picture frame, they are likely to play an important role in the battle between Harry and Voldemort. For example, the former heads of Hogwarts live in Dumbledore's office and are sworn to assist him. As Headmaster, he enlists their support with the Order of the Phoenix's business. Thus, it is logical to assume other portraits will assist the Death Eaters. Could a former Headmaster break ranks and assist the Death Eaters? What a tangled web!

The Headmasters and Headmistresses

Armando Dippet

Dippet sounds a great deal like dippy, which means not sensible or foolish. This is a fitting name for Armando Dippet, who was Dumbledore's predecessor. He is a frail looking wizard. Dippet was the Headmaster who expelled Hagrid, but was willing to listen to Dumbledore and keep Hagrid on as gamekeeper. Dippet also liked Tom Riddle. It was upon Tom's word, which he expelled Hagrid. Before the death of Myrtle, Dippet was actually considering allowing Tom to stay at Hogwarts over the summer. Thus, he is easily manipulated.

Dilys Derwent

Dilys looks and sounds like dilly, which is a word for one who is remarkable or extraordinary. Again this fits because Dilys was one of the most celebrated Headmistresses of Hogwarts. She was an elderly witch with long silver ringlets. Dilys was a St. Mungo's Healer, 1722-1741 and Headmistress of Hogwarts School of Witchcraft and Wizardry, 1741-1768.

Everard

Everard is a masculine name meaning strong as a wild boar[1]. He, like Dilys, was a celebrated head. He is a sallow-faced wizard with short, black bangs. He has a painting in the atrium in the Ministry of Magic. His appearance is similar to Snape. Also, the readers were not given his last name. When all the other headmasters and headmistresses were introduced they were given both first and last names. Perhaps he is Snape's ancestor. What do the detectives think?

Phineas Nigellus

Nigellus is Latin for blackish, which can either be taken literally, as he is a member of the Black family, or could suggest he is a member of the dark side. Phineas is a clever looking wizard. He was in Slytherin House and is extremely proud of this fact. He is also Sirius' great-great-grandfather. Sirius explained Phineas was the least popular Hogwarts Headmaster in the history of the school[2]. The Detectives are in no doubt why. It appears Phineas dislikes students and does not understand their thinking or even care how they feel.

What most intrigues the Detectives about Phineas is where he went the night Sirius died? Remember, to be a Black is to be almost royal and their house elf ended the Black line. Did the portraits hold court and force Kreacher to commit suicide? Or is Phineas really evil? After all, he calls Voldemort, the Dark Lord, which is a mark of a Death Eater. So, did he give Kreacher the order to kill Sirius? The Detectives doubt it. Kreacher's actions ended the Black family line, which is not something Phineas would have supported. The murder of Sirius could either free Phineas to actively help Voldemort or force him to change sides and willingly assist the Order, only time will tell.

Other Headmaster and Headmistress Portraits

The former headmasters and headmistresses are honor-bond to serve the current Headmaster. These paintings are different from the other paintings throughout Hogwarts. They do not just move throughout each other's frames, but they are free to move between their own portraits in other buildings. Also, they are typically feigning sleep and rarely speak to students. Another headmaster who spoke was a corpulent, red-nosed wizard called Fortescue, who could be related to the ice cream parlor owner. A gimlet-eyed witch with a thick wand, which resembled birch rod, also spoke to encourage Phineas to comply with Dumbledore's request. The Detectives wonder if she was the Headmistress, when Phineas attended Hogwarts, due to the implication she would cane Phineas if he failed to comply.

Other Portraits Throughout the Castle

The portraits may prove to be very useful. They have hung in the castle for years. The combination of all the portraits can tell the entire history of Hogwarts. Thus, they possess a wealth of knowledge. It is not clear what role they will play in the ensuing battle. Since the subjects can move between paintings throughout the castle, they would be more than capable of sounding an alarm. The Detectives believe they will be very useful in later books.

The Fat Lady

The Fat Lady is the portrait, which guards the entrance to the Gryffindor common room. She has been there for years and recognizes all the students who should be in the tower. The Fat Lady does not hesitate to tell students off for getting in late or for wasting her time. In addition, she will not let anyone in without the password. As evidence, she refused to allow Sirius Black to enter without the password, even though she probably recognized him. The name J.K. Rowling selected for this portrait is interesting because it is unconventional. It reminds the detectives of the saying when something appears to be hopeless, "it's not over until the *fat lady* sings." This could be code for it is not over until Harry, a Gryffindor, defeats Voldemort the heir of Slytherin.

Sir Cadogan

Frank Cadogan Cowper was a British painter, who did immense research on his subjects. Some of his paintings hang in the House of Commons[3]. It would be fitting for a portrait, who interrogates people, to be named after him. Sir Cadogan is a short, squat knight in a suit of armor. He has a fat gray pony. Sir Cadogan was probably a Gryffindor, since he was allowed to guard the entrance to the common room in year 3. It is his habit to challenge anyone who passes his paintings to a duel. As Harry discovered in the third year, the only thing that will distract Sir Cadogan is a quest. While guardian of the tower entrance, Sir Cadogan changed the password continually, thinking of ridiculously difficult passwords. Sir Cadogan was fired after allowing Sirius to enter the tower since he had all the passwords. Thus, he strictly abides by the rules. And McGonagall did not like this? Hmmm, the irony! In is important to note Bill remembers Sir Cadogan. Is it possible they developed a relationship and he will be loyal to Bill?

Violet

Violets represent faithfulness, virtue, modesty, and simplicity. Thus, the Detectives can assume Violet will assist those with what is right and protect Hogwarts. Her portrait hangs in a room off of the Great Hall and she is the Fat Lady's friend. The Detectives know very little about her at this point.

Chapter 4

Ghosts & Other Creatures at Hogwarts

Ghosts in General

There are many ghosts at Hogwarts, but the readers know the names of very few. Not every witch or wizard who dies becomes a ghost. Also, it is clear that the happiest of people are not the ones who become ghosts, case in point, Moaning Myrtle. Nick explained at the end of Book 5 he had become a ghost because he was afraid of death. Also, he had no idea what lay ahead in the afterlife. He choose to stay in the inbetween, rather than move from life to afterlife.

Nearly Headless Nick

Sir Nicholas de Mimsy-Porpington is the resident ghost of the Gryffindor tower. Nick is nearly headless due to a blotched beheading. He died on Halloween in 1492 and celebrated his 500th death day in

Harry's second year. Interestingly enough, this is exactly 489 years before James and Lily Potter's death. As a rule, Halloween is not a good day for Gryffindors.

Nick was petrified by the basilisk and therefore prevented Justin from being killed in year 2. The ghosts know a great deal about Hogwarts and Nick is more than willing to share his knowledge with the Gryffindor students as long as they do not offend him when he is sharing the information. Nick and Harry have developed a close relationship during Harry's tenure at Hogwarts. Harry was the only living person invited to Nick's death day party although, he was permitted to bring Hermione and Ron. In addition, Nick frequently gives Harry warnings as to what tricks Peeves is up to, so Harry will not be his victim. Finally, in Harry's second year, Nick talks Peeves into causing a disturbance in order to get Harry out of trouble. Is this normal? Does Nick typically get students out of trouble with Filch or does he have a special bond with Harry? The Detectives believe a pattern has been formed and Nick will prove to be an asset in the ensuing battle. As a ghost, he can appear without warning and has shown a willingness to manipulate others and use his knowledge in order to assist Harry.

The Bloody Baron

The Bloody Baron is the resident ghost of Slytherin House. He is completely covered with transparent silvery blood, but no one has asked how he got covered in all of that blood. Also, the Bloody Baron is the only one who can control Peeves, the poltergeist. Or is he really? He has been seen walking around near the north tower at around the time as Sinastra. Are the two of them up to something? This is a long way from the dungeon. The Detectives would like to know what he was doing so far from his region of the castle. Perhaps finding Peeves, but possibly something else. The Bloody Baron will play a larger role in future books. Hopefully, we will find out how and when he got covered in so much blood. The Detectives want to know even if the other ghosts do not.

The Fat Friar

The Fat Friar is the Hufflepuff ghost. The Fat Friar is a forgiving man. In the first book it was clear he wanted to give Peeves a second chance. The Friar seems to have a bit of Dumbledore's personality of forgiveness and a belief in second chances. Unfortunately, he does not seem to realize Peeves has not made any changes.

Moaning Myrtle

Moaning Myrtle is an extremely sensitive ghost who spends most of her time crying in the girls' bathroom on the first floor. The basilisk killed Myrtle the first time the Chamber of Secrets was opened. Therefore, she was for all intents and purposes the first victim of Voldemort. Myrtle has proved herself willing to help Harry on three separate occasions. First, she tells Harry how she died and where she saw the big yellow eyes. Thus, she helped him to find the entrance to Chamber of Secrets. In Book 4, Myrtle helped Harry by telling him to open the egg under water and told him he was correct that he had to find the Mermaids. Then, in the lake, Myrtle told Harry which direction he needed to go. This forms a pattern of events demonstrating a willingness to help Harry. Given a choice, the Detectives have no doubt that Myrtle will choose to help Harry, instead of Voldemort, the man responsible for her death.

Peeves

Peeve means annoyance. For example, a pet peeve is something, which annoys a person. Well, J.K. Rowling named Peeves correctly. Even so, Peeves is a great character. In fact, he is one of the Head Detective's personal favorites. He loves chaos and is called the Master of Chaos. Peeves wreaks havoc on the castle. He is always bouncing up and down breaking things, and constantly throwing things around. So, why does Dumbledore allow Peeves to stay in the castle? Perhaps, he is useful. In theory, Peeves would make a good alarm. Another idea is Dumbledore will or does use Peeves when he needs to distract everyone for a little while.

One interesting point about Peeves is he treated Lupin like dirt. Why? (See section on Lupin) The Detectives believe Peeves really liked James, Sirius, and Remus. They were troublemakers and wreaked havoc on the castle, just like Peeves. Later, Peeves doesn't tell anyone Sirius is in the castle, but gleefully tells Dumbledore he was there when asked who slashed the painting? Why didn't he say something at the time? Why was he waiting around to tell them all about it? Well, he liked Sirius and was happy to see him back to cause a little more trouble.

Furthermore, Peeves never got Fred and George in trouble. Why? They cause trouble, so he liked them. When Umbridge comes to the castle, Peeves hates her. He does everything he can to make her miserable. Now maybe we know why Peeves is around. In addition, when Fred and George were departing, Fred told Peeves to "give her hell from us[1]." Clearly, Fred, George, Peeves were kindred spirits, since Peeves had never been known to take an order from a student, but at these words from Fred, he sprang into a salute. Upon Umbridge's departure, Peeves chased her gleefully from the castle hitting her repeatedly with McGonagall's walking stick and a sock filled with chalk.

The Detectives expect Peeves will be a key player in the ensuing battle. As a poltergeist, he cannot be killed. This is a benefit! Also, when he wants to help people, he is capable of doing so. Unlike the ghosts, Peeves can move objects. Also, in spite of his love of chaos, he did not like Umbridge, although she put the school into complete chaos. Thus, Peeves does have some sense of loyalty, not just a love of chaos.

Fluffy

Fluffy is a three-headed dog who falls to sleep when music is played. Hagrid bought him in a pub, probably the Hog's Head. He lent him to Dumbledore to guard the Sorcerer's Stone in year 1. The Detectives wonder where Fluffy went at the end of Book 1. It is doubtful he will play a role in the battle because both sides know how to calm him.

Aragog

Aragog is an Acromantula, which is a "monstrous eight-eyed spider capable of human speech[2]." Their legs can reach up to fifteen feet and its pincers have a poisonous secretion. The Acromantula was a wizard-bred creature and has near human intelligence[3]. Aragog was Hagrid's pet in school. He was the reason Hagrid was expelled from Hogwarts. Aragog was thought to be the monster from the Chamber of Secrets. Aragog escaped to the forbidden forest, but was blinded by Tom Riddle's curse. Hagrid found Aragog a wife, Mosag. They had many children. In the second year, Harry and Ron met Aragog. At the time, Aragog said his children did not harm Hagrid upon his orders, but this does not apply to other humans, who wonder into the forest. Will this change after Hagrid was released from Azkaban and he tells Aragog what happened? The Detectives think so. The only reason Harry and Ron were not eaten was because the Weasley's car came to their rescue just in time. Then in the fourth year, one of Aragog's children was in the final stage of the maze and unintentionally injured Harry's leg. No doubt the spiders had been told not to hurt any of the students, since the spider had only picked Harry up and did not hurt him until Harry had injured the spider. It was very interesting the secretion did not affect Harry. It is poisonous, but the poison running through his veins does not bother Harry. The Detectives believe this is due to the combination of Basilisk poison and Fawkes' tears. This may have formed an antidote in Harry's blood. The Detectives believe Aragog, his wife, their many children and grandchildren will play a major role in the ensuing battle. Hagrid visits him in the forest and will have told him Voldemort has returned. Voldemort is also the reason Aragog is blind and Hagrid was expelled. Aragog undoubtedly hates Voldemort. This is enough of a reason to want revenge. Aragog will join the fight against Voldemort and will be a key player.

Thestrals

A thestral is a winged horse invisible to most people. Only people who have seen death can see the thestrals. Thus, many wizards consider them unlucky. They have an outstanding sense of direction. Hogwarts has the only domesticated herd in England. The thestrals pull the school carriages and take Dumbledore on long trips when he doesn't want to apparate. The Detectives believe the thestrals took Mrs. Figg to Harry's hearing. Also, it was the thestrals who took Harry and the others to the Ministry of Magic. The role the thestrals will play in the future will be one of emergency transport for both Harry and Dumbledore.

The Centaurs

The centaurs are half-man and half-horse. They consider their intelligence to be superior to human intelligence. Hagrid calls them "ruddy stargazers[4]." When unicorns were being killed in their forest, the only answer they are willing to give Hagrid to his question about whether they had seen anything odd is "Mars is bright tonight[5]." Other than Firenze, there are only three others the readers know by name—Bane, Ronan, & Magorian. The Centaurs' leader is Magorian. He has long black hair, high-cheek bones, and a chestnut body. Magorian is firm, but only believes in attacking the guilty. Also, he does not believe in harming the innocent. Bane means annoyance or to cause misery[6]. Bane's beard, hair and body are black and he has a terrible temper. Also, Bane was furious with Firenze for saving Harry in the Forbidden Forest. Ronan has red hair and a red beard, and a chestnut body, with a long, reddish tail. Ronan is much more even-tempered. He was not as angry with Firenze and suggested Firenze felt he was acting for the best. The Detectives suspect that Magorian is the father of Bane and Ronan given Magorian's features are a combination of the two. Another centaur who was described is a hard-faced gray centaur with a temperament similar to Bane. When Firenze agreed to help Dumbledore and teach at Hogwarts, the herd banished Firenze due to their belief that working for humans is entering into servitude. Since Hagrid prevented the herd from kicking Firenze to death, the centaurs turned on Hagrid as well. The Detectives suspect the centaurs, like the people from the Middle Ages, will move in Firenze's direction.

The Dementors

The word Dementor sounds a great deal like demented, which means insane or mentally ill. This is fitting since J.K. Rowling says the Dementors represent mental illness or depression[7]. The Dementors are large, dark creatures, which glide when they move. They guarded the wizard prison of Azkaban until the end of Book 5. When Dementors approach, all the lights go out and a horrible cold sweeps the area. They have the power to force their victims to relive the worst memories of their lives. Their last weapon is known as the Dementor's kiss. They clamp their jaw over their victim's mouth and suck the soul out of the body. As dark creatures, Voldemort considers them his natural allies. The Dementors joined Voldemort and can be expected to attack those fighting against him.

The Giants

The Giants are about 20 feet tall; some of the larger ones are 25 feet tall. As a rule, they are extremely violent in nature. Giants, like trolls and dragons, have something in their blood or skin that makes them extremely difficult to attack with a spell. Their weak point is their eyes, just like the dragon. Even Hagrid, who was only half-giant, did not feel Harry and Hermione pushing him and was not stunned by the stunning spells. They do not like wizards, especially when magic is used against them. In the last century, the Giants had driven themselves almost to extinction during the Giant Wars. Those who remained joined Voldemort. The Aurors killed a few, but after Voldemort's fall, the Giants went to live in the mountains. Voldemort clearly stated during his rebirthing ceremony he would recall the giants. Upon hearing this plan, Dumbledore immediately took action. Dumbledore sent his own envoys to the giants, Hagrid and Madam Maxime, both of whom are half-giant. They left immediately after year 4 and took gifts to Karkus, the Gung, the leader of the giants. The name, Karkus, sounds like carcass, which is appropriate, since Hagrid and Madame Maxime took him gifts and gave him Dumbledore's messages for two days before the giants had a battle amongst themselves and killed him. The new Gung, Golgomath, was not interested in what Dumbledore's messengers had to say and dangled Hagrid by his feet. Madam Maxime performed magic on them, which means they will never be able to visit the

Giant camp again. Hagrid and Madam Maxime remained and observed the camp. They saw Voldemort's envoy meet with Golgomath and realized they were allies. Hagrid and Madam Maxime went from cave to cave to talk to the giants who had not wanted the new Gung. They had seven or eight convinced to join Dumbledore, until the cave was raided. Afterwards, those who survived were not interested. The hope is the message will be remembered and some will come when they get tired of being beaten up or enslaved.

Grawp

Grawp is Hagrid's half-brother. He is sixteen feet tall. Hagrid brought him back with him when he returned from his mission to the giants. Hagrid hid Grawp in the Forbidden Forest. Grawp is violent, but Hagrid is determined to teach him English. When it appeared Hagrid would lose his job, Hagrid introduced Grawp to Harry and Hermione. This proved to be useful given Grawp saved them from the Centaurs. Grawp had missed Hagrid and wanted to know where he was. The Detectives believe Grawp will prove to be very useful to the Order. Perhaps Hagrid had a second reason for introducing Grawp to Harry. As the Giants had heard of Dumbledore and Voldemort, thus, they had probably heard of Harry Potter. Hagrid probably hoped Grawp would be able to recognize Harry and protect him in the future. Hagrid has befriended and tamed several monsters, which the rest of the wizarding world thought impossible to do. As a result, they are extremely loyal to him.

Goblins

Goblins are short, clever creatures, with pointed beards, long fingers and feet. In History of Magic, Hogwarts students have learned a great deal about the Goblin Rebellions, but as Harry doesn't pay attention, we do not know what happened. They are capable of handling wizards, but have never achieved equal rights. There are still treated as second class citizens in the wizarding society. The Ministry of Magic has a Goblin Liaison Office and Mockridge is in charge.

Goblins are obsessed with gold. They run Gringotts, the wizarding bank. On Harry's first trip to Gringotts, Griphook took Harry down to his vault. Dumbledore mentions Griphook again, as the contact goblin for wizards wishing to make a donation to Comic Relief, in Fantastic Beasts and Where to Find Them[8]. This suggests Griphook works with noble causes. Later, the Goblins made several bets with Bagman, which he lost and never paid. Ragnok "reckons the Ministry did a cover-up[9]." Thus, he is feeling anti-wizard according to Bill Weasley, who has been trying to reach out to Ragnok for the Order. Perhaps the Goblins will take a stand in the upcoming war, since they suffered the last time Voldemort took power.

<u>Chapter 5</u>

<u>Hogwarts Students</u>

The Hogwarts students are a very important group of characters. The students are sorted into four houses, Gryffindor, Hufflepuff, Ravenclaw, and Slytherin. Harry Potter will spend up to seven years with his fellow Hogwarts Students. Thus, this group of characters will grow up with the famous Harry Potter.

<u>Gryffindor</u>

Gryffindor is the combination of two words; griffin and d'or. A griffin is a mythological creature with the head and wings of an eagle and the hindquarters of a lion. D'or is French for gold. Thus, Gryffindor literally means Griffin of gold. Gryffindor House is known for bravery, daring, nerve, courage, and gallantry[1]. Their symbol is the lion and their colors are scarlet and gold, which resembles Scotland's flag. Albus Dumbledore, himself, was a Gryffindor.

<u>Katie Bell, Alicia Spinnet, & Angelina Johnson</u>

Bell, Spinnet, and Johnson are the Chasers on the Gryffindor Quidditch team. Very little is known about them, thus far. Johnson becomes the Captain in year 5 and she seemed to be channeling Wood's spirit of win or else. Johnson has a bad temper, similar to that of both Harry and McGonagall. She, also, has a redeeming quality; she is willing to give someone who shows potential and comes from a family of good Quidditch players a chance. In this respect, she differs from Wood. Ron could have easily blown the season for Gryffindor, but Angelina was willing to give him a chance to prove himself. Johnson and Spinnet will both graduate this year. So, Katie Bell will be Captain of the team during year 6.

Lavender Brown

The flower, lavender represents faithfulness. It is also aromatic and used in both medicines and perfume. This could suggest Lavender has a future in healing. Lavender is the best friend of Parvati. She went to the Yule Ball with Dean Thomas. Lavender has shown she is really does belong in Gryffindor House. She is brave. She, like Dean, helped Hagrid when the skrewts ran amuck, instead of running and hiding in Hagrid's cabin like the majority of the class. However, Lavender did not initially believe Harry and Dumbledore that Voldemort had returned. She did come around and even joined the D.A. when it was formed.

Colin & Dennis Creevey

Colin and Dennis are brothers from a muggle family. They were placed in Gryffindor House. Both are very short and have mousy hair. They regard Harry as their hero. Colin is famous for taking pictures all the time, particularly of Harry. Colin was the first person the basilisk petrified in the second year. He was only saved because he saw it through his camera lens. Dennis is a year younger than Colin and fell in the lake on his way to the Sorting Ceremony. Harry tries to avoid the Creevey brothers whenever possible because he finds the constant staring at his scar and their hero-worship annoying. The Detectives believe Colin and Dennis could prove to be very useful indeed. The fact they clearly adore Harry and were placed in Gryffindor could make them an asset to both Harry and the Order. The Detectives would advise Harry to be kind to the Creevey brothers because he may need them in the future.

Seamus Finnigan

Seamus is in the same year at Hogwarts as Harry. His best friend is Dean Thomas. Seamus is known for catching things on fire when he is casting spells. As his name suggests, Seamus is Irish. Seamus's mother is a witch and his father is a muggle. Harry met Seamus' mother at the World Cup. Unfortunately, the Finnigan's are some of the people who believed Harry was crazy and Dumbledore was senile. Seamus has allowed himself to be swayed by his mother and the newspapers instead of trusting four years of evidence he personally collected while living in the same dormitory with Harry. Had Harry not been so hotheaded he probably could have swayed Seamus back to his side simply by answering Seamus's question regarding what happened in the graveyard. The Detectives do not believe it was all that unreasonable. Seamus did eventually believe Harry. Interestingly enough, it was after he got his question answered. He went further than just telling Harry he believed him. Seamus sent the article to his mother in order to bring her around. So, after Seamus saw the light, he started converting others. Not a bad person, just a doubting Thomas. Next, Seamus joined the D.A. Unfortunately, they were exposed that night, so he did not get much practice.

The other important thing to note about Seamus is even when he did not believe Harry he never told Umbridge on him. They lived in the same dormitory, ate at the same table, and had all the same classes together. Don't try to tell the Detectives Seamus never heard anything for which he could not have turned on Harry or noticed the absence of half of the Gryffindor House. We know for a fact he heard about Harry giving *The Quibbler* interview because Seamus was sitting at the table, when Neville, Dean, and Harry were discussing it. Surely, the D.A. was discussed in the dormitory. The fact still remains Seamus never turned them in to anyone. Why? Possibly he was reserving judgment until he got his question answered. Maybe it was a situation like Ron in the fourth year and he really missed having Harry as a friend, but he could not bring himself to admit he was wrong and then there was the whole issue of his mother finding out about it. The Detectives don't know, but the fact is Seamus only questioned, he never betrayed Harry. This shows he can be trusted in the future.

Lee Jordan

Lee Jordan is Fred and George's friend. He commentates the Quidditch matches in a biased way, often risking having his megaphone taken away by McGonagall. Like the twins, he is a troublemaker, but seems to know where to draw the line. Lee was more than willing to help the twins get their joke shop off the ground. He assisted in helping to test their merchandise. Lee was a member of the D.A. In regards to Umbridge, he was one of the vocal students and paid the price for it by attending one of her hand slicing detentions. In addition, he put two nifflers in her office by levitating them through the window. This suggests Lee is a skilled wizard because he is capable of levitating large objects. Lee may prove to be an asset to both Harry and the Order in the future. Year 5 was Lee's seventh year at Hogwarts, the Detectives would not be a bit surprised if Fred and George brought him into the Order of the Phoenix following graduation.

Hermione Jane Granger[2]

Hermione's name come from Shakespeare's *A Winter's Tale.* She was the beautiful, virtuous, kind, and persuasive Queen of Sicily. Each of these characteristics represents the Hermione in the *Harry Potter.* Jane is the name of a brilliant author, Jane Austin, which is appropriate because Hermione is so intelligent and well read. Granger hid Scotland's crown jewels from Oliver Cromwell until his death, then returned them to the people. This represents Hermione's loyalty and protection.

Hermione is one of Harry's best friends. She is muggle born and has long curly hair. Hermione is an extremely hard worker, with a photographic memory, and quite bossy. She has a cat named Crookshanks. This is an interesting name. A crook is one who makes a living by dishonest means or a part bent like a hook. This is a frightening thought. A crook is living with Hermione. Now that is disturbing, but course, there are crooks in the Order. A shank is the shaft of a key. So are Hermione and her cat the key which will help Harry win the war?

Hermione is the equivalent of Lupin. She, like the others, is highly intelligent, but for the most part, even-tempered, rational, and clear thinking. Hermione has been an essential part of most of Harry's dangerous adventures, the exception being in the second year when the basilisk petrified her and of course, neither she nor Ron, were in the graveyard in year 4. After seeing the way Winky was treated at the Quidditch World Cup, Hermione started S.P.E.W., which shows her attempt to persuade people to change their ways. During the Triwizard Tournament, Hermione met Viktor Krum and started dating him. They still keep in touch and the Detectives question whether Hermione will bring him into the Order.

It was Hermione who discovered Rita Skeeter was an unregistered animagus, and how she was able to listen in on private conversations. Then, Hermione blackmailed Rita and prevented her from writing for the Daily Prophet for one year. It is a good thing Hermione caught her when she did. Had Rita published an article about the last conversation she overheard it would have been deadly. Rita heard Dumbledore's orders to Snape, saw Sirius, and the parting of the way between Dumbledore and Fudge. Later, when the ten Death Eaters escaped from Azkaban, Hermione wrote to Rita

Skeeter and persuaded her to write an article about Voldemort's rebirth. It was also Hermione's idea for Harry to secretly teach other students Defense Against the Dark Arts, in order to defend themselves against Voldemort and his Death Eaters. This lead to the formation of Dumbledore's Army.

Hermione took part in the battle with the Death Eaters in the Department of Mysteries. She was doing well during the battle, proving she is not just book smart. Ultimately Dolohov knocked her unconscious. As Hermione has been such a key part of each of Harry's adventures, the Detectives believe she will continue play a key part in the ensuing battle.

Neville Longbottom

Neville is a short, plump, round-faced, blond-haired boy. He is a pureblood wizard with a terrible memory. The Detectives wonder if this is due to someone putting a memory charm on him when he was very young. If so, who placed it on him? Was it Lucius Malfoy? Was he part of the group who tortured Neville's parents and did not want Neville to be able to identify him? Or was it Neville's Gran because she wants to save Neville from more pain. Neville has a pet toad named Trevor, a gift from his Uncle Algie for getting into Hogwarts. The Detectives wonder if Trevor is an animagus. He is always wondering off, but never fails to return to Neville's side.

Neville is the dark horse in the Harry Potter series. Neville is a friend of Harry, Ron, and Hermione. He, like Harry has suffered at the hand of Voldemort and his Death Eaters. His parents, like Harry's, had narrowly escaped Voldemort three times. Then, they were tortured into insanity by Crouch, Jr. and the Lestranges. Neville's parents, Frank and Alice Longbottom are still in St. Mungo's. As a result, Neville's Grandmother raised him. Neville has been along for a couple of the dangerous adventures, including the encounter with Fluffy, the Forbidden Forest, and the battle with the Death Eaters at the end of the fifth year.

Neville is Snape's least favorite student, second only to Harry. Snape is always harassing Neville in potions and giving him detentions. This is a very important clue. Snape is forcing Neville to learn because he knows it is a matter of personal safety for Neville, like Harry. Neville's worst fear is Professor Snape. In the third year, Neville's boggart turned into Professor Snape. This is interesting. The boggart is Snape, not the Lestranges. The Detectives believe this is interesting because Snape has caused him no harm and the Lestranges have put his parents in St. Mungo's for life.

Neville's favorite and best subject is Herbology. Thus, it is no surprise he received a plant from his Great-uncle Algie for his fifteenth birthday.

However, the plant he received is quite intriguing. It is called Mimbulus mimbletonia. It appears to be a small gray cactus covered in boils, not spines. This plant is from Assyria and extremely rare. Uncle Algie seems to have traveled far and wide for this year's birthday gift, didn't he? It seemed important to him Neville had this plant. The reason for this could be due to it's "amazing defensive mechanism[3]." When Neville prods it the plants it sprays him with Stinksap, which is not poisonous. The Detectives wonder if this defense mechanism not only protects the plant, but also its owner. Perhaps this would explain why Uncle Algie was insistent Neville have this plant immediately following the return of Voldemort. The Detectives suspect it is the worst fear of Neville's relatives that he will meet the same end as his parents. It is also important to note McGonagall makes Mimbulus mimbletonia the password for Gryffindor tower for the fifth year. This means McGonagall had talked to Neville's grandmother or someone in his family and discovered Neville has received this plant as a gift. Thus, he would be likely to remember it as the password. This took ammunition away from Umbridge.

At the end of Book 5, Neville goes to the Department of Mysteries with Harry, Ron, Hermione, Ginny, and Luna. Neville's wand was broken as he tried to get to Hermione when she was knocked unconscious. At this point, Neville reveals he has been using his father's wand. Wow, this is huge! Mr. Ollivander told Harry in Book 1 "you will never get such good results with another wizard's wand[4]." So, this is the root of Neville's problem at school. He is still performing well, but his work would be much better with his own wand. The Detectives believe Neville will show remarkable improvement in the sixth year. Furthermore, Neville is the last student fighting other than Harry. This was a Bludger. Neville is a powerful wizard, just as powerful as Harry, in fact. Neville meets Bellatrix and is tortured by her. In spite of this, the Death Eaters never knock out Neville.

The mystery surrounding Neville is finally answered in Dumbledore's office. As it turns out the Detectives are right, Neville is truly the Dark Horse. The prophecy was made in June of 1980, could have applied to either Harry Potter or Neville Longbottom. The only reason Harry is the famous one is because Voldemort chose him. This leads to several questions. What is it these two babies had in common even before they were born? Well, they both had parents in the Order of the Phoenix who had escaped Voldemort three times. But would this alone allow them to defeat the most powerful dark wizard of all time? The Detectives doubt it. So, what else could two baby boys born on the same day have in common? Could the key be in their genetics? Who would have the power to defeat the heir of Slytherin? The other founders united and defeated Salazar Slytherin, particularly the heir of Godric Gryffindor. It would make sense the combination of their blood into two heirs would produce the power to defeat the heir of Slytherin. The Detectives believe Neville is an heir of both Gryffindor and Hufflepuff. Alice Longbottom, who has prematurely aged, resembles Albus Dumbledore, who the Detectives believe is Gryffindor's direct descendent. Since, Neville is a pureblood wizard his genealogy should be easy to trace. The Detectives also believe Neville is a descendent of Hufflepuff. This is based on the fact Neville is extremely loyal. The Sorting Hat took a long time to decide where to place Neville. This could be the reason why. The Detectives believe Neville will be one of the most important characters in the ensuing battle. Neville will also avenge his parents' insanity and overcome the possible memory charm. (See Section of Bellatrix Lestrange)

Parvati Patil

Parvati's name comes from Hinduism. She is the goddess of plenty[5]. Parvati is considered the most beautiful girl in her year. Her twin, Padma is in Ravenclaw. Parvati went to the Yule Ball with Harry and thoroughly enjoyed sitting at the head table and being the center of attention on the dance floor for the opening dance. Parvati does have redeeming qualities, though. In year 1, Neville fell off of his broom in their first flying lesson and Malfoy made fun of him. It was Parvati who told Malfoy to "shut up[6]." It was also Parvati who jumped to defend Harry when McGonagall came running outside. Thus, Parvati showed early on, she is brave and willing to defend "weaker" people. In the fifth year, Parvati joined the D.A.

Dean Thomas

Dean is in Harry's year at Hogwarts and shares his dormitory. Dean comes from a muggle family and is Seamus's best friend. He is a West Ham soccer fan. The readers have been told in each book, Dean is good at drawing. We do not know why this is important, but it clearly will become so because it has been mentioned with such frequency. His boggart was a severed hand, possibly because if he lost his hand he would no longer be able to draw. Regardless of the reason, the Detectives strongly advise Dean to stay away from Wormtail due to the fact Wormtail's new hand was a gift from Voldemort and could easily be jinxed. When Voldemort placed the new hand on Wormtail's arm he said, "May your loyalty never waver again, Wormtail[7]."

The Detectives would not put it past Voldemort to put something in that hand to make sure if Wormtail's loyalty wavered, he did not get to keep his nice powerful hand. So, watch out Dean and stay away from Wormtail!

Another point important to note is even though Dean was Seamus's best friend, he did not turn against Harry when Seamus did. This shows strength of character. Dean joined the D.A. without Seamus, but when Seamus was ready to see the truth, he brought him along. The Detectives believe Dean has leadership potential. Another trait the Detectives particularly like about Dean is that he stood up to Umbridge regarding Lupin. When she referred to dangerous half-breeds, he was quick to say Lupin was the best teacher they ever had. Dean was also willing to help Hagrid when the skrewts had gone wild and most of the rest of the class had run to hide in Hagrid's cabin. Again, the Detectives believe Dean Thomas will prove to be an asset and a future member of the Order of the Phoenix.

Fred & George Weasley

Fred and George Weasley are a pair like no other. They are known as the school troublemakers. In fact when they leave Hogwarts, it is said the position of Troublemakers-in-chief has been recently vacated. It has also been said these two could give another set of troublemakers, James Potter and Sirius Black, a run for their money. Like Sirius, the twins make rash decisions. It was through one of these rash decisions the twins stole the Marauder's Map from Filch's office. The Detectives wonder if Fred and George ever discovered Sirius was one of the authors. The twins gave this map to Harry in the third year so that he would be able to go to Hogsmeade. Surprisingly, they only received three O.W.L.s each. The reason why is a great mystery to everyone. The twins are extremely talented. Their inventions range from a swamp to the creation of extendable ears. Their dream is to open a joke shop. They placed a bet at the World Cup betting their entire savings hoping they would then have the money to start their joke shop. After winning the Triwizard Tournament, Harry gave the twins his gold, making their dream to start the joke shop a reality. The Detectives believe this is the reason for their loyalty to Harry. Fred and George have been dealing with Mundungus in order to get some of the ingredients for their inventions. Again, this is another trait of Sirius'. The Detectives believe after Sirius's death, Dung will be turning to the twins for support and will be loyal to them.

When Umbridge took over Hogwarts, the twins did their best to make her miserable. After they dropped out of Hogwarts, the Detectives believe that it is clear Fred and George joined the Order of the Phoenix, as they wanted to join the Order before their seventh year. The Detectives believe the inventors will develop something the Order will be able to use against Voldemort and the Death Eaters. Unfortunately, it is likely one will die in the ensuing battle.

Ginny Molly Weasley[8]

Ginny Weasley will play a major role in the series. She is the only daughter and the youngest child in the Weasley family. Ginny has bright brown eyes and, like all her brothers, flaming red hair. She is a year behind Harry and Ron. In the second year she was possessed by Tom Riddle and taken into the Chamber of Secrets. She had a crush on Harry until his fifth year. Ginny went to the Yule Ball with Neville, where she met Michael Corner and started dating him. In the fifth year, Ginny was part of the group in Umbridge's office who escaped. Ginny hit Malfoy with the Bat Bogey hex. She then went on to the Department of Mysteries, with Ron, Harry, Neville, Hermione, and Luna. Size is not an indication of power in the words of Fred Weasley. This definitely applies to Ginny. The Detectives believe Ginny will definitely play a key role in the ensuing battle. Lucius Malfoy targeted her, in the second year, and Ginny has shown herself willing to help, both in the Order of the Phoenix and with Harry Potter. The Detectives believe Ginny will survive, join the Order after her graduation and marry Neville Longbottom.

Ron Bilius Weasley[9]

Ron is one of Harry's best friends. Ron comes from a family of pureblood wizards, who are extremely poor. He has five brothers and one sister. He had a pet rat, who turned out to be an animagus, named Peter. Ron now has an owl, named Pigwidgeon, who was a gift from Sirius. The word pigwidgeon is a word referring to anything small. Ron's dream of playing Quidditch for Gryffindor came true, in his fifth year, when he started playing Keeper.

Ron was one of the first people Harry met on the train to Hogwarts and has been a partner in many of Harry's dangerous adventures. Like Harry, Ron is extremely lazy. The Detectives believe he has a great deal of talent, but like many talented people does not apply himself. He is an excellent wizard chess player. Chess is considered a war game and "for thousands of years, chess and variants of chess were used by civilian and military personnel alike for entertainment, education, for 'simulation[10].'" Ron's skill at chess saved Harry, Ron, and Hermione's lives during the first year.

The Detectives believe Ron's expertise at chess is a sign Ron is equipped for the battle ahead.

Ron is terrified of spiders and his fear increased in the second year when he and Harry ventured into the forest after Hagrid had given them the clue to follow the spiders. This was when they came in contact with Aragog, the acromantula. This adventure could have proven deadly had the Weasley's flying car, not shown up to rescue them. During this adventure, the readers saw Ron's fear incapacitate him, so the Detectives believe Voldemort and the Death Eaters will use this fear against him in order to reach Harry.

Ron is the equivalent of Sirius. He is Harry's best friend and would give his life for him. This became evident in the third year, when he told Sirius Black he would have to kill all three of them if he wanted to kill Harry. This was brave, but not the smartest thing to say to someone convicted of murdering 13 people with a single curse, who had just kidnapped you and had your wand. However, this earned Ron the respect of Sirius.

In the fifth year, Ron was a member of the organization he, Hermione, and Harry created—Dumbledore's Army. Also, Ron was part of the group in Umbridge's office who organized the escape and made it possible for the group to go to the Department of Mysteries. Then, Ron battled the Death Eaters for the first time. One of them put a spell on Ron that made him go funny. The Detectives believe Ron will be one of the most important players in the ensuing battle. Ron has played a part in each of Harry's adventures. The Detectives also believe Ron will marry Hermione. The signs have been there for a while, but they have not dated yet.

Oliver Wood

Wood is a dense area containing trees or a strong material used for building. This could be a clue to Oliver Wood's character. He is clearly strong. Wood is a pureblood wizard based on the fact he had never heard of basketball. Wood was the Captain of the Gryffindor Quidditch team for years 1-3 and is absolutely obsessed with Quidditch. As long as his team won the cup it did not matter who got hurt in the process or even if a famous mass murderer was after his seeker. With this personality, the Detectives question, why the Sorting Hat placed Wood in Gryffindor. Yes, he is brave when it comes to Quidditch, but will he get his priorities in order like McGonagall suggested. Wood made the reserve team of Puddlemore United. Harry, Ron, and Hermione ran into him at the Quidditch World Cup. The Detectives expect to see Wood again, as his flying skill and drive could be an asset to Harry.

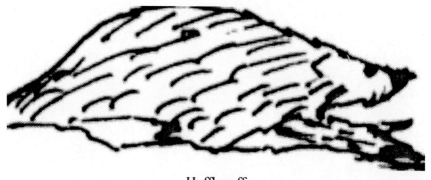

Hufflepuff

Hufflepuff House is known for being patient, just, loyal, and hard working[11]. Its symbol is the badger. The colors are yellow and blue.

Hannah Abbott

Hannah is one of the Hufflepuff prefects in year 5. In addition, she is the first to receive the Calming Draught in the O.W.L. year. Also, Hannah is a member of the Dumbledore's Army and she helps to defend Harry on the train back to King's Cross Station. The Detectives believe she will become a member of the Order of the Phoenix.

Susan Bones

Susan is the niece of Madam Bones and a member of Dumbledore's Army (D.A.). Voldemort and the Death Eaters directly affected the Bones family. Susan had an uncle, aunt, and cousins killed by the Death Eaters. The Detectives gather Susan is very close to her aunt, possibly because she is one of her only remaining nieces. The reason for this theory is Susan knew about Harry's hearing and about his Patronus. On the train back to King's Cross Station, Susan helped to defend Harry when Malfoy, Crabbe, and Goyle attacked him. The Detectives believe Susan Bones will be a key player in the ensuing battle against Voldemort and his Death Eaters due to her family history and her eagerness to join the D.A. She will also be a future member of the Order of the Phoenix. Strong bones are the essential part of body, which enable a person to stand and they are also the last part of the body to deteriorate in the grave. Thus, it is an appropriate name for one who had family members put in an early grave by Voldemort. It is also logical to interpret the Bones' family will help the Order to stand strong.

Cedric Diggory

Cedric was both the Captain and Seeker on the Hufflepuff Quidditch team. In addition, he was Cho's boyfriend. He was one of the Triwizard champions from Hogwarts. He and Harry helped each other throughout the tournament and particularly in the maze. Cedric was loyal, kind, and valued fair play. Sadly, Cedric was killed the night Voldemort rose again. His echo, like the other echoes which came out of Voldemort's wand, helped to save Harry's life.

Justin Finch-Fletchley

Justin is a curly haired boy who comes from a muggle family, like Hermione. In the second year, he was petrified and nearly everyone believed Harry was responsible. This is because of an incident, which occurred during the dueling club. When a snake came out of Malfoy's wand and turned toward Justin, Harry in desperation told the snake not to attack Justin. The problem was he had said this, not in English as he thought, but in parseltongue. The next person to be petrified was Justin. Thus, people believed Harry was responsible. In the fifth year, Justin became a member of the Dumbledore's Army and defended Harry when he was attacked. The Detectives believe Justin is a future member of the Order of the Phoenix due to his readiness to defend Harry as exhibited in this instance

Ernie Macmillan

Macmillan is the name of an old and famous British publishing company, which suggests Ernie Macmillan comes from one of the oldest and wealthiest pureblood wizard families. Ernie is a pompous, arrogant boy, who is nonetheless good to have on your side. Ernie also became a prefect in year 5. He was willing to say loud and clear he believed Harry and Dumbledore when it was not the popular opinion. He states, "My family have always stood firm behind Dumbledore, and so do I[12]." Ernie becomes a member of Dumbledore's army and defended Harry on the train back to King's Cross Station when Malfoy, Crabbe, and Goyle tried to hex Harry. The Detectives believe Ernie will become a member of the Order of the Phoenix for two reasons. First, he was one of the few to stand up and say he believed Dumbledore and Harry; and second, he was willing to protect Harry, when he was attacked. It is also interesting, Ernie knows the Malfoy family and seems to really dislike them for some reason. The Detectives are curious as to why? Granted most people dislike the

Malfoys, which could have something to do Lucius threatening to curse peoples' families in order to bend them to his will. It would be interesting to know what the Malfoys have done to the Macmillans, especially what Narcissa has done, since Ernie's comment was directed at her. "I must say, I'm looking forward to seeing Malfoy's mother's face when he gets off the train[13]."

Zacharias Smith

Smith was a member of the Hufflepuff Quidditch Team. He overheard the planning meeting for Dumbledore's Army, so he was given a grudging invitation. He is not well-liked and is critical of Harry. But he comes to all the meetings and is not the one who tells Umbridge about the organization. Given Smith was on the Hufflepuff Quidditch team his attitude may have a very simple explanation. Possibly, he was a good friend of Cedric Diggory. Maybe that is why he wants to know how Cedric died and why he is in the D.A, learning to defend himself. This could explain his attitude toward Harry. It is possible he resents that Harry came out alive, when Cedric died. Smith may surprise the Detectives and become a member of the Order of the Phoenix.

Ravenclaw

Ravenclaw House is known for students who are the most highly intelligent and witty[14]. Their symbol is the eagle, which is a bird of prey and represents strength and freedom. Their colors are blue and silver.

Terry Boot & Anthony Goldstein

Both Boot and Goldstein are in Ravenclaw House. They both joined Dumbledore's Army and are friends of Michael Corner. Goldstein is also a Ravenclaw prefect. An important item to note about Terry Boot is he has been in Dumbledore's office. There are a limited number of students who have been in the Headmaster's office, including Tom Riddle, Harry Potter, and the Weasley children. Also, the reason people go to that office are very few, either something is gravely wrong, they have done something outstanding, or the person is in serious trouble. So, why was Boot in Dumbledore's office? The other key point is one of the headmaster's portraits spoke to Boot. This is exceptional. The portraits did not even speak to Harry until the end of his fifth year. Why would the portrait speak to Boot? Is Boot a descendent of the portrait? They are always pretending to sleep when Harry is in the office. This implies Boot was left alone in Dumbledore's office. Again, this suggests Dumbledore trusts Boot. The Detectives recommend keeping a close eye on Boot. Also, on the train back to King's Cross Station when Malfoy, Crabbe, and Goyle tried to hex Harry, Boot and Goldstein were members who defended Harry by raining hexes and jinxes down on the three troublemakers. The Detectives believe they will become members of the Order of the Phoenix due to their readiness to defend Harry exhibited here. After all that is one of the Order's primary objectives.

Cho Chang

Cho is a pretty girl who Harry had a crush on for a couple of years. He wanted to go to the Yule Ball with her, but Cedric asked her first. Consequently, she became Cedric's girlfriend. She, of course, was heartbroken when he was killed. In year 5 she is known for crying all the time. Ironically, Harry gets his chance to date Cho in his fifth year and even gets his first kiss from her. It appears Cho has turned to Harry for comfort, since she thinks he is probably dealing with similar internal problems. After all, Harry was the one with Cedric when he died. The Detectives are skeptical, they think Cho simply likes famous wizards. Cedric was famous, Harry is famous and she has dated them both. Hmmm, seems fishy to the Detectives. Also, she stands by her sneak friend Marietta. Cho point blank refuses to accept Marietta sold the whole group out, including her. Instead, she criticizes Hermione for the jinx. Again, she refuses to acknowledge without the jinx, she, along with the rest of the group, would have been expelled. So, keep an eye on Cho! She is not trustworthy!

Penelope Clearwater

Penelope comes from Greek mythology and she was the wife of Odysseus. She waited 20 years after Odysseus had sailed to Troy for him to return to her. Penelope did not give up hope. She had many suitors during this time period, but refused to marry any of them[15]. Penelope Clearwater was a Ravenclaw prefect in the same year as Percy. In addition, she was Percy's girlfriend. It is unknown if this relationship continued after Hogwarts. In the second year, the basilisk petrified her with Hermione. Percy was extremely distraught when she was petrified. The Detectives are skeptical about Penelope. Perhaps Percy is just a suitor with whom Penelope is toying.

Michael Corner

Michael is Ginny's boyfriend throughout most of year 5. They met at the Yule Ball. After he and Ginny split up, he started dating Cho. Michael is a member of the D.A. The Detectives are undecided about whether or not he will join the Order of the Phoenix. They believe it is likely he joined the D.A. for two reasons. One explanation is because he was dating Ginny and the second reason is so he could pass his O.W.L. Clearly, very few people believed Umbridge's classes were going to sufficiently prepare them for the exam. Michael's future role in unclear at this point.

Roger Davies

Davies is the Captain of the Ravenclaw Quidditch team. Very little is known about his character except he has appeared in each book and took Fleur Delacour to the Yule Ball.

Marietta Edgecombe

Marietta was a friend of Cho Chang. Her mother works for the Ministry of Magic in the Department of Magical Transportation, Floo Network, and was helping to "police" the Hogwarts fires[16]. Cho dragged her along to the D.A. meetings. Marietta eventually sold out the group. She went to Umbridge and planned to tell her about the group and its meetings. Fortunately, Hermione had jinxed the list they had all signed. So, she was only able to tell her it was in the Room of Requirement that evening before her face was covered with spots forming the word sneak. Apparently, they have not yet found a counter curse given she is still keeping her face covered. One can only hope Marietta has now learned her word is truly her bond and it is to her advantage to keep it.

Luna Lovegood

Luna means moon or in alchemy, silver. In Roman mythology, she was the goddess of the moon[17]. Luna Lovegood appeared for the first time in Book 5. Harry learned Luna's mother died when she was nine and her father, who is the editor of the magazine, *The Quibbler*, raised her. Luna is odd to say the least. She believes in many things for which there is absolutely no proof. Luna was a member of Dumbledore's Army, which was the Defense Against the Dark Arts group where Harry was secretly teaching people to defend themselves against Voldemort and his Death Eaters.

Luna may be eccentric, but she is clearly highly intelligent, given she is in Ravenclaw. Luna went to the Department of Mysteries with Harry, Ron, Hermione, Neville, and Ginny. She was also one of the last people standing among the kids, right behind Harry and Neville. The Detectives assume from this she is not only clever, but also a very powerful witch. She appears to be more powerful than either Ron or Hermione. It is also noteworthy, after the death of Sirius, Harry is unable to talk to Ron, Hermione, Dumbledore, or even Hagrid. Amazingly enough, Harry is able to talk to Luna because he realizes she too is able to see the thestrals. This strange bond formed between Harry and Luna at the end of Book 5 leads the Detectives to believe that there may be a Snitch involved. Luna may be Harry's soul mate and as her name suggests his love. The Detectives would not be surprised if Harry and Luna end up married.

Padma Patil

Padma is Parvati's twin sister. She went to the Yule Ball with Ron. Padma was a prefect in the fifth year and also a member of the Dumbledore's Army. As the twin of Parvati, who lives in the same dormitory as Hermione, she will be privy to a great deal of information other Ravenclaws will not receive.

Slytherin

Slytherin House is known for its selection of pureblood wizards. It is also known for the number of wizards to have gone to the Dark Side. Voldemort himself was in Slytherin House. The symbol is the serpent and the colors are green and silver. The Sorting Hat states; Slytherins are cunning folk, who will use any means to achieve their goals and they will make their *real friends* in Slytherin House[18]. Poor Snape. Dumbledore tells Harry about some of the other qualities Slytherin prized in his students, strength, resourcefulness, determination, a certain disregard for the rules, and parseltongue. In the fifth year, the Inquisitional Squad becomes important. All the hand-picked members are in Slytherin. Why? There could be a couple of reasons. First, was the whole house selected? It does not say, so the Detectives assume this is not the case. Umbridge, herself, was in Slytherin, so that explains at the very basic level why the whole squad came from Slytherin. Second, how did Umbridge select who was loyal to her? Are these possibly the children of her Death Eater friends? Clearly Malfoy, Crabbe, and Goyle were on the squad. Did Lucius help Umbridge make the selections?

Millicent Bulstrode

Millicent sounds a great deal like Maleficent, the wicked witch in Disney's Sleeping Beauty. Her personality certainly fits with that of Disney's wicked witch. Millicent Bulstrode has been a persistent character throughout the series. Hermione dueled with her in the dueling club in year 2. Actually, it turned into "muggle dueling" as McGonagall would call it or a catfight. Then in year 5, Bulstrode was on the Inquisitional Squad. During the scene in Umbridge's office, she was the member who was restraining Hermione. The Detectives look for Bulstrode to join the Death Eaters.

Vincent Crabbe & Gregory Goyle

Crabbe and Goyle are Malfoy's best friends. They really appear to be Malfoy's bodyguards more than anything else, perhaps this is the same role their fathers' play for Malfoy's father and they are simply in training. The readers know Malfoy tells Crabbe and Goyle information based on the time when Harry and Ron took the polyjuice potion. Like Malfoy, their fathers are Death Eaters, who managed to weasel their way out of Azkaban when Voldemort fell from power. Ironically, Malfoy, Sr. and Goyle, Sr. are now in jail, yet Crabbe Sr. is not. Crabbe and Goyle were members of the Inquisitional Squad Umbridge created to control the rest of Hogwarts. Crabbe and Goyle have been raised to be evil, but, unlike Malfoy, neither of them is overly intelligent. They epitomize the cliché, "dumber than a bucket of bolts." The fact they are large and stupid could prove to be beneficial to Harry.

Draco Malfoy

Draco Malfoy's name, like his father's gives the Detectives a clue as to what to expect from his character. Draco is Latin for dragon or serpent. Appropriate that he is in Slytherin house. Malfoy is French. Mal means bad or evil and foi means faith. Thus, the readers have been warned with his name to watch out for Draco Malfoy. But could there be an even deeper meaning to Draco's name. There is a constellation in the Northern Hemisphere called Draco near Cepheus and Ursa major. The detectives should note where this is located. In Greek Mythology, Cepheus is the father of Andromeda. Andromeda is Draco's good aunt. This could lead to an argument indicating Draco will turn good in the end. Also, Draco was the name of an Athenian politician who enacted Athenian laws, which were praised for impartiality. But the code was extremely unpopular because of its severity. (It prescribed death for almost every offense.) So, will a life-changing event turn Draco good, like Snape? This is a possibility. Harry had a dream his first night at Hogwarts and the Detectives believe Harry is a Seer. In this dream Draco turned into Professor Snape. Well, this is interesting! James saved Snape's life. Snape was a Death Eater, but deserted and became a spy for the Order. Thus, if this dream is foreshadowing then Draco will abandon his evil upbringing.

Draco Malfoy is a thin, blond haired boy with a pointed nose. He is the only son of Narcissa and Lucius Malfoy, who are Death Eaters. His two best friends are Crabbe and Goyle, whose fathers are also Death Eaters. Harry saw both Draco and his father in a dark arts shop in Knockturn Alley. Lucius was selling items he did not want the Ministry to find if they raided his house. By taking Draco with him, he is including his son in his dark activities. Also, Draco took it personally when Harry put his father in Azkaban and informed Harry, he would make him pay. So, will Draco attempt to join the Death Eaters after his fifth year? Will he take Crabbe and Goyle with him? Will Voldemort take him before he finishes his education? Voldemort does not exactly have the moral fiber that the members of the Order have in not allowing underage wizards and witches join. He would not care about the dangers associated with joining him. The Detectives are sure Lucius would be opposed until Draco is of age since he has discouraged Draco from picking fights with Harry for years. Lucius will be furious when he gets out of Azkaban, if Voldemort agrees to let Draco join before he reaches adulthood. Heaven help those who encourage this idea.

Draco Malfoy and Harry Potter have been enemies, since the first train ride to Hogwarts. Incidentally, Draco was the first wizard Harry met who was his own age. They met in the robe shop in Diagon Alley on Harry's 11th birthday and Harry got a small taste of Draco's pureblood mania at that point. Draco stated, he did not think kids who came from muggle families should be allowed in Hogwarts. Later, Draco informed Harry he should not make friends with filth like the Weasleys and he could help him discern which wizards were good and which were bad. This was the beginning of a relationship similar to the James/ Snape animosity. In fact, on the train ride at the end of the years 4 and 5, Draco, Crabbe, and Goyle, attempt to hex Harry. They were not successful on either occasion and ended up in a terrible state.

In the second year, Draco's father buys his way on to the Slytherin Quidditch Team rather than letting him earn the position. This shows another personality trait of Draco. He would rather have things handed to him, than work for them. Draco plays Seeker for Slytherin. Draco is highly intelligent and very popular among the Slytherin students. He is Snape's favorite student. In the third year, Draco does his best to get Hagrid fired. He does not pay a bit of attention to what Hagrid says about Hippogriffs and the result is he was slashed. He milks the injury for months in order to allow his father time to take the case to the Disposal of Dangerous Creatures and the Governors of Hogwarts School. This shows Draco will use any means necessary to get what he wants. In his fifth year, Draco was prefect and leader of the Inquisitional Squad.

It is always interesting to note how people are addressed. Both Umbridge and Snape address Draco by his first name. Draco also brags that they both know his father very well. One who knows Lucius "very well" would know about his role as a Death Eater. So, does this mean they are both Death Eaters with Lucius? So, do they both come to the Malfoy house for Sunday dinner? Also, Draco does not knock on Snape's door. He just walks in. This is extremely important. It suggests a whole new level of familiarity. Typically, if one does not knock on a door and just walks in, they are either family or very close friends. The Detectives believe this would describe Snape's relationship with the Malfoy family. Snape has known Lucius since his first year at Hogwarts, thus he probably met Draco when he was born. If this were an American book, Draco would probably address Snape as Uncle Severus in private. Draco will be a key player. If the Detectives have predicted the foreshadowing correctly, Harry will save Draco's life and he will turn to the side of good. If we are wrong, watch out because he is an evil little git.

Montague

Montague is the Captain for the Slytherin team and plays the position of Chaser. He was two years ahead of Harry Potter. Montague was on Inquisitional Squad, but when he attempted to take points from Fred and George Weasley they forced him head first into the Vanishing cabinet. Montague did not appear for a while and when he did he was jammed inside a toilet on the fourth floor and was very confused. Madam Pomfrey was either unable or unwilling to cure Montague, but he was not sent to St. Mungo's. It should be noted, the Montagues and the Capulets were the two warring families in Shakespeare's play, Romeo and Juliet. In the play, the death of both, Romeo and Juliet is an indirect result of the families' feud. The Detectives wonder whether Montague will be one of the family members fighting for evil in the battle or if he will fall in love with a girl on the side of good.

Theodore Nott

Very little is known about Nott. He is in the same year as Malfoy and his father is a Death Eater. The Detectives believe his father managed to stay out of jail for a second time because he was injured early on and presumably left the battle at that point. The Detectives are wary of Nott because he is living in the dormitory with Malfoy, Crabbe, and Goyle and after *The Quibbler* article was talking to them more. As the battle rages, Nott will have very little choice, but to turn to them because they will be the only people who will understand what he is going through. They, also, will all be facing the same question, on joining the Death Eaters.

Pansy Parkinson

Oh, dear old Pansy. Hermione's favorite Slytherin girl is Pansy Parkinson. She is named for a flower, which means thoughtfulness. This is interesting, since the readers have yet to see Pansy being thoughtful. In her fifth year, Pansy became a prefect. She went to the Yule Ball with Malfoy. Interestingly enough she was the only other person, other than Malfoy, Crabbe, and Goyle who was giving Rita Skeeter interviews about Harry and Hermione. Pansy was also on the Inquisitional Squad in year five and was the one to run into the Room of Requirement and get the list of the names of the D.A. members. The Detectives expect Pansy will play an active role in future dark activities.

Warrington

Warrington is a bloodthirsty Chaser for the Slytherin Quidditch team. He is also a member of the Inquisitional Squad. Warrington includes three words, war, warring, and ton. Thus, it is logical to assume he will participate, a great deal, in the war.

Chapter 6

The Ministry of Magic

The Minister of Magic

Cornelius Oswald Fudge

The name Cornelius has an interesting historical reference. When the exiled Saint Cornelius, the Bishop of Rome, died, Pope Lucius I was installed. This is definitely intriguing, as Cornelius Fudge is the Minister of Magic. The leader of the magical world has been given an interesting name. In addition, the choice of surname is humorous to say the least. Fudge means nonsense, fake, evasion, or go beyond the proper limits of something. Wow, the Detectives may assume Fudge is not an honest politician, but for the first several books this was not clear. Even with this Bludger regarding his name, Fudge is a difficult character to decipher. The Detectives are still trying to determine whether he is a Death Eater or sympathizer. For example, in Book 2, Fudge knew Hagrid was innocent, but bowed to pressure and sent Hagrid to Azkaban Prison. In contrast, in Book 3, Fudge takes it upon himself to ensure Harry Potter's safety when Black escapes. What makes this sketchy or even suspicious is Fudge was one of the first law enforcement wizards on the scene and modified several muggle memories after getting their testimonies. Well, clearly this appears logical, even necessary, and without any of Fudge's other actions the Detectives would think nothing of it. But could there be something he was in a hurry to cover up? Did he know Sirius was innocent?

The Goblet of Fire unearths several facts about Fudge, including a friendship between the Fudge and Crouch families. In addition, Fudge got the position of Minister of Magic, due to the embarrassment of Crouch's son being caught as a Death Eater. Until then Crouch was expected to be the next Minister of Magic. In the Order of the Phoenix the Detectives learn Fudge has been Minister of Magic for five years. We learned in Book 1 the wizarding community wanted Dumbledore to take the job, but he refused. This, incidentally, was the same year Harry started at Hogwarts.

It is not until the Goblet of Fire that the Detectives become extremely suspicious of Fudge. After the return of Voldemort, Fudge goes from Dr. Jekyll to Mr. Hyde. According to Snape, "When we told Mr. Fudge that we had caught the Death Eater responsible for tonight's events...he seemed to feel his personal safety was in question. He insisted on summoning a dementor to accompany him into the castle. He brought it up to the office where Barty Crouch...[1]." There are several interesting points in this statement and the Detectives make several assumptions. Snape probably told Fudge who the Death Eater was, that they had given him Veritaserum, and a "cliff notes" version of his testimony. In addition, he undoubtedly told him where Crouch was tied up and McGonagall was standing guard. We know McGonagall and Snape are extremely powerful wizards. One would assume to become the Minister of Magic, you would be a highly skilled wizard, as well. So, why would Fudge feel his personal safety was threatened? Crouch is tied up and without a wand. In addition, there are two powerful wizards prepared to defend him. The only explanation is Fudge is not afraid of a wand, but rather what could come out of Crouch, Jr.'s mouth. What is it Crouch, Jr. could expose? Another key point is, as soon as, the Dementor and Fudge entered the room the Dementor performed the kiss on Crouch, sucking his soul from his body. Note: Dementors are only supposed to perform the kiss when ordered. They usually follow this rule since they have not sucked the souls out of the prisoners at Azkaban, nor did it attempt to perform the kiss on McGonagall or Snape. Thus, it logically follows Fudge ordered the Dementor to perform the kiss before they entered the room. Apparently it was crucial for Fudge to prevent Crouch from exposing any information about him. It is apparently something so damaging it could cost him everything--- his career, his way of life, etc.. So, what was it? Does Winky know? If so, can we get her talking? The Detectives have a couple of theories of what this could be. When Crouch, Sr. was out of his mind he was talking about going to a concert was with his wife, son, and *Mr. and Mrs. Fudge.* This suggests Fudge was around both the wife and the son quite a bit. One option is Fudge was the Death Eater who recruited Crouch, Jr. and would thus, be exposed. There could be a couple of explanations as to why Snape has not told Dumbledore about Fudge. The first possibility is Voldemort is the Secret Keeper for the Death Eaters, so Fudge's name would be kept confidential. If you managed to convert the Minister of Magic it would be kept top secret. Fudge does fit the profile of a Death Eater. He is an upper class pureblood. In addition, he is prejudiced against half giants and those who "lack proper wizarding pride" Also, Fudge is surrounded by Death Eaters. The Malfoys seem to be good friends of Fudge. When Harry gives him the names of the Death Eaters he had seen at Voldemort's rebirthing celebration, Fudge defended each one of them saying they had been cleared. Well, who cleared them? The Detectives suspect Fudge cleared them. Why not admit he could have made a mistake? To err is human. Again, he could still either be a Death Eater or a sympathizer, like France. There is not enough evidence to convict him of being a Death Eater, at this point. France would never admit to making a mistake. Malfoy's money is probably keeping him in power because in the words of Hagrid, Fudge is a "bungler if ever there was one" and Fudge clearly loves power[2]. So, even if Fudge is not a Death Eater, they could be blackmailing Fudge, in order to bend him to his will.

Another option is Fudge knew all along Crouch, Sr. had smuggled his son from Azkaban and possibly aided in giving his wife the polyjuice potion until her death. This would be the end of his career and Crouch, Jr. would have known this information. But why would he want to expose it? As Crouch's assistant at the Ministry and a close personal friend it is possible Crouch, Sr. would have trusted Fudge beyond any of his other friends. However, if this were the case it is odd he did not turn to Fudge in the end. Instead, Crouch turned to Dumbledore. In addition, we know from Book 3, Fudge makes frequent trips to Azkaban and sometimes slips things to prisoners. After all, he gave Sirius his newspaper. Thus, it would not have been very difficult for him to give Crouch's son/wife a flask. No one would have thought anything about his visit, since he inspects the prison with some frequency. This is also questionable. As the Minister of Magic, he could delegate this unpleasant task to a subordinate. Why does he want to go to Azkaban? What does he really do out there? The who's who of the Death Eaters are all there and he visits frequently. It is important to note Crouch, Sr. put those Death Eaters in Azkaban and then, after his son was caught, Fudge cleared the rest. So, Fudge visits those in prison and socializes with the Death Eaters outside of prison. Hmmm, this does not look good for Fudge. This could certainly be a case for guilt by association. It is also possible Fudge made sure Crouch, Jr. was caught and hence, another reason he fears for his personal safety. He benefited in several ways from Crouch, Jr.'s arrest. The first was Crouch, Sr.'s fall in popularity and his getting the job of Minister of Magic. The second is the ability to prevent the rest of the Death Eaters from going to Azkaban. When Fudge took over Crouch's job, he was able to clear his friends, possibly in exchange for not being exposed himself. Although the Detectives are not sure which of these theories are correct, they lean most heavily on the "made man" theory. (A "made man" is one who owes his success to a group, such as the Mafia.)

There are two other incidents at the end of Book 4, which support the Death Eater theory. Dumbledore's statement, "The only one against whom I intend to work is Lord Voldemort. If you are against him...[3]." Is there any question? Again, Fudge could merely be a sympathizer. Historically, France plays the sympathizer role in each war. They refuse to stand up to evil in exchange for the hope their comfortable lives will not be disrupted. The next thing is how Fudge reacts to Snape. They have always gotten along very well, like Fudge gets along with all the other Death Eaters. Fudge even wanted to give him the Order of the Merlin First Class for catching Sirius Black. When Snape shows Fudge the Dark Mark on his arm Fudge "recoiled." So, why did he flinch? He knew Snape had been a Death Eater because he had been at the trials. So why was this a surprise to him? Perhaps the mark was not the surprise. Maybe, he, like the other Death Eaters, thought Snape was a spy for them and yet he backed up Dumbledore. This would be a frightening thought for any Death Eater. Terrifying, in fact. Fudge just stares, "apparently repelled by the ugly mark on Snape's arm." Fudge then states "I don't know what you and your staff are playing at, Dumbledore[4]." Fudge immediately left saying he must return to the Ministry. Fudge has been faced with solid evidence, which he point blank refuses to acknowledge or accept. So, where does

Fudge really go? Does he go to Malfoy? If so, Snape was not far behind him. Malfoy would tell him that the Dark Lord says his faithful servant is a Hogwarts. Clearly Malfoy thinks this is Snape and Fudge cannot exactly tell him, he disposed of one of their best Death Eaters. In Book 5, Snape is again being treated well by the ministry, so Malfoy managed to convince Fudge that Snape was on their side. Stupid git!

Sr. Undersecretary to the Minster

Dolores Jane Umbridge

See Hogwarts Professors

Jr. Assistant to the Minister/ Court Scribe

Percy Ignatius Weasley

Perceval, one King Arthur's knights, is credited with finding the Holy Grail. Through Perceval's ignorance, he was responsible for the death of his uncle and his mother. Percy Weasley is the third son. Like his father and Ron, Percy is tall and thin. He is highly ambitious and wants to be the Minister of Magic. In fact, at the beginning of Book 2, he was reading *Prefects Who Gained Power*[5]. The Detectives wonder if Tom Riddle is mentioned in this book or if he is conveniently omitted. Nonetheless, it gives the readers a flavor of Percy's mentality and he not only wants to be successful, but he wants power. This is dangerous! Power leads to corruption. Percy was a prefect and Head Boy at Hogwarts and has an owl, named Hermes. Now, this is interesting! Hermes was Zeus' messenger. He was one of the shrewdest and most cunning gods and a Master Thief[6]. Percy, who is highly intelligent and well read, would have known this. So, why did he select this name for his pet and messenger? Perhaps he thinks of himself as Zeus, the most powerful of the gods? Again, this tells the readers a great deal about Percy Weasley. However, the Detectives do not believe Percy is evil. If he were, the Sorting Hat would have broken the family tradition, as it did with Sirius, and placed him in Slytherin. Percy is simply misguided and following his dreams. Percy does have a heart and does care about someone other than himself, which means he does not fit the profile of a Death Eater.

Upon graduation, Percy landed a job working for Barty Crouch. Percy idolized Crouch because he was the epitome of what Percy wanted to be. They were both rules oriented, highly successful, and extremely ambitious people. Under normal circumstances, Crouch would have adored Percy and taken him under his wing. Percy was the son Crouch had always wanted. Perhaps this is why Crouch could not be bothered to remember Percy's name; he was a bitter reminder of the disaster his own son had made of his life. It is Percy's ambition that Voldemort takes advantage of in Book 4. Since all purebloods are interrelated, one can assume Crouch might be his uncle, of whom Percy was responsible for the death, like Perceval. Likewise, Percy fails to notify his superiors of Crouch's strange behavior, while there was still time to prevent his murder. Then in Book 5, Percy puts his ambition before his family and common sense. He becomes Fudge's personal assistant and severs the ties with his family and Harry Potter. Percy believes this is the best course of action for his career goals and deludes himself into believing Fudge is correct. Thus, Percy aligns himself with Fudge, instead of Dumbledore.

Percy does have one redeeming quality, which is going to save him from turning totally evil. Unfortunately, the Detectives believe it will be too late for his mother. His foolishness will cost Molly her life, just as it cost Crouch his life. Percy loves Ron more than anything else. He puts Ron before his career, his image, and even, his ambition. This says a great deal for someone who wants to be the Minister of Magic. The first time this is seen clearly is at the lake, when Harry and Ron emerged from the surface after everyone thought they had drowned. Percy, in front of the entire school and members of the Ministry, "looked very white and somehow much younger than usual, came splashing out to meet them… Percy seized Ron and was dragging them back to the bank ('Gerroff, Percy, I'm all right!')…Madam Pomfrey had gone to rescue Ron from Percy's clutches[7]." Percy was so afraid Ron had drowned that he did not even wait for him to get out of the water. Then, he would not let go of him. Clearly, Percy cares a great deal about his youngest brother. The next major incident is the letter he sent Ron during the fifth year, when he has supposedly cut off all contact with his family. Fudge told Percy that Ron had been made a Prefect and that he was still a friend of Harry Potter. Fudge knew exactly what Percy would do given he undoubtedly had heard about what had happened during the second task of the Triwizard tournament. He clearly thought it might be good to try to sway Ron to the Ministry's side and knew Percy would try to protect this brother. It should also be noted Fudge and Umbridge knew not to touch Ron. She attacked Fred and George, but left Ron alone. This shows they were not willing to risk pushing Percy away because they needed him for some reason. From Percy's prospective, sending Ron the letter was risky, yet he sent it anyway. Percy says he sent it in the evening rather than in the morning, so Ron could read it away from "prying eyes and avoid awkward questions[8]." Since Percy knows Ron always spends his evenings with Hermione and Harry and sometimes even Fred and George, clearly Percy is more concerned Umbridge would recognize his owl. Again, this shows how much Percy cares about Ron. He warns Ron about several things and gives him the best possible advice Percy believes he can give. Percy wants Ron to become Head Boy and stay out of trouble. He does not seem to realize his advice will lead Ron directly into danger. Again, the Detectives believe Percy will rejoin the side of good. Or in the words of Sirius, "Don't worry about Percy…He'll come round[9]." Unfortunately, the Detectives believe his mother will be dead and Ron will be gravely injured before that time comes.

Head of Magical Games & Sports

Ludovic Bagman

Ludo is the beginning of ludicrous, which means foolish. This would definitely describe Ludo Bagman. A bagman is one who carries money for the mob. Interesting name, for a man accused of passing secrets to Death Eaters. Ludo Bagman has round blue eyes and short blond hair. He is tall and muscular, but has a bit of a stomach. He is a jovial man. Bagman played Quidditch for England and was a Beater for the Wimbourne Wasps. His nose appears to have been broken quite a few times. This is cause for concern among the Detectives. As a Beater the mediwizards would have been there to fix any injuries sustained during the match, so they wonder when, where, and what exactly Bagman was doing when he got his nose broken. Perhaps it has something to do with stealing people's money when they place bets with him.

After the fall of Voldemort, Bagman was accused, tried, and acquitted of passing information to Death Eaters. Bagman was part of Rookwood's network outside the ministry. At Bagman's trial, he stated Rookwood was an old friend of his father and kept promising to get him a job at the ministry, after his Quidditch days were over. Bagman was cleared of the charges, due to his fame as a Beater for the Wasps. The Detectives believe Bagman may have been cleared due to his fame as an athlete; this is extremely common. There was DNA evidence, but OJ Simpson was still cleared, thus it is highly probable the same standard applied to Bagman. Of course, there is the possibility Bagman did not knowingly help the Death Eaters on round one. There are only three arguments the Detectives can think of to support this point of view. First, it is highly convenient Bagman fits the criteria of a dumb jock. Second, Dumbledore was not prepared to convict him, when Harry asked if he was guilty. One should note he did not say Bagman was innocent or he trusted Bagman, Dumbledore simply said, he "has never been accused of any Dark activity since[10]." Well, this is meaningless since Voldemort was no longer in power and the Death Eaters, who are not in Azkaban, are all pretending to be respectable citizens. Frankly, the Detectives cannot think of a better cover than a boyish Head of the Department of Magical Games and Sports. The final reason, Bagman may not have been knowingly passing secrets to the Death Eaters is he would not have needed the money. If professional Quidditch players are like most professional athletes, he was not short on cash during Voldemort's reign. However, on round two, it is probable he will be corrupted with the full knowledge of what he has joined as a direct result of his gambling problem and many debts.

Bagman has a severe gambling problem. The goblins are angry with him because he owes them a lot of money. During the Triwizard Tournament, Bagman attempted to help Harry to win in order to repay his debts. The Detectives wonder if this was his only reason for wanting to help Harry. This shows Bagman is willing to use unethical and illegal means to accomplish his goals. Bagman seems likely to work for or, be blackmailed, by the Death Eaters because of his gambling problem. Most governments will not hire people with gambling problems or high debts for exactly this reason. There is also the likelihood Bagman's fame as a Beater combined with his likable personality saved him from a well-deserved sentence in Azkaban. That was clearly the opinion of Crouch, Sr. and the Detectives are inclined to agree—Ludo Bagman is a Death Eater. Consider the evidence, all of which is circumstantial and hearsay for the Detectives, but Crouch, Sr. may well have had enough for a conviction. First, there are several people who have a less than favorable opinion of Bagman for reasons other than being a poor Head of his Department. Rita Skeeter states, "I know things about Ludo Bagman that would make your hair curl[11]." It should be noted she uses the word *things,* which is plural. This suggests she knows more than one thing about Ludo Bagman, thus it is not only his trial. She also says, "[Bagman] was always a bad liar[12]." Always? So, they must go back a fair number of years. It should also be noted when Harry walked in for the weighing of the wands Ludo and Rita were talking and they were on a first name basis. The next individual who clearly dislikes Bagman is Winky. She states "Mr. Bagman is a bad wizard! A very bad wizard! My master isn't liking him, oh no, not at all[13]." This is very interesting. One question comes to mind. Which Master Crouch, Sr., Jr. or both does not like Bagman? We know what Crouch, Jr. hated most was a Death Eater who walked free. So if Bagman is a Death Eater, he would despise him. Though Crouch, Sr. did not believe he should have gotten off, he is willing to work with him and attempts to keep him on track. After the World Cup, Bagman was hiding deeper in the woods than the goblins. In fact, he was near Barty Crouch, Jr., right before Bagman saw Harry, Ron, and Hermione and heard about the riot. Thus, the Detectives wonder if he heard Winky and Crouch, Jr. arguing and offered his assistance to Crouch, Jr. in exchange for money to help repay his debts. This would explain why when Winky was asked if she saw anyone she looked from Diggory, to Bagman, to Mr. Crouch. If she had not seen Bagman why would she have looked at him? He was not questioning her nor was he her master. Also, he is someone for whom she had no respect. Another interesting comment from Bagman is after hearing about the riot he says, "Damn them[14]." This makes it sound like he knew who had caused it and he had asked that they not do it. Why? Well, because he was in charge of the World Cup and it would make him look like a complete fool. Also, he was late after the Dark Mark was conjured and was "looking breathless and disorientated[15]." All the other wizards disapparated immediately and apparated at the site pronto. Why didn't Bagman? Did he follow the Death Eaters and then the Ministry wizards? If so, it's no wonder he is getting tired! The final and most convincing piece of evidence is the fact he ran for it after the third task. Supposedly, the goblins were after him. Well, Bagman doesn't exactly have a track record of honesty. Are we sure the Dark Mark didn't burn on his arm and he had to run so he could get somewhere in order to apparate to Voldemort? Everyone would have known Harry and Cedric had disappeared with the cup because they were gone for quite a while. The potion to restore Voldemort to his body took a fair amount of time and the cup was just supposed to lift them out of the maze. Panic had probably set in at Hogwarts and everyone was trying to figure out where they had gone. Karkarff ran for it! Bagman, also, ran for it, and when Fred and George demanded their gold and he made up a story quickly about Goblins. They would be willing to believe and even have been amused Bagman was in trouble with the goblins. He would have looked scared to death because all the Death Eaters would have been scared out of their skin about Voldemort's return. Another point to consider is the goblins would not be likely to attack the Head of a Department at a major event. They would be up in front of the Regulation and Control of Magical Creatures for a crime like that.

The Detectives would also like to consider the possibility Bagman, like Rita Skeeter, is an unregistered animagus. A wasp appears right before Harry has the vision planted in his head about Sirius being tortured in the Department of Mysteries. Well, Harry noticed a beetle in Book 4. Also,

Bagman is known for playing for the Wasps and frequently wears his old wasp robes. It is something to consider. Could this be another "secret" Bagman passed for the Death Eaters?

Department of Mysteries

Bode

Bode means to predict or foretell. The character works in the Department of Mysteries and is an Unspeakable. He worked in the Hall of Prophecies. Bode knew Arthur Weasley, but was not a member of the Order. Bode was the victim of Malfoy's Imperius Curse. Malfoy wanted him to steal the prophecy regarding Harry and Voldemort, but only the persons they pertain to can lift the prophecies from their shelves. The spells protecting the prophecies from theft caused Bode to go mad. He was not capable of speech and went to St. Mungo's. He was killed by a Devil's Snare plant in St. Mungo's Closed Ward, when he started to show signs of improvement. This makes the Detectives wonder if St. Mungo's is controlled by the Death Eaters? After all St. Mungo's is Malfoy's favorite charity.

Croaker

Croaker is another Unspeakable, who Mr. Weasley points out to the children with him at the World Cup. The Detectives know very little about him at this point. He was with Bode at the Quidditch World Cup.

Department of Magical Law Enforcement

Department Head—Amelia Susan Bones

Amelia Bones is the Head of the Department of Magical Law Enforcement. She has short gray hair, a square jaw and wears a monocle. Madam Bones was on the panel for Harry's hearing, and wanted to know more about the Dementors. Bones made it clear she believed Mrs. Figg. Likewise, she was impressed with Harry's ability to produce a Patronus. At the end of the hearing, she voted to clear Harry. This sequence of events shows Madam Bones is not under Fudge's or the Death Eaters' control. She is simply interested in fairness, which is what Tonks, who works in her Department, told Harry. It is also important Madam Bones is friendly to Arthur Weasley, even when Fudge has made it clear he has been blacklisted. Perhaps, Madam Bones realizes Fudge is an idiot.

Madam Bones has an interesting family history. She is the sister of Edgar Bones, who the Death Eaters murdered, along with the rest of his immediate family. She is also the aunt of Susan Bones, who is in Hufflepuff and joined the D.A. In addition, Madam Bones told Susan about Harry's hearing and his Patronus. This, again, shows she speaks highly of Harry Potter, when the majority of the wizarding world thinks he is a lunatic. Madam Bones may be useful in the battle of good and evil.

Mafalda Hopkirk

Mafalda Hopkirk works for the Improper Use of Magic Office and has sent all of Harry's notices regarding violations of the Decree for the Reasonable Restriction of Underage Sorcery. In the second year, she sent an owl, which did not go directly to Harry, as is customary for owls, or even to his "parents," but to the muggle guests. This would seem to be a violation of the Statute of Secrecy and makes the Detectives wonder if Hopkirk is trying to cause more trouble. In the fifth year, she was willing to expel Harry from Hogwarts and have Harry's wand destroyed without a trial. These actions make the Detectives question whether Hopkirk belongs in the category of sympathizer or Death Eater.

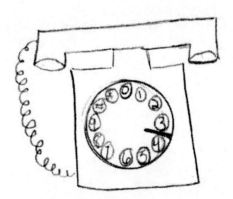

Misuse of Muggle Artifacts

Section Head—Arthur Weasley

See the Order of the Phoenix

Perkins

Perkins is an elderly wizard and Mr. Weasley's assistant in the Misuse of Muggle Artifacts Office. It is interesting someone so old is an assistant to someone, as young as, Arthur Weasley. The office he and Mr. Weasley share is decorated entirely to Mr. Weasley's taste and there was no mention of Perkins having any family photos. Perkins loaned Mr. Weasley tents for the World Cup, which looked and smelled like Mrs. Figgs' house. The Detectives question whether he and Mrs. Figg are not related in some way. Until Harry left for Hogwarts, the Dursleys would only leave him with Mrs. Figg when they were gone, perhaps to protect him. Could this have been a part of Dumbledore's protection so Harry would be safe at the World Cup? Mr. Weasley would not have known about the tents, but Perkins could have slipped them to him just by trying to be a nice coworker. Maybe Harry would have been better served staying in the tent, than roaming free in the woods. Both the tent and Mrs. Figgs' house smell like polyjuice potion or the apothecary where all the potion ingredients are purchased. So, could Perkins be in disguise? If so, why? Who is he hiding from? Is there a reason someone, or a certain group of people, does not need to know he is still alive? In addition, Perkins was in a panic about Harry's hearing. Why did he take such an interest in the hearing of a boy he has never met? Or has he met Harry and Harry does not know it? Another interesting point is Professor Binns, who is a ghost, always calls Harry Potter, Perkins. Granted Binns does not get any of the students' names correct, but the Detectives believe he addresses the students by their relatives' names. For example, when Hermione had her hand raised, Binns had to ask for her name because her family did not go to Hogwarts. He later selected another muggle-born girl's name by which to address her. Another question, the Detective have in regard to Perkins, is whether Perkins is a first or last name? Arthur Weasley typically addresses people by their first name, so the Detectives are inclined to believe that someone with whom he works with on a daily basis would definitely be addressed by his first name. If so, what is Perkins' last name? Could it be Potter? Or could he be related to the Potters? This would explain the potion and the disguise.

Aurors

Dawlish

Dawlish, a tough-looking wizard with very short, wiry gray hair, appeared for the first time in The Order of the Phoenix[16]. He is an Auror, which is an elite branch of magical law enforcement, designed to catch dark wizards. Interestingly, Fudge and Umbridge bring Dawlish on special missions. He was present in the attempt to expel Harry and consequently, to arrest Dumbledore. In fact, Dawlish was the only one who gave Fudge a nod of support and moved toward his wand showing he was willing to take on Dumbledore. This can be interpreted two ways, either Dawlish is very loyal and brave or extremely foolish. The readers are told at this point, Dawlish received Outstanding on all of his N.E.W.T.s[17]. Thus, he is a skilled and powerful wizard. It should also be noted Dawlish was the first to awaken after Dumbledore's spell and immediately began to search for him.

Dawlish also accompanied Umbridge on her attempt to ambush Hagrid. While Hagrid was under the attack of approximately five people, Dawlish told him to "Be reasonable[18]!" This implies he is quite familiar with Hagrid, maybe they went to school together. The Detectives wonder if Dawlish may be in the wrong field. He is targeting the Order, not the Death Eaters. Yes, he is doing it on orders, but are his actions justified? Later, Fudge sent Dawlish and Williamson to the Department of Mysteries to see if Dumbledore was correct that several Death Eaters had been detained inside. Thus, Fudge clearly trusts Dawlish. The Head Detective says, "Beware!" In the words of Hamlet, "Something is rotten in the state of Denmark[19]."

Kingsley Shacklebolt

See the Order of the Phoenix

Nymphadora Tonks

See the Order of the Phoenix

Williamson

Williamson is an Auror, seen only once. He had a ponytail and was wearing a scarlet robe. Detectives should note the color of his robe is the color of Gryffindor House. The night of Voldemort and Dumbledore's duel, Williamson arrived with Fudge in the atrium of the Ministry of Magic. Williamson said, "I saw him, Mr. Fudge, I swear, it was You-Know-Who[20]." Williamson made this statement before anyone else had spoken, which shows he is willing to stand up for what is right even if his reputation could suffer. Fudge later sent Williamson and Dawlish to the Department of Mysteries to see if Dumbledore was correct about several Death Eaters being detained there. Thus, Fudge trusts Williamson. The Detectives believe Williamson could act as a liaison between the Ministry and members of the Order. He has shown, in one scene, he has the potential to play a part on the side of good in the battle of good versus evil.

Watchwizard

Eric Munch is a badly shaven watchwizard, who seems to be bored with his job. He checks the wands of visitors to the Ministry of Magic. In addition, Munch was the one who arrested Sturgis Podmore when he was attempting to enter the Department of Mysteries at 1am. It is unclear at this point which side Munch will join.

Department for the Regulation & Control of Magical Creatures

Culthbert Mockridge

Head of the Goblin Liaison Office

Mr. Weasley pointed Mockridge out at the World Cup, but his significance is unknown at this point in the series. The Detectives suspect he will become more important when the Goblins enter the battle.

Bob

Bob appeared in Book 5 and had found a "breach of the Ban on Experimental Breeding[21]." He and Mr. Weasley seemed to be pretty friendly, which is saying a great deal given the current climate in the Ministry of Magic. The Detectives believe he is someone Arthur Weasley will reach out to, in the upcoming books, to join the fight against Voldemort.

Gilbert Wimple

Wimple means ripple or is the name for the "covering of the head, neck, and sides of the face, worn by women in medieval times[22]." So, what is Gilbert Wimple covering up? Wimple is on the Committee on Experimental Charms and has horns on his head. Could this mean he represents the devil or was just the recipient of a charm that went awry? If this is the case, why can't it be reversed? Wimple's name and horns imply a connection with darkness, so the Detectives are wary of him.

Department of Magical Accidents & Catastrophes

Arnold Peasegood

Arnold Peasegood is an Obiviator for the Accidental Magic Reversal Squad, who Mr. Weasley pointed out.

Department of Magical Transportation

Madam Edgecombe

Madam Edgecombe works in the Floo Network Office and has been helping Umbridge to police the Hogwarts fires[23]. Her daughter, Marietta, was the student who tried to snitch on her fellow members of the D.A., but was stopped due to the hex Hermione had put on the parchment, which all the members signed. Like her daughter, Madam Edgecombe is not to be trusted.

Basil

Basil is a culinary herb and also, the name of a Saint, who saved his church in Greece[24]. Two other significant Basil's were Basil I, the Macedonian, who murdered two rivals to obtained the throne, and Basil II or Bulgaroctus, whose reign consisted of continuos warfare and expansion... and he inflicted great suffering on the Bulgarians[25]." The Detectives would recommend watching out for this man. The only time Basil has been seen, thus far, was when he was organizing the arrival of the Portkeys at the World Cup, where the Bulgarians were playing. Scary, eh?

Department of International Magical Cooperation

Barty Crouch, Sr.

Bartemius Crouch, Sr. is an elderly man with short gray hair and a mustache. He has a very crisp appearance and dresses to the nines. He comes from an old wealthy, pureblood family. Crouch is well known for his rigid compliance with rules, which was the reason Percy Weasley adored him "He spoke as though he wanted to leave nobody in any doubt that all his ancestors had abided strictly by the law[26]." In addition, Crouch speaks over 200 languages, including Mermish, Gobbledegook, and Troll[27]. Sirius describes him as "a great wizard, Barty Crouch, powerfully magical—power-hungry...always outspoken against the Dark Arts[28]."

An interesting characteristic about Crouch, Sr. is he is very concerned about Bertha Jorkins, who hasn't worked for him in years. In contrast, he cannot remember his assistant's name, even though he is familiar with his father. " If you want to know what a man's like take a good look at how he treats his inferiors not his equals[29]." Failing to remember the name of someone suggests the person does not matter to you. The Detectives believe it is unfortunate Crouch met Percy so late in life. They suspect if his life had turned out differently, Crouch would have really liked Percy. Percy is exactly like him and undoubtedly the way he wished his son would have turn out.

During Voldemort's last attempt to take power, he was Head of the Department of Magical Law Enforcement. Fudge was in his department and they seemed to have been friends, as Crouch, his wife, and son went out with Mr. and Mrs. Fudge in the evenings. This is interesting to note, because Crouch, Sr. was the presumed heir for the position of Minister of Magic until his son was caught with the Death Eaters. As a result, Fudge got the position of Minster of Magic. This makes the Detectives question whether or not Fudge had anything to do with Crouch's downfall. Instead, Crouch was made Head of International Cooperation, which was very insulting. Instead of becoming Prime Minister, he was named Head of an organization, like the United Nations, which exists only for appearances. Crouch had a great deal of support for his firm stance against the Dark Arts. "Crouch fought violence with violence, and authorized the use of the Unforgivable Curses against suspects. I would say he became as ruthless and cruel as many on the Dark Side[30]." He put people in Azkaban without a trial; thus he subscribes to the mentality of guilty until innocent. He gave the Aurors new powers, "power to kill rather than capture[31]." This is interesting because to crouch means to stoop and according to Sirius, Crouch, Sr. stooped to the Death Eater's level. In addition, Crouch ran the trials of the Death Eaters. He believed Bagman was guilty of being a Death Eater and only got off because of his fame. As a result, when Bagman was appointed Head of Magical Games and Sports, Crouch criticized the way he ran it.

Crouch was a workaholic. Before being controlled by the Imperius Curse, it is doubtful he ever took a day off work for illness. He never took the time to get to know his own son. Even when Crouch, Jr. earned 12 O.W.L.s, the highest number possible; he could not get his father's attention. Crouch, Sr. said he was proud and returned to work. Thus, when his son was caught with the Lestranges, Crouch held a trial and sentenced his own son to life in Azkaban. He even disowned his own son at his trial. One can assume this is what Crouch was referring to when he said, "I trust you remember the many proofs, I have given, over a long career, that I despise and detest the Dark Arts and those who practice them[32]?"

Crouch, Sr. is not all bad, interesting enough the rules obsessed man smuggled his son out of Azkaban as a last favor to his dying wife. In addition, he had Winky, the family house-elf, nurse his son back to health. Later, he controlled him under the Imperius Curse and forced him to wear an invisibility cloak. The Detectives believe the fact Crouch returned his son to good health, instead of letting him die at home proves he loved his son a great deal. He even allowed him go to the Quidditch World Cup as a special treat because his son had always loved Quidditch. It seems Crouch had not accepted his son was beyond redemption and was trying to make up for the void in his childhood.

Late in life, Crouch was "obsessed with catching Dark wizards[33]." He went so far as to act as if Harry, Ron, and Hermione were guilty of conjuring the Dark Mark without stopping to think they were far too young. When Winky was found under the mark, he was furious and treated her terribly. Since Winky failed him, Crouch gave her clothes and set her free. It is interesting to note, Crouch gave Winky a full outfit, not simply a sock. Also, he did not throw her out of the house right away; instead he waited for Dobby to take her with him to Hogwarts. This suggests Crouch cared a great deal about the elf. She had been treated as an equal in his house and a partner in making decisions about his son. Perhaps Crouch realized his son was going to become a danger and wanted his elf to be free, out of danger, and able to tell Dumbledore what had happened if things got out of hand. Crouch fought the Imperius Curse and wanted to confess what he had done to Dumbledore. The Detectives believe Crouch and Dumbledore were close, due to the fact he is one of the few people in the series to address him as Albus. Unfortunately, he was not able to deliver the message because his son found him first, killed and buried him. This was a sad end for a man who had fought evil his entire life.

<u>Chapter 7</u>

<u>The Order of the Phoenix</u>

The Order of the Phoenix is a secret organization formed during Voldemort's last reign of terror. Dumbledore is both the founder and leader of the Order. Upon Voldemort's return to his body, the Order was recalled. Its mission is to stop Voldemort from getting hold of the power he seeks and to fight him every step of the way. In the fifth year, the Order tried to protect the prophecy made about Voldemort and the one with the power to destroy him—Harry Potter. The other mission of the Order of the Phoenix is to protect Harry from Voldemort and his Death Eaters. This means Harry has an around-the-clock guard watching him when he is not at Hogwarts. The Detectives believe those who are entrusted with this job are those who Dumbledore and/or Sirius Black trust above all other members. In addition, every member is aware they may be required to give the ultimate sacrifice. The Order is comprised only of adults, who have left school. Its headquarters is at number 12 Grimmauld Place. The Detectives believe the Order of the Phoenix never really disbanded. It is likely they continued to meet occasionally, to protect Harry and to keep tabs on Death Eaters. However, they did not have an official headquarters and were not actively recruiting members. So, what happened to the old headquarters and where was it? Clearly they cannot use it anymore because of Wormtail's betrayal.

Founder

Albus Dumbledore

See Hogwarts Professors

Sirius Black

Sirius is a star in the Constellation Canis Major and the brightest star in the sky. It is also called the Dog Star, Sothis. Sirius "is powerful almost to the point of being destructive to the individual…it is transforming and makes sacred all that it touches, whether this be to the betterment or detriment of the individual[1]." The selection of this name provided the Detectives with a great deal of information about Sirius in order to solve the mystery in Book 3, long before it was revealed. It is also interesting he is the brightest star in the sky. He could have been the best, if fate had been kinder. The word black has several meanings. It means dirty, soiled, evil, wicked, dark, and marked by anger or sullenness. Most of these definitions provide the readers with more insight into the Black family, but the last definition definitely describes Sirius. It is easy to see from the range of definitions why the Detectives were confused about Sirius Black in the beginning. He clearly could have been evil, if he had chosen that path. Sirius Black is a tall, thin man whose face was hollowed from Azkaban, although the vestiges of good looks remain. He has a loud bark like laugh. Like Dumbledore, Harry, and Lupin, Sirius uses Voldemort's name and is insistent Peter does the same. This tells the Detectives Sirius is a brave man. In addition, Sirius, like James, Lily, Remus, and Peter was an original member of the Order. Sirius was James Potter's best friend at Hogwarts and they were the leaders of their gang. Lupin and Pettigrew were the other two members. Sirius and James were quite the troublemakers. In fact, they drew the Marauder's Map and signed it with their nicknames. Lupin was

Moony; Sirius, Padfoot; James, Prongs; and Peter was Wormtail. Black and Potter tormented Snape during their tenure at Hogwarts. They were extremely talented wizards and James was excellent at Quidditch. Sirius and James were arrogant as kids, no doubt because they were "the best in the school at whatever they did and everyone thought they were the height of cool[2]." They also had the reputation of jinxing and hexing anyone who annoyed them. An example of how talented James and Sirius were is the fact they managed to become animagus after only five years of magical education. This is an extremely difficult piece of magic. James, Sirius, and Peter never registered, as the Ministry requires. Yet, they managed to do it after only five years of magical education. James transformed into a stag; Sirius, a dog; and Peter, a rat. After Hogwarts, Sirius was the best man at James and Lily's wedding, named Harry's godfather, and appointed Harry's guardian if anything happened to the two of them.

Following Voldemort's murder of the Potters, Sirius went to the Potters' house and tried to persuade Hagrid to give Harry to him. Hagrid had his orders from Dumbledore to take Harry to his aunt and uncle's and Sirius eventually relented. He even lent his magical motorcycle to Hagrid to carry Harry to safety. The Detectives believe this was the breaking point for Sirius. First, he lost his best friend. Second, Dumbledore overrode James and Lily's wishes and took Harry away from Sirius. What gave Dumbledore that right? Why did Sirius agree? Does Sirius know something about Dumbledore? In effect, Sirius had lost it all. The Dursleys would never let him near the baby. Thus, he cracked. Sirius went to kill Peter Pettigrew, who Sirius alone knew had been the Potters' secret keeper. Peter outsmarted Sirius by shouting for the whole street to hear that Sirius had betrayed the Potters. Then, before Sirius could curse him, Peter cut off his finger, blew up the entire street, transformed into a rat, and ran down the sewer. Sirius stood there and laughed. No doubt he could not believe Peter had the brains to do such a thing. As a result, Sirius spent twelve years in Azkaban, the wizard prison. Sirius escaped from Azkaban after learning Peter was not only still alive, but at Hogwarts in the perfect position to hand Harry over to the Death Eaters if he got the slightest hint the Dark side was reforming. So, he escaped to kill Peter. Unfortunately, he did not succeed and Sirius had to go on the run. He was able to tell his story to Dumbledore, Lupin, Harry, Hermione, and Ron.

Sirius was not permitted to raise Harry after the death of James and Lily, which caused a great deal of resentment. Since he has gotten to know Harry as a teenager, which was the same time period he got to know James, many believe Sirius is confusing the two. The Detectives disagree. Sirius believes Harry is not a child. The Detectives also believe since

Sirius was James's best friend, he was privy to information, which the other characters were not. Also, since he knew James so well and Harry is so much like his father, Sirius knows it is better and safer to give Harry the facts rather than let him discover them. Thus, when Harry arrived at headquarters Sirius wanted to tell him everything. Lupin and the Weasleys stopped him because Dumbledore did not want Harry to know anything beyond a certain point. The Detectives believe telling Harry would have prevented Sirius's death and then he could have taught Defense Against the Dark Arts. Picture it: Snape and Sirius, both teaching at Hogwarts. What fun would that have been! The Head Detective is still bitter. Sirius Black was her favorite character! Alas, she saw it coming, but it did not make it any easier!

The readers learn a great deal about Sirius in Book 5. Sirius comes from a line of extremely wealthy pureblood wizards. Apparently, it was expected Sirius would be placed in Slytherin House, just like the rest of his family. Undoubtedly it was a great disappointment when they heard he was sorted into Gryffindor. On Harry's first train ride to Hogwarts, Ron was faced with a similar situation. His whole family had been in Gryffindor and he says to Harry. "I don't know what they'll say if I'm not. I don't suppose Ravenclaw would be too bad, but imagine if they put me in Slytherin[3]." Well, in Sirius' case, the Sorting Hat did exactly that as far as his family was concerned. It put him in the rival house. The equivalent of a family of University of Michigan fans having a kid go to The Ohio State University. Fortunately, in Ron's case the Buckeye stayed in Columbus. Sirius's placement in Gryffindor House was probably one of the reasons he was constantly reminded that his younger brother was a much better son. So, at the age of sixteen, Sirius ran away from home and went to live with James. His Uncle Alphard had left him some gold. So, at seventeen, he was able to get a place of his own and look after himself. According to Kreacher, the house-elf, he broke his mother's heart. Is this why or was there something else?

The readers are given the opportunity to see the Black Family Tree in Book 5. The Black family believed "to be a Black made you practically royal" and subscribed to the same pureblood mania as the Malfoy family[4]. Whenever the Black family produced a decent witch or wizard they were disowned and blasted off the family tree. Sirius' parents were not Death Eaters, but they were all for the purification of the Wizarding race and having purebloods in charge. The Detectives wonder if the Blacks went to school with Tom Riddle? If McGonagall would ever start talking we would find out. They thought Voldemort had the right idea in the beginning, but when they saw what he would do to gain power, they had a change of heart.

Sirius gives a brief summary of his family history, which may prove to be useful, so the Detectives will repeat it is as follows. His great-great-grandfather, Phineas Nigellus was the least popular headmaster of Hogwarts ever. His mother's cousin, "Araminta Meliflua…tried to force through a Ministry Bill to make Muggle hunting legal…Aunt Elladora started the family tradition of beheading house-elves[5]." Sirius also tells Harry, Molly Weasley is his cousin by marriage and Arthur Weasley is his second cousin.

Sirius's favorite cousin, Andromeda, was disowned because she married muggle born, Ted Tonks. The detectives have met their daughter, but wonder where her parents are and whether or not they know what is going on. It is really Andromeda's sisters who are fascinating. They are Narcissa Black, who married Lucius Malfoy, and Bellatrix Black, who married Rodolphus Lestrange. Sirius is particularly touchy about the issue of Bellatrix. Why? He has calmly discussed the rest of his insane relatives without any sign of being bothered, but when Bellatrix was mentioned, it was a different story. Sirius was short with Harry when he told him they were in Azkaban. He even snapped at Harry when he commented about Sirius' failure to mention she was his cousin. This is not normal behavior for Sirius and suggests there is something very deep here, possibly a Snitch. Furthermore, the Detectives believe Harry had a good point. Sirius wasted no time in telling Harry, Ron, and Hermione that Snape had been friends with Bellatrix, but neglected to mention she was his cousin. Hmmm, that is odd. Sirius's strange behavior does not stop there. "Does it matter if she's my cousin?" snapped Sirius. "As far as I'm concerned, they're not my family. *She's* certainly not my family[6]." Wow! That is deep. What has Bellatrix done to Sirius? They clearly hate each other. Isn't it interesting she is the one who takes his life?

Well, the answer may lie in the only other relative Sirius was irritable during the discussion of—his brother. Sirius had a younger brother, Regulus Black, who died fifteen years ago, the same year Harry was born. Is there a connection? The Detectives certainly would not rule out the possibility. Regulus joined the Death Eaters and was either killed by Voldemort or on his orders. Regulus, like Sirius, is named for a star. It is one of the four royal stars of Persia and represents "success without revenge[7]." Regulus was also a Roman general, who was "captured by the Carthaginians… sent on parole to Rome to negotiate peace, but he "advised the senate against accepting the Carthaginians terms. On his return to Carthage he was tortured to death[8]." The Detectives believe it is likely Regulus Black suffered the same fate at the Death Eaters' hands. According to Sirius, his brother "got in so far, then panicked about what he was being asked to do and tried to back out. Well, you don't just hand in your resignation to Voldemort. It's a lifetime service or death[9]."

Hmmm, let's think about this for a minute. Your two cousins and their husbands are in this organization and so are a bunch of your friends from school. If this were simply a case of nerves and panic, one would assume a network like this would help you work through the issues bothering you. Voldemort would prefer to resolve this problem rather than eliminating one soldier since his army was not very large. So, what was it Regulus was being asked to do? Was it something he would not be able to work through? Perhaps it was an issue, which would not only turn him, but his parents against Voldemort. Move them from the sympathizer category to a movement fighting against him. What order would that be? It would either prove his loyalty or alienate him completely? Kill Sirius! Kill your brother! The Detectives believe Regulus refused to kill Sirius and his refusal cost him his life. The Detectives also believe Kreacher knows. When he says Sirius broke his mother's heart, he is referring to several things. First, of course is his being in Gryffindor and leaving home. Then, his decision to fight Voldemort, caused him to be placed on the hit list, which not only endangered his life, but his brother's life. The Detectives believe Kreacher blames Sirius for Regulus's death and the misery it caused his mistress. If Voldemort did not kill Regulus himself, then he ordered Bellatrix to do it. Perhaps this is the reason Kreacher does not respect her anymore.

Sirius's death was part of a well-organized plan at the end of Book 5. Narcissa and Kreacher were working together. The object was to get both Harry and Sirius to the Department of Mysteries. Then, Harry would lift the prophecy off of the shelf and allow the Death Eaters the chance to kill Sirius. The Detectives believe no one is allowed to kill Harry, except Voldemort himself. Why? It would be a threat to his power. Even Malfoy says to be gentle with Potter, but he doesn't care what they do to the others. It should be noted no one tried to kill Sirius, except Bellatrix. Why? The killing curses were heading his way from her wand all night. The killing curse is the only curse we know that has a jet of green light. She manages to kill him on her third attempt. Interestingly, she made no attempt to kill anyone else, nor did any of the other Death Eaters. Why? Was he their target? Were there two missions that night? Perhaps Bellatrix had to do Regulus's job and Narcissa had to plan it to prove their loyalty. After all, Narcissa had escaped justice. Bellatrix seemed to feel she needed to tell Voldemort why she did not know what happened to the prophecy and who she was fighting. Voldemort took her with him when he escaped. Perhaps this was a reward for accomplishing one of the missions.

Finally, where do wizards go if they do not fear death and choose to stay behind as ghosts? Dumbledore says the ones we love never truly leave us. They live inside us. The Detectives believe they go on and offer a protection for the living. Could this be the real reason Sirius had to die? Or is Sirius really dead at all? He simply fell behind the curtain and is presumed dead. No one saw him die or his dead body. Could Sirius simply be trapped behind the iron curtain, like countless others who were trapped after WWII? This curtain could simply lead to another dimension? If so, with whom is he trapped? The Detectives wonder if Dumbledore knows the answer, but also realize Harry must be angry in order to kill Voldemort. The Detectives believe Sirius will reappear if Book 8 is written, given Books 1-7 are meant for children and the concept would be far to difficult for them to grasp.

Dedalus Diggle

Daedalus, which is only one letter off of Dedalus, was a character in Greek Mythology. He was a renowned craftsman, sculptor, inventor and the builder of the labyrinth. Daedalus fashioned the wings with which he and his son Icarus escaped from Crete after their imprisonment by Minos[10]. Thus, the Detectives can assume Diggle is innovative and talented. Diggle is a tiny old man with a squeaky, wheezy voice. He is very clumsy. He was also an original member of the Order and knew Lily and James well. Diggle has been appearing briefly ever since Book 1. First, it was the issue of the shooting stars in Kent. This annoyed McGonagall and she stated that he had never had much sense. On the day after Lily and James were killed, Diggle was outside Vernon's office and Vernon knocked him down. Was this a coincidence? There are no coincidences. Diggle proceeded to hug Vernon and actually calls him "dear sir[11]." Why did he hug Vernon? Did he put a protection spell on him? The Detectives believe this is exactly what Diggle did. This would have been quite innovative, don't the detectives think? And to call Vernon "dear sir?" Who would call Vernon a dear man? Perhaps Petunia's protection was voluntary, but Diggle did something extra to Vernon when he hugged him, so Harry would be safe with him too. Later, Diggle bowed to Harry in a shop. This is part of the reason the Detectives do not believe the Order was ever completely disbanded. Later, Harry remembered Diggle when he was introduced to him in the Leaky Cauldron. The Detectives believe Diggle is close to

Dumbledore based on the photo of the original Order. This is assuming Dumbledore would be standing between two close friends. The other alternative is Dumbledore, the leader, was standing in between his two deputies. Either way, Diggle would be highly trusted. Diggle was also a part of Harry's guard from the Dursleys. The Detectives expect to see quite a bit of Diggle in the future.

Elphias Doge

The name Doge comes from the man who was elected chief magistrate of the former republics of Venice and Genoa. Thus, the Detectives may assume he is a powerful wizard and possibly a leader. Other than this the Detectives know very little about Doge. He is a wizard with a wheezy voice and silver hair and he knew Harry's parents. In addition, he was one of the original members of the Order of the Phoenix and part of Harry's guard.

Aberforth Dumbledore

Aberforth Dumbledore is the brother of Albus Dumbledore. He was an original member of the Order of the Phoenix. Moody says Aberforth is a "strange bloke[12]." This is evident in his brother's comment, Aberforth was "prosecuted for practicing inappropriate charms on a goat[13]." The goat reference makes the Detectives wonder if Aberforth is the bartender in the Hog's Head. The bar smells like goats. Also, the man is described as a tall, thin, "grumpy-looking old man with…long gray hair and beard[14]." This physical description sounds a lot like Albus Dumbledore. Furthermore, someone in the Hog's Head protected Dumbledore and threw out the eavesdropper when Trelawney gave the prophecy. Aberforth has been mentioned in both Books 4 and 5, so the Detectives question when we will meet this wizard or be formally introduced to him? It is possible he is similar to Sherlock Holmes' brother and is very bright, or powerful, but does not apply himself.

Arabella Doreen Figg

Dear old, Mrs. Figg. Her name like so many others may be a clue as to her character. Arabella Stuart was the cousin of James I of England and a descendant of Henry VIII's sister[15]. The Arabella was also the ship John Winthrop and the Puritans sailed on to the New World in search of religious freedom. Her name suggests Arabella Figg could be a relative of James Potter and will be instrumental in the fight for freedom in the wizarding world. The word fig means not literal or figurative and a fig leaf is something that conceals or camouflages. So, the Detectives must ask what is she concealing and if she is not literal, then who is she really? The Detectives knew Mrs. Figg was important because she kept appearing in the series and Aunt Petunia would not allow Harry to go to anyone else's house despite the alternatives suggested by Vernon. This was a snitch not all detectives may have caught. Harry also says the Dursleys always left him with Mrs. Figg. Thus, this proves to the Detectives, the incident in Book 1 was not isolated. Mrs. Figg was clearly part of a protection network. If the Detectives had any doubt, it was removed when Sirius was sent to various people, including Arabella Figg. So, she is a friend of Sirius too. In addition, she knew he was innocent, which means she met with someone, either Dumbledore or Lupin. Mrs. Figg lives in Harry's neighborhood and was Harry's baby-sitter. Clearly, Dumbledore trusts her a great deal. She was one of the first people to whom he sent an owl, after Lily and James were killed. "None of them noticed a large, tawny owl flutter past the window[16]." This also means Mrs. Figg lived in the neighborhood before Harry arrived. Mrs. Figg is obsessed with cats. Why? Mrs. Figg is a Squib and like Filch, has a cat. The Detectives believe this is a form of ancient magic designed to protect Squibs, the non-magic children of a witch and wizard. Also, the Detectives have a theory as to how squibs came about. Retardation, typically, is seen in the child of two highly intelligent parents. Thus, it would logically follow a squib would come from two extremely powerful wizards. Thus, the Detectives wonder, who are Mrs. Figg's parents? Harry tells the readers her house always smells like cabbage. Again, why? What else smells like cabbage? The Apothecary smelled like cabbage and so does Polyjuice potion. Could Mrs. Figg be taking Polyjuice potion? Why would she do that? Who is she really? What is her real name? In the fourth book, the tent Mr. Weasley borrowed from Perkins was decorated like and smelled the same as Mrs. Figg's house. This seems strange. Could the tents belong to Mrs. Figg? Furthermore, the Detectives have never met Mr. Figg. Where is he? Is he dead? Or has he just been hidden in plain sight? Who is he? Could Perkins be her husband? Or could she be Perkins? Her house smells like Polyjuice potion. Another question, is who are Mrs. Figg's parents? Are they the reason she takes the potion? Does she have children? Perhaps they are the reason she takes the potion.

The Detectives were given a Snitch as to who her mother is in Book 5. When Mrs. Figg came running into the alley she was wearing "tartan carpet slippers[17]." This was such an exciting clue. Well, whom do the detectives know who wears tartan dress robes and whose every accessory is tartan? Who is obsessed with tartan? As if that is not enough of a clue, she follows up with a Bludger. Mrs. Figg tells Harry she is a Squib, she says, "I've never so much as transfigured a teabag[18]." Hmmm, Let's think about this for a minute. McGonagall is obsessed with tartan, a Transfiguration teacher, and she can turn into a cat. (Mrs. Figg is obsessed with cats.) So, the Detectives have found McGonagall's other child. Harry says Mrs. Figg is old. Well, what is old to a child? Someone who is older than your parents or aunt and uncle is old. They are in their thirties. So, someone in her forties or fifties would definitely be old. McGonagall is in her seventies. If they were sisters, this would be a bit much to ask Mrs. Figg to watch Harry when he was a baby for weeks at a time. Further evidence Mrs. Figg's parentage is important is at Harry's hearing. Fudge tells her to leave her parentage with Percy after the hearing. When she got up to leave, she "cast a frightened look from Fudge to Dumbledore[19]." Why was she frightened? She did not leave the details as Fudge requested either. In fact, after Harry was cleared, Dumbledore left abruptly with Mrs. Figg, without even stopping to tell Mr. Weasley Harry had been cleared. Why was Dumbledore in such a big hurry to get out of there with Mrs. Figg? Why didn't he want anyone to know who her parents were? Apparently, no one knows McGonagall had a baby. Could Mrs. Figg be McGonagall's child? The Detectives are sure Minerva McGonagall is her mother. Who is Arabella's father? The Detectives are not as clear about this. Is she Tom Riddle's baby? She cannot be because J.K. Rowling confirmed Voldemort has no children[20]. But there are others who could be her father. Mrs. Figg has Moody's grizzled gray hair. This of course could have to do with the potion she is taking, but she could be Moody's daughter. She could also be Dumbledore's daughter. He would not want this revealed because Voldemort and the Death Eaters would make her a target. They would want to do anything to hurt Dumbledore. Or could McGonagall be Minerva's married name? This is the theory the Detectives believe is most likely. Again, does Mrs. Figg have children? We asked earlier what Mrs. Figg's real name was. So what is it? What is Perkins' last name or is Perkins his last name? Also, Sirius is sent to tell her about Voldemort's return, along with Lupin and Mundungus. Sirius told Harry the Potters had adopted him as a second son and he was always welcome at their house. Arabella Figg and Perkins cannot be the Potters because J.K. Rowling says all of Harry's grandparents are dead[21]. But could they be the related to the Potters, possibly first cousins, as her name suggests? The Detectives believe James Potter was named for King James, so a Snitch would suggest Arabella was his first cousin as well. This theory will be explained thoroughly in the section on Harry Potter.

Mundungus Fletcher

Mundungus literally means a stinking tobacco and a fletcher is one who makes arrows. Gee, he is not someone the Detectives would want to be around, but definitely would be useful, especially if you needed tobacco or arrows. Mundungus Fletcher is a petty criminal, whose name appeared in two books before the readers finally got to meet him in Book 5. He is loyal to Dumbledore because Dumbledore helped him out of a tight spot. He is also a friend of Sirius. In addition, he apparently knew Sirius was innocent since Sirius went to tell him Voldemort had returned. Interestingly enough, he doesn't pay much attention during the meetings, but will side with Sirius when asked for his opinion.

Mundungus was off buying stolen cauldrons when the Dementors attacked Harry. He is also helping the Weasley twins get the illegal, or hard to obtain, ingredients they need for their inventions. The Detectives expect Mundungus to play an important role. He seems like a sketchy character, but in the words of Sirius, he is useful. Every government knows when it is time to infiltrate, you work with people with whom you would not ordinarily associate because they hear and know things others do not. The point is people like Mundungus sometimes prove to be extremely useful. Mundungus was banned from the Hog's Head 20 years ago. Why? Who is the barman anyway? With Sirius gone, Mundungus will turn to the twins because they like Sirius will be his friends in the order. The twins, like Sirius, are interested in keeping Harry alive. Look for Mundungus to continue to supply them with ingredients for their inventions.

Rubeus Hagrid

See Hogwarts Professors

Hestia Jones

Hestia is from Greek Mythology. She is the Goddess of the Hearth and the sister of Zeus[22]. Very little is known about Jones. She has pink cheeks and black hair. Jones was a member of Harry's guard from the Dursleys.

Remus John Lupin

See Hogwarts Professors

Madame Olympia Maxime

Olympia sounds a great deal like Olympus, which is a mountain in Greece. It is also where the Greek gods were said to have lived. Maxime is French for principle. This could either mean she is a principled woman or she is the principal or Headmistress of Beauxbaton. In addition, Maxim was the name of a family of inventors, who invented weapons[23]. Madame Maxime, like Hagrid is a half-Giant. Madame Maxime and Hagrid are openly smitten with each other. The Detectives believe it is clear Madame Maxime joined the Order. At the end of the year 4, Dumbledore met with both Maxime and Hagrid. Over the summer, he sent them to find the giants in order to persuade them to join the Order as opposed to joining Voldemort. Their mission was not successful. In addition, Madame Maxime knew Hagrid had brought Grawp back with him, but kept silent. This show Madame Maxime is loyal to Hagrid and willing to take part in dangerous missions. The Detectives expect she will build the French Resistance, or the Order in France.

Minerva McGonagall

See Hogwarts Professors

Alastor "Mad Eye" Moody

Alastor is Greek for an avenging deity or spirit[24]. Moody means a frequent change in mood or temperamental. This is clearly a clue as to Moody's brusque personality. Moody has a wooden leg, his face is severely scared, and he has a large chunk missing from his nose. He has a magical blue eye that can see through the back of his head and other solid objects. He is extremely distrusting and paranoid. Moody was one of the original members of the Order of the Phoenix. He is retired from the Ministry of Magic, but was considered the best Auror of all time. Moody is famous for rounding up more Death Eaters than any other Auror. Thus, the Death Eaters fear him. In Book 4, he was captured and imprisoned in his own trunk by Barty Crouch, Jr. and Wormtail. This was the perfect cover. Everyone thinks Moody is eccentric, so strange behavior would go unnoticed. Also, Moody and Crouch, Jr. had something in common. They both hated Death Eaters who had walked free. Well, Moody hated all the Death Eaters without conditions. Crouch, Jr. did not even have to act on this one. He could torment the same people Moody would have tormented and get away with it. Even better, under the cover of being Moody, he knew the people he was tormenting were so terrified of Moody, they were powerless to do anything about his harassment.

Moody had a photo of the original Order of the Phoenix. The Detectives wonder, who took this picture? Was it done by magic? It may not be important. In the photo, he was pictured standing next to Dumbledore. The Detectives believe there could be several reasons for this. First, the leader of the organization, Dumbledore would, in theory, be standing between his deputies. The alternative is Dumbledore would be standing between his two closest friends. Both could be correct. We already know Moody is one powerful wizard. We also know from Dumbledore's pensive of the trials, Moody is one of the very few wizards who addresses Dumbledore as Albus, which suggests a close relationship. In addition, Moody was one of Harry's guards, which once again suggests he is one of the most highly trusted members of the Order.

Sturgis Podmore

Podmore is a square-jawed wizard with straw colored hair. Podmore was another original member of the Order. Unfortunately, Malfoy hit Podmore with an Imperius Curse while he was standing guard for the Order of the Phoenix. Then, while under the curse, he got Podmore to attempt to enter the Department of Mysteries. Podmore was caught by the Ministry of Magic and was sent to Azkaban for six months. According to a letter from Percy, Podmore was considered a "great friend of Dumbledore[25]." Podmore was also a member of Harry's guard from the Dursleys and was supposed to be guarding him to King's Cross Station. The Detectives expect to see Podmore again, but it is doubtful he will be entrusted with Harry again because he will be considered easy prey for the Death Eaters.

Kingsley Shacklebolt

Charles Kingsley was a British cleric and writer famous for novels of social criticism, notably Alton Locke (1850). It is key J.K. Rowling named this character after this particular writer. Charles Kingsley was widely known "as the most outspoken and powerful of those who took the side of the labouring classes, at a critical time[26]." This is a Bludger. Shacklebolt is powerful and has joined the Order at a *critical time*. Also, in Kingsley's story of Dreamland, he tells a short story of a revolution of the oppressed and starving to "put down these riotous and idle wretches[27]." After the revolution, he encouraged them to divide the land equally between the rich and poor and work the land as God intended, as opposed to hoarding and resorting to crime and sloth. This suggests Shacklebolt will not only help to fight the battle, but will also participate in the reconstruction effort, mainly helping to keep order after the fighting has ended. The surname is equally noteworthy. A shacklebolt is the bolt that holds the shackle together, which is a metal fastening to confine the ankle or wrist of a captive. Wow, the Detectives are certainly glad he is on our side. This is definitely a clue as to Shackebolt's character. He is hindering the Ministry's search for Sirius and their attempt to arrest Dumbledore. Shacklebolt, as a Senior Auror, is a trusted employee of the Ministry of Magic and is also an undercover spy for the Order. He was not one of the original members of the Order; thus, the Death Eaters had not discovered his existence in the beginning of Book 5. Unfortunately, after the battle, Shacklebolt will have been exposed as working for the Order. We shall see how the Ministry treats him. If Voldemort's spies are any good, there will be no change.

Shacklebolt is a tall, bald, black wizard. He wears a single gold hoop earning and has a deep, slow voice. From the encounter when the advance guard picked Harry up, it was clear Shacklebolt knew James. He thinks Harry looks exactly like James. The Detectives believe Shacklebolt went to Hogwarts with Remus, James, and Sirius. This makes the Detectives wonder why on earth the Ministry would assign him to the search for Sirius. Not smart. Assign an old friend to look for an escaped friend. We are with Snape on this one. No way! Shacklebolt is leading the search for Sirius. So, he is feeding the Ministry a bunch of misinformation. Good man! He will be in big trouble if he is caught. Shacklebolt is clearly high up in the Auror hierarchy because Fudge brought him with him when he intended to expel Harry. Also, you would not place a rookie on the search for the most wanted criminal in the wizarding world. Umbridge either respected Shacklebolt's opinion or feared losing his support. The Detectives expect to see a great deal of Shacklebolt in the following books.

Severus Snape

See Hogwarts Professors

Nymphadora Tonks

Nymphs exist in both Greek and Roman mythology. They are numerous minor deities. Typically, they are beautiful maidens inhabiting and often personifying nature. They are able to blend in with their surroundings. This is definitely a clue into Tonks' character. She is a master of disguise. After all, she is a Metamorphmagus, which means she can change her appearance at will. She is also a rookie Auror, a Dark Wizard Catcher.

It is lucky she is on our side. This is an interesting job for a person to choose, whose aunt and uncle are serving a life sentence in Azkaban for their role as Death Eaters, don't you think? Tonks is an extremely clumsy, young woman and a new recruit to the Order. She is a member of the Black family, but her mother, Andromeda was blasted off the family tree for marrying muggle born, Ted Tonks. It is also interesting the Ministry hired her. Amazingly, Tonks has been a part of all of Harry's guards, even though she is so new to the order. Perhaps this is because she is so good at disguising herself, therefore giving the Death Eaters the false impression the Order has more people than they really do. Nonetheless, this tells the Detectives someone, either Dumbledore or Sirius, trusts Tonks a great deal. At the end of Book 5, Tonks fought and was injured in a battle with Bellatrix. She was sent to St. Mungo's, but Dumbledore said she would make a full recovery. Since she was on guard duty by the end of term we assume that she did. It is important to note Bellatrix hurt Tonks, but did not attempt to kill her niece. Why? Bella hasn't gone soft on us, has she? She wanted to kill her cousin. The Detectives believe that was indeed her mission. So, why not make a clean sweep? Get rid of all those relatives who have "disgraced" the Black Family. Or did she think her sister would come after her if she killed her daughter? If her sisters, cousin, and daughter are any indication, Andromeda is a powerful witch. Perhaps, Bella just doesn't want to infuriate her. "Hell hath no fury like a woman scorned[28]." Or did she think that if she killed Tonks she would not get the opportunity to kill Sirius because he would then realize she really was capable of killing her own flesh and blood?

Emmeline Vance

Vance is described as a stately looking witch who wore an emerald green shawl. She was an original member of the Order and a member of Harry's guard. The Detectives know very little about Vance, but expect her to continue fighting Voldemort and his Death Eaters.

Arthur Weasley

Arthur is a good strong name. The Detectives suspect that he was named for King Arthur the legendary British hero of Camelot, who was famous for his Knights of the Round Table. Arthur Weasley is a tall, thin, balding, red headed man. He has scars from the night he got caught being out of bound by the Hogwarts gamekeeper. Will these scars turn out to be useful? Remember Dumbledore said they sometimes do. Mr. Weasley is married to Molly and has seven children. Their home is called "the Burrow" which means a hole dug in to the ground for habitation or a snug place. This certainly describes their home. Arthur loves muggles and is fascinated by all of their gadgets. This explains why he works for the Ministry of Magic in the Misuse of Muggle Artifacts Office. Mr. Weasley is the Head of his office, which consists of two people. His assistant is Perkins. For the World Cup, Mr. Weasley borrowed a tent, from Perkins. This tent was decorated, looked, and smelled exactly like Mrs. Figg's house. Hmmm, who suggested this tent? Was it protected, since Harry was going to be staying it? Perkins is an old wizard. More on this theory was discussed in the section on Mrs. Figg.

Voldemort's snake bit Mr. Weasley while he was on guard duty for the Order. Fortunately, Harry saw this in his dream and was able to alert the Order and save Mr. Weasley's life. Mr. Weasley fully recovered, despite his experimentation with muggle remedies—stitches. The Detectives believe that Mr. Weasley will survive the series and become the Minister of Magic. The basis of this is Ron's statement, "we've got about as much chance of winning the Quidditch Cup this year as Dad's got of becoming Minister of Magic[29]." This could be foreshadowing given that a strange twist of fate lead to Gryffindor winning the Quidditch Cup. This statement combined with McGonagall's statement, "There may well be a new Minister of Magic by the time Potter is ready to join[30]!" If Arthur Weasley were the new Minister of Magic, he would certainly employ Harry Potter. Also, Dumbledore does not want the job, but would recommend someone who is loyal to him.

Bill Weasley

Bill Weasley is the oldest of the Weasley brothers. He is built like his father. Bill has long red hair and an earring with a fang. While at Hogwarts, he was Head Boy. Bill was a curse breaker for Gringotts in the Egyptian tombs. After Voldemort's return, Bill transferred to England. In addition, he is dating Fleur Delacour. Will he bring her into the Order?

Charlie Weasley

Charlie is the second oldest Weasley son. He is built like the twins. Charlie was both a Seeker and Captain for the Gryffindor Quidditch team and could have played for England. Charlie is studying dragons in Romania and works as a dragon tamer. He and Hagrid got along very well because they shared a love for dangerous creatures. Charlie came to Hogwarts with the other dragon trainers during the Triwizard Tournament.

Following Voldemort's return, Charlie remained in Romania, but is joined the Order. Dumbledore says, he wants as many foreign wizards brought into the Order as possible. Thus, we assume Charlie is recruiting wizards abroad.

Molly Weasley

Molly Weasley is the wife of Arthur and the mother of seven red haired children. In addition, she has somewhat adopted Harry and feels he might as well be another one of her sons. Clearly, Dumbledore knows and trusts the Weasley family. It is possible he is even related to them, provided of course, Dumbledore is a pureblood. Surely all detectives have noticed Harry spends a great deal of time at the Weasley household. Hopefully, these same detectives have noticed Dumbledore is very particular about where Harry spends his time, either 4 Privet Drive, Hogwarts, the Leaky Cauldron, Headquarters of the Order, or the Weasley's House. What do these places have in common? 4 Privet Drive is Harry's aunt's house where Voldemort cannot touch him. Many spells and protections surround Hogwarts to protect its inhabitants, along with Dumbledore himself. Many wizards are able to keep an eye on Harry in the Leaky Cauldron. The Headquarters of the Order of the Phoenix is probably the safest place in England. In addition, it is located in Sirius' house and he is living there. So, why is Harry allowed to stay at the Weasley home? It does not fit with the rest. Clearly, Dumbledore has decided it is all right or he would not continue to allow Harry to go to the Weasley's house. Keep in mind; Aunt Petunia has prevented Harry from staying places in the past, so she would be capable of doing it again. Thus, Dumbledore trusts the Weasleys, even if Sirius does not like Molly. The Detectives believe this animosity is due completely to the fact they both want to raise Harry and Dumbledore will not allow either of them to do so.

Finally, the Detectives believe Mrs. Weasley's boggart is foreshadowing future events. First, the boggart was Ron's dead body. Then, Bill, who was followed by Mr. Weasley. Next, dead twins followed by dead Percy, and finally dead Harry. The boggart represents Mrs. Weasley's worst fears. Hence, she fears losing her family. "Half the family's in the Order, it'll be a miracle if we all come through this[31]." Well, the Detectives quite agree, Mrs. Weasley, and are so glad you brought up the subject, so we don't appear to be ogres. The Detectives note a couple members of her family are noticeably missing from this sequence. Ginny's body does not appear. She nearly lost Ginny during her first year at Hogwarts. The Detectives believe Ginny will indeed survive the series. Next, there was no dead

Charlie. Why not? Charlie works with dragons, which is not exactly a safe job, but she does not fear his death. Why? Since Charlie is abroad, she thinks he is safer than the others. Possibly he is not even suspected to be a part of the Order. Then Mr. Weasley's body, since Harry saw the would be fatal attack on him, the Detectives believe Arthur will survive the series. The Detectives believe there is a strong possibility Bill and one of the twins will die before the end of the series. Harry will clearly live. This boggart has another effect. An unspoken understanding passes between Sirius and Molly. They share the same fear—losing Harry. Then there is the issue of Percy. The Detectives are undecided about whether or not Percy will survive the series. His chances of survival went down markedly when he chose to play with fire and side with Fudge, instead of Dumbledore and his family. J.K. Rowling gets many of her characters' names from legends and history. Many times this is key to the character's role. Percy's name comes from Percival from the Knights of the Holy Grail. Through his ignorance he was responsible for the death of his uncle and his mother. Given all purebloods are interrelated, one can assume Crouch, Sr. was the uncle. Thus, it is logical to assume Molly will die before the series ends. The question is, will Percy be killed when he attempts to leave the sympathizer category or, will he make it to safety? This issue will be discussed more thoroughly in Percy Weasley- The Ministry of Magic.

Chapter 8

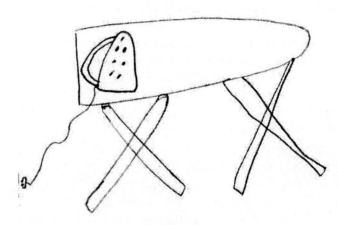

House-Elves

House-elves are bound by the enchantments of their kind. A house-elf cannot disobey a direct order from his or her master. They serve only one family. They are bound to the family and to the family home. They can, however, leave the home if they really want to. They are typically found in very old, wealthy, families and very old, large houses. When a house-elf does something that his master would not like, the elf must punish itself. The house-elves live with the family and keep the family secrets. A house-elf can only be freed, if his master presents him with clothes. Elves are not allowed to carry a wand, but they are magical. They seem to be able to perform magic through their fingers.

Dobby

Dobby was the Malfoy family's house-elf. Dobby has large, green eyes. He left the Malfoy house to warn Harry Potter of an evil plot. Dobby did not want Harry to return to Hogwarts because he was afraid he would be in danger. Dobby proceeded to continue to leave the Malfoy home to give Harry warnings and attempt to force him to leave Hogwarts. Harry did not realize at the time that Dobby was doing this at great risk to himself. Each time he warned Harry he had to punish himself. Then it was Dobby who told Harry Lucius had given Ginny, Tom Riddle's Diary. At the end of the year, Harry discovers Dobby serves the Malfoy family and tricks Lucius into giving Dobby a sock. This deepened Dobby's adoration for Harry. Lucius, then, attempted to harm Harry and Dobby pointed his finger at him and sent him flying down the stairs. Wow! So, the house-elves have powerful magic. Possibly this is why wizards are so keen to keep them enslaved. Lucius is afraid of Dobby after he is free and he is unwilling to challenge Dobby. Clearly, Lucius believes that Dobby's magic is stronger than his own.

Dobby enjoys his freedom. For this reason, the Detectives believe he will help Hermione with S.P.E.W. After hearing Winky has been freed, Dobby comes up with the idea they should try to get work together. Dobby wants to keep wearing clothes and to be paid, as well. This is the reason he has not been able to find work, as most wizards do not believe this is the purpose in having a house-elf. Winky pointed out there were not many places with enough work for two elves. This gave Dobby the idea to come to Hogwarts. Dumbledore hires both of them and says he will pay Dobby. In addition, Dobby likes Dumbledore and is proud to keep his secrets. The Christmas after Dobby comes to Hogwarts he gives Harry a pair of socks, which he made himself. Is there protection in them? If the Detectives had any doubt in Book 2, none remains after Book 4. Dobby will do anything to help Harry. When Dobby heard Harry had not found the information he needed for the second task, he rushed to Harry's aid. Dobby steals the gillyweed from Professor Snape's office. This shows he will do anything if it will help or save Harry Potter. Now, that is loyalty! Dobby is also the only elf trying to help Winky. Will Winky tell Dobby her story eventually? The Detectives believe the answer is yes.

Dobby is loyal to Harry and will not be loyal to anyone who intends to harm Harry. There is no doubt of this after the fifth year. When Umbridge tells the house-elves not to warn the students in the Room of Requirement, Dobby immediately warned Harry. This time, Dobby has not skirted the orders he has been given, but broken them completely. Dobby was determined to save Harry!

Dobby is a key character. The Detectives wonder what Dobby will do to Kreacher. Kreacher has hurt Harry deeply by killing Sirius. Will this lead to a battle between the elves? Will Dobby kill Kreacher? Dobby has a very bad reaction anytime anyone hurts or even insults his Harry Potter. This was seen when Winky called Harry nosy. This reaction is similar to that of Hagrid when someone insults Dumbledore. The Detectives also believe Dobby will leave Hogwarts when Harry leaves. Again, Dobby is only loyal to Harry. He will be Harry's house-elf. Money will not be an issue for Dobby and he will not care, if Harry can pay, as much as, Dumbledore or even if he can pay at all. Dobby's only desire is to assist Harry Potter.

Kreacher

Kreacher was the Black family's house-elf. He, like the majority of the Black family, fits in with the dark wizards. Kreacher adored Mrs. Black. Likewise, he hates Sirius and blames him for breaking his mother's heart. Kreacher is a servant, but still considers himself to be better than Hermione, which tells the readers a great deal about his mentality. Kreacher also calls Voldemort "The Dark Lord." This should have been a Bludger to everyone.

Kreacher left 12 Grimmauld Place and went to Narcissa Malfoy willing to help her in anyway he could. He wanted to destroy Sirius. Kreacher then lied to Harry and told him Sirius had gone to the Department of Mysteries. Therefore, Kreacher was indirectly responsible for Sirius's death. The Detectives are curious as to what will happen to Kreacher. Will he be killed by Dobby? After all Kreacher has hurt Harry and Dobby seems to have a negative reaction when people harm Harry. Or will the portraits in number 12 Grimmauld Place take care of Kreacher? He killed Sirius; the last of the Blacks and "to be a Black made you practically royal[1]." Kreacher has ended the Black family's bloodline to which he was sworn to serve. Kreacher has now done exactly what he hated Sirius for doing— breaking his mistress' heart. This could be enough to kill Kreacher. The Detectives can hope! Especially if the portraits held court after Phineas Nigellus arrived at 12 Grimmauld Place telling them their house-elf was responsible for the murder of the last of their line.

Winky

Winky was the Crouch family's house-elf. Before Winky was freed she had a tea towel draped like a toga. When she was freed she was given a skirt, shirt, and hat, which are now covered in butterbeer and soot. Winky has been drinking a great deal since she was freed. Winky knows many secrets, but is hesitant to reveal them. So, when will Winky reveal her secrets? Winky knew Barty Crouch, Jr. had been smuggled out of Azkaban and he was fighting the Imperius Curse, but she was horrified to learn he had murdered his father. Winky loved both of them dearly. After, the Dementors kissed Barty Crouch, Jr., Winky is forced to accept what Dobby has been telling her. Dumbledore is now her master. The Detectives believe Winky knows what Fudge was afraid Barty Crouch, Jr. would reveal. So, will Winky reveal this information? The Detectives believe she will reveal this information. The real question is to whom will Winky reveal the information? Dobby?

Mary C. Baumann

<u>The Hogwarts House-Elves</u>

There are over one hundred Hogwarts House-Elves. They all wear the same uniform draped like a toga with the Hogwarts crest stamped on it. They work in the kitchen, light the fires, and clean the common rooms. They show the mentality of the house elf populous. The Hogwarts House-Elves believe both Dobby and Winky are a disgrace to their kind. They have both been freed. In addition, Dobby is not "properly ashamed of freedom" and is even being paid[2]. Although, Winky is ashamed of her freedom, she is drinking a great deal and miserable without Mr. Crouch. These house-elves will do whatever they are told by the Hogwarts' Headmaster. These elves were more than happy to provide Ron and Harry with extra food and were delighted when they were complimented on their service. Perhaps this is the key to winning their loyalty. The elves do not seem to like Hermione at all. She told them, they should help Winky and try to cheer her up. At this they informed her Winky had no right to be unhappy because there was work to be done. Hermione went further and told them that they had the right to be unhappy, to wear clothes, and to earn wages. At this point, the house-elves determined Hermione was dangerous and pushed her, Harry and Ron out of the kitchen. The Hogwarts House-Elves have no desire for freedom and are offended even from the suggestion. However, they are loyal to their master and will assist him as best they can. Thus, as long as Dumbledore is the master the Hogwarts House-Elves can be counted on to assist in the fight for good.

__Chapter 9__

The Death Eaters

The Death Eaters are an elite organization of Dark wizards who have sworn eternal loyalty to Lord Voldemort. It is a lifetime commitment or death in the words of Sirius. They each have the Dark Mark burned into their left forearm. This is reminiscent of two important references, the sign of the beast and the Holocaust. Revelations 13:16 states the sign of the beast would be burned into the individual's right hand and those individuals would never be able to enter the Kingdom of Heaven[1]. Also, Hitler had ID numbers tattooed on the left forearm of those imprisoned in the Nazi Concentration camps. As Voldemort's character is so similar to that of the Devil and Hitler, this is yet another chilling reference. The Death Eaters refer to Voldemort as the Dark Lord and address him as Master. The organization operates in the utmost secrecy and Voldemort alone knows all of their names. Below are the names and analysis of the known Death Eaters and a few the Detectives have discovered. There were 30 Death Eaters at the rebirthing celebration. In addition, 10 were in Azkaban plus the one who performed the rebirthing task and the three Voldemort mentions and knows the reason for their absence, so the Head Detective would like to note this list is by no means conclusive. There should be 44 on a complete list and there are only 22 listed below.

Avery

The character Avery is intriguing. Avery went to Hogwarts with Snape, Bella, and Rodolphus, and they were mates. He was clearly in Slytherin, just like the rest, but that is not what makes Avery interesting. Avery wormed his way out of Azkaban on round one by saying he was acting under the Imperius Curse. Also, Avery was the only Death Eater who Voldemort tortured during his rebirthing ceremony. Why? Avery was simply asking for forgiveness. What guilty secret was Avery hiding? All the Death Eaters had abandoned Voldemort, but he only tortured Avery. He also stated that he did not forgive. What is it Avery has done? Clearly, Avery screwed up something. What was it? The Detectives believe Avery was the eavesdropper, who got caught half way through the prophecy, therefore bringing about the downfall of Voldemort. This would explain why Voldemort was angrier with Avery than with the rest of the group. Also, in the dream Harry has about Rookwood, Voldemort discovers Avery has again gotten the information wrong. Could it be Avery is still trying to remedy the situation regarding the prophecy? Again, Voldemort tortures Avery. Poor Avery, he is frequently Voldemort's victim. Avery was part of the raid in the Department of Mysteries. He was paired up with Macnair. At the end of Book 5, Avery, like many other Death Eaters was sent to Azkaban. The Detectives believe Avery will appear once the Death Eaters break out of Azkaban again. The question is will he be killed for his many failures?

Ludo Bagman

See the Ministry of Magic

Borgin

Mr. Borgin owns a large Dark Arts shop, called Borgin and Burkes. It is located in Knockturn Alley, which is a street totally devoted to the Dark Arts or the ghetto of the wizarding world. Mr. Borgin has poor posture, oily hair, and a voice to match. He appears to do business with Lucius Malfoy regularly, but seems to both dislike and fear him. When Draco walks in with his father, Borgin is excited to see the young Malfoy, undoubtedly due to the fact that Draco's presence is good for business.

The Detectives believe there is a strong possibility Borgin is a Death Eater or in some way indebted to them. He probably ranked much lower than Malfoy in the hierarchy, which could be another reason for the strong dislike. In the encounter between Borgin and Malfoy in Book 2, there are several incidents where Malfoy becomes angrily impatient and Borgin quickly appeases him. Borgin uses an "oily voice," he bows to Malfoy, and makes it clear he needs no explanations[2]. As soon as Malfoy exits the store Borgin's attitude changes, "Good day yourself, *Mister* Malfoy, and if the stories are true, you haven't sold me half of what's hidden in your *manor[3]*." Again, this suggests to the Detectives, Borgin is in close contact with other Death Eaters and has a very good idea with which artifacts Malfoy was entrusted. Another noteworthy point is the stress on the word "Mister." This causes the Detectives to ponder what Borgin called Malfoy in the past. As Borgin is the source of many poisons and other dark arts relics, it is logical he will appear again, possibly using the items which he sells.

Crabbe

Crabbe is an especially large Death Eater. Crabbe is named for a sea animal with pincers or a grumpy person. Either would be appropriate, as is a friend of Lucius Malfoy, who acts primarily as a bodyguard. He is the one to hold the victim, while Malfoy attacks. Crabbe's son Vincent is in the same year as Draco Malfoy. Clearly, Lucius Malfoy and Crabbe keep in touch, given Draco knew Vincent on the first train ride to Hogwarts. Perhaps they had been childhood friends.

Crabbe was a part of the mission at the Department of Mysteries. Perhaps he is not as dumb as we might think, since Voldemort entrusted him with this task. Crabbe was the Death Eater who picked Neville up and wanted someone to stun him. He was teamed up with Rabastan when Malfoy was pairing up the Death Eaters in the Department of Mysteries. Crabbe, like the others went to Azkaban. The Detectives are sure Crabbe will appear again in the ensuing battles.

Barty Crouch, Jr.

See Hogwarts Professors

Antonin Dolohov

Dolohov has a long, pale, twisted face. He was convicted of the brutal murders of Giden and Fabian Prewett. He is famous for the torturing of countless muggles and many witches and wizards who did not support Voldemort. Dolohov's favorite curse seems to include a slashing movement and a purple flame coming from the wand. This completely knocks out the victim. Dolohov performed this curse on Hermione and tried to do it to Sirius. The consequence of being on the receiving end of this curse is taking ten different potions a day. Dolohov went to Azkaban, but will certainly be a key Death Eater to watch in future books.

Goyle

Goyle is a large Death Eater. He is, also, a friend and/or bodyguard of Lucius Malfoy. This is appropriate given his name sounds like gargoyle, which is a stone statue that wards of evil or protects. Goyle does not ward off evil, but he does protect Lucius. Goyle has a son Gregory, who is in the same year as Draco. Like Crabbe, Lucius and Goyle kept in touch, given Draco and Gregory knew each other on the train ride to Hogwarts. Goyle, Sr. was not involved with the events at the Department of Mysteries. So, one must question, what he was doing at this time? Or is Goyle just too stupid to be trusted with such an important mission? Fortunately for Goyle he stayed out of Azkaban. As a result, he will have to take on more responsibility until his fellow Death Eaters break out of prison.

Jugson

Jugson has only been seen one time. He was the Death Eater who got his head caught in the jar of time and kept reverting to a baby and then an adult. Due to the fact he was trapped, the Detectives assume he was sent to Azkaban. The other Death Eaters did not seem to have any ideas for freeing him, but we are sure someone who works in the Department would be capable of doing so. Jugson was paired up with Dolohov in the Department of Mysteries.

Igor Karkaroff

Karkaroff is a tall, thin man with short white hair, a goatee and a weak chin. He has a fruity voice and his teeth are yellow. Karkaroff's eyes are cold and shrewd. He wears a cloak of a sleek, silver material. The Detectives suspect this cloak is made from Demiguise, which is the same material spun into Invisibility Cloaks. Further evidence to this theory is when Harry was walking in the dark covered in an Invisibility Cloak, Karkaroff did not see him and walked right into him. The question is why didn't Harry see Karkaroff? Well, the Demiguise can make itself invisible and the fur is spun into the Invisibility Cloaks. Perhaps this is how Karkaroff is avoiding Voldemort's capture. After all, he is the "one, too cowardly to return…he will pay[4]."

Moody caught Karkaroff after the fall of Voldemort. He was released from Azkaban because he made a deal with the Ministry, meaning he said he had seen the error of his ways and named names. These included Dolohov, Rosier, Travers, Mulciber, Rookwood, and Snape. It is interesting to note who was given up by Karkaroff. Snape was his last resort. It is equally interesting whom he did not give up to the Ministry. The Detectives surmise Karkaroff knew Malfoy was a Death Eater as well, but did not reveal him to the Ministry of Magic. Why? Perhaps Karkaroff feared the repercussions. Karkaroff and Malfoy are friends, given Lucius considered sending Draco to Durmstrang. But then, Karkaroff considered Snape a friend, but as a last resort was willing to sell him out for his own freedom.

After Karkaroff's release from Azkaban, he became the Headmaster of Durmstrang. The school is located in the far north. The name is fascinating. It is the combination of Strum und Drang, which was a literature movement popular in Nazi Germany. This is appropriate given Karkaroff's role as a Death Eater and Durmstrang's reputation. Durmstrang has a terrible reputation because it teaches the Dark Arts to the students not the Defense Against the Dark Arts. Karkaroff's favorite student was Victor Krum, the famous seeker. The Detectives expect to see Karkaroff again. He will not be able to avoid Voldemort forever. Karkaroff will be caught and forced to rejoin the Death Eaters.

Bellatrix Black Lestrange

Bel is the root for the word beauty in many languages, i.e. belle in French. Bellatrix, like her sister, was named for beauty. It is no surprise she is physically attractive, but like her maiden name suggests inside she black as night. Bellatrix is also a star in the constellation, Orion. The name means female warrior, but "signifies quickly coming or swiftly destroying[5]." From this the Detectives believe Bellatrix's role will develop quickly and she will destroy many people and things. The star's influence includes, "military honor, but danger of sudden dishonor…wealth…and gives a high-pitched, hard, sharp voice[6]." This clearly fits Bellatrix Lestrange. Furthermore, her married name Lestrange, is the combination of two word, le is French for "the" and the English word, strange. Like the name suggests she is strange.

Bellatrix is pure evil. Bellatrix Black Lestrange believes herself to be the Dark Lord's most faithful servant. This is interesting because when the star, Bellatrix is combined with Mars, the planet most visible in the sky at the present time, there is success as a soldier[7]. When combined with

Saturn, the presumed sign of Voldemort, Bellatrix lives a secluded life and "the married partner may die young, no children[8]." Again, this is fitting because Bellatrix spent a large portion of her life in Azkaban and she and Rodolphus have no children. He needs to watch out because this foretells an early death for him. Bellatrix Lestrange is tall, thin, and has heavily lidded eyes. She, like Sirius, retained the vestiges of good looks after her years at Azkaban. Like Lucius, Bellatrix thinks she is the leader of the pack. The Detectives sense a rivalry and possibly an explosion later in the series over this issue. She went to Azkaban for torturing the Longbottoms into insanity when Frank would not give her information regarding the whereabouts of her exiled master, Voldemort. She was one of the four seeking to find Voldemort and restore him to power. Bella clearly enjoys torturing people. The Detectives believe Crouch, Jr. may have been telling a half-truth that it wasn't him who tortured the Longbottoms. The Detectives have no doubt it was Bellatrix who did the torturing. The others were just there waiting for the information of Voldemort's whereabouts. Thus, they were accessories to the crime. In the Department of Mysteries, she suggests torturing Ginny and orders the Death Eater next to her, presumably her husband, to seize Ginny. Then she looks around at the group of Death Eaters, who she apparently thinks are less than thrilled with the idea of torturing a child and says, "I'll do it." A bit eager, don't you think? It was also Bellatrix who tortured Neville, when the other Death Eater wanted to stun him and get him out of the way. Thus, the Detectives assume Bellatrix enjoys torturing people. She is clearly deranged. Keep in mind: she has been in Azkaban for a long time, so she hasn't been able to have her version of fun in quite some time. The Detectives also learn from Bella that in order to do the Cruciatus Curse effectively, righteous anger is not enough to cause pain for long, you must enjoy causing pain. This puts the Longbottoms' insanity into perspective. Bellatrix's Cruciatus Curse is more effective than others' because she is so unhinged.

Bellatrix is a member of Black Family. She was the youngest daughter. She fits in very well with the rest of the family. They were dark wizards and went into Slytherin House. Bellatrix was the same age as Sirius. Cousins who are the same age, typically are either very close or absolutely hate each other. The Detectives believe it is safe to say the latter applies in this case. Sirius was very touchy about the subject of Bellatrix. Sirius goes so far as to say, "*She's* certainly not my family[9]." Wow! That is deep. What has Bellatrix done to Sirius? They clearly hate each other. Isn't it interesting she is the one who takes his life? Well, the answer may lie in the only other relative Sirius was irritable during the discussion of—his brother. Sirius had a younger brother, Regulus Black, who died fifteen years ago. Interestingly enough, Harry is 15 years old. Is there a connection? The Detectives certainly would not rule out the possibility. Regulus joined the Death Eaters and was either killed by Voldemort or on Voldemort's orders. According to Sirius, "he got in so far, then panicked about what he was being asked to do and tried to back out. Well, you don't just hand in your resignation to Voldemort. It's a lifetime service or death[10]." Hmmm, let's think about this for a minute. Your two cousins and their husbands are in this organization with you along with a bunch of your friends from school. If this were simply a case of nerves and panic, one would assume a network like this would be able to help you work through the issues bothering you. Surely, Voldemort would prefer this given his army was not that large. So, what was it Regulus was being asked to do? Was it something he would not be able to work through? Perhaps it was an issue that would not only turn him, but his parents against Voldemort and force them to fight against Voldemort. What order would that be? It would be an order, which would either prove his loyalty or alienate him completely? Kill Sirius! Kill your brother! The Detectives believe Regulus refused and was killed, as a result, possibly by Bellatrix. Kreacher may even know this. This would also explain why Kreacher does not respect her anymore. He still loves her and keeps a picture of her as a young woman up in his room, but he does not *respect* her anymore. Then Bellatrix kills Sirius. He was her target all evening. She made no effort to kill anyone else, but green light was flashing over Sirius's head all night from her direction. Why? Also, no other Death Eater made any effort to kill Sirius or anyone else. Again, why? Was Sirius their target and was Bellatrix ordered to do the job? Perhaps this was to prove she would not allow blood to interfere with her loyalty to the Death Eaters, unlike Regulus. It should also be noted Narcissa was the one who planned how to get Harry to the Department of Mysteries, knowing it would trap Sirius as well. Perhaps, she too had to prove her loyalty. Further evidence, Voldemort takes the time to save Bella when fleeing the Ministry of Magic after hearing she had been fighting Sirius and finding out from Harry's head that Sirius was indeed dead. She did one of her jobs, so he saved her. Nice guy! The Detectives expect Bellatrix to play a major role in the ensuing battle. It is possible she will unintentionally assist in bringing about her master's downfall. By taking the time to grab Bella, Voldemort allowed the people pouring into the Ministry of Magic to see him. This was an uncharacteristic sign of caring from Voldemort. He allowed the rest of his Death Eaters to go to jail, but not Bella. Why? He is starting to care and to care is to be human. Since it was Bellatrix he cared about, then she will inadvertently cause his downfall. Bellatrix's downfall may, also, be seen in the stars. When Bellatrix, the star, is combined with Neptune, there will be "many narrow escapes, but eventual violent death[11]." Wow! Both Harry and Neville were born under Neptune. Apparently, one will kill her, possibly using her choice method of torture. It would be far more appropriate for this to be Neville's destiny, since she is the reason he does not know his parents. Perhaps killing her will reverse his parents' insanity magically.

Rabastan Lestrange

Rabastan is a thickset man who had a blank stare at his trial. His brother, Rodolphus, is married to Bellatrix. He went to Azkaban for torturing the Longbottoms, in order to discover the whereabouts of Voldemort to restore him to power. In Book 5, he was part of the raid at the Department of Mysteries. Then, he went back to jail. The Detectives expect he will play a minor role in the future books.

Rodolphus Lestrange

Rodolphus was a thin, nervous looking man. Rodolphus is married to Bellatrix. He and Bella were friends with Snape and Avery at Hogwarts. He, like Bellatrix, went to Azkaban for torturing the Longbottoms. In the Department of Mysteries' mission, Rodolphus is unsurprisingly paired up with his wife, Bellatrix. The Detectives think Malfoy assumes her husband might be able to exercise some control over her or at least reason with her. Keep her from harming Potter, until we get the prophecy, OK Rodolphus? You married her, so you must be able to reason with her. Rodolphus went back to Azkaban. Now the Detectives have to ask about the logic here. If these ten Death Eaters escaped from Azkaban once, why would the Ministry of Magic send them back again? If I caught these clowns twice, I would execute them. If they escaped once, they can do it again. Think about it for a minute. Vernon is right on this issue. "Hanging's the only way to deal with these people[12]." Now if they want to send those who have never been to Azkaban before, OK. That is reasonable, even logical. But kill those who have already escaped once or history will repeat itself.

Walden Macnair

Macnair worked for the Disposal for Dangerous Creatures, as an executioner. He was also the envoy to the giants for Voldemort. He persuaded the giants to join Voldemort. Macnair was also part of the group of Death Eaters on the mission to the Department of Mysteries. Macnair, like the others, was caught and sent to Azkaban. Thus, his cover was blown and he can no longer be a spy for the Death Eaters in the Ministry of Magic. This means we will see his character change and become more brutal.

Lucius Malfoy

Lucius Malfoy is exactly as his name suggests. Lucius is named for Lucifer or the Devil himself and Malfoy comes from French. Mal means bad or evil and foi means faith. So, the devil is combined with bad faith. The Detectives would suggest Dumbledore, Harry, and even Voldemort, keep a close eye on this man. His name alone tells us he is definitely bad news..

Lucius Malfoy is clearly a very cunning, clever, and wealthy man. The combination of these three traits undoubtedly kept him out of Azkaban prison the first time. The Detectives also suspect he and Fudge may have sold out the Lestranges and Crouch, Jr. in exchange for Malfoy's freedom and Fudge getting the top job. Nice thing to do to your in-laws! Lucius is an extremely wealthy man and, due to his money, is very well connected. He gives to many causes, which helps him demand favors. He also uses bribery when he needs it. St. Mungo's is Lucius Malfoy's favorite charity. The Detectives are very suspicious about this. Is it possible the reason the Longbottoms are not getting well is because Lucius Malfoy is making sure they do not get well? The Detectives think so. After all, they are in the same closed ward where Bode was murdered because he was improving and would have been able to reveal what Malfoy had done. Well, it would be highly suspicious to murder two people, but no one would think anything of the fact neither was ever able to recover, right? Maybe a Healer in this ward is a Death Eater and she or he is deliberately keeping Mr. and Mrs. Longbottom from getting well because they would be able to incriminate Malfoy. Also, if they recovered, they might be able to continue to fight Voldemort.

The scene at Hogwarts is so easy to imagine. Picture it! Lucius graduated from Hogwarts in 1967. Undoubtedly, by their seventh year he and Narcissa were already dating. Narcissa's baby sister, Bellatrix, came to Hogwarts in 1966. She was sorted into Slytherin, unlike their disappointing middle sister and cousin, who entered Hogwarts the same year. Clearly, Narcissa was going to look out for her baby sister. Well, little Bella had made friends with another boy, who was fascinated with the dark arts and knew more about them, than most kids in their seventh year. Narcissa tells her boyfriend, possibly fiancé, about this boy. Lucius takes little Severus under his protective wing and offers him a guiding hand. They were truly a match made in Hell. After Hogwarts, Severus leaves and takes his place with the Death Eaters, which Lucius has prepared for him. As a spy, Severus deals with Lucius who still trusts him a great deal. Draco thinks he knows Snape well. Why, because Snape is practically family? He grew up with Snape visiting the house. So, the only question that remains is why didn't Severus marry Bella? Perhaps this is yet another reason for Snape to hate James. The other point to note is Lucius had a foe at Hogwarts, Arthur Weasley. This pairing of good versus evil began with Tom and Hagrid, and continued with James and Severus, and now Harry and Draco. This hatred has carried forward into the wizarding world at large. When Lucius decided to plant Tom Riddle's diary at Hogwarts, he slipped the diary to Ginny Weasley. This plan had several benefits. Hagrid would go to Azkaban, and Arthur Weasley would be ruined and with any luck, Ginny would be killed. The Detectives are still wondering what it is Lucius has done to Hagrid. Hagrid hates Lucius and the entire Malfoy family. Maybe Malfoy's father went to school with Hagrid and the grudge has been passed down like Snape's grudge passed down from James to Harry. Hagrid says that the whole Malfoy family was a bad lot. The Detectives also believe it will be Lucius who kills Molly Weasley, as well as any of the Weasley children who die in future books.

Lucius Malfoy married Narcissa Black. They had one son, Draco. Draco is his father's prince. Anything Draco wants, Lucius will give him. Also, Lucius fancies himself as a leader among the Death Eaters. This was seen in the Department of Mysteries. It was clear that Lucius had given Bellatrix orders about how they were going to accomplish this task. They were not going to attack Harry! Then, he orders the whole group to gather around him and gives them instructions. This tells the Detectives Lucius thinks of himself as the leader. Fortunately, Lucius was caught and sent to Azkaban. As a result, he will not be able to carry on with the front of a respectable member of the wizarding community. When Lucius escapes from Azkaban, he will continue to play a key role in the Death Eaters.

Narcissa Black Malfoy

Narcissa Malfoy has not been officially named a Death Eater, but the Detectives believe these clues qualify as Bludgers. We have only seen Narcissa once, but we have heard a great deal about her. In addition, Narcissa's name tells us a great deal about her. She is named for a Greek God; Narcissus, who pines away in love for himself and in death was transformed into the flower which bears his name[13]. He was extremely vain. In all the artwork depicting him he is looking in a mirror admiring his reflection. Also, Narcissus was created to help Zeus' brother, the lord of the *dark* underworld[14]. We know Narcissa grew up in the Black family; a family obsessed with being pure blood. She is also the sister of Bellatrix. Like Bellatrix, she is beautiful and evil.

If her marriage and sister were not enough to convict Narcissa, there are other actions, which would clearly put her under suspicion. In the Goblet of Fire, Harry, Ron, and Hermione, see Draco in the woods "Where are your *parents*?" asked Harry "Out there wearing masks, are *they*?" Draco's response, "Well… if *they* were I wouldn't be likely to tell you, would I, Potter[15]?" It is important to note it is "parents" in the plural not parent as in father. Narcissa is not protecting Draco. Of course, he is safe. The Death Eaters are not going to harm any one of their children. Draco has as good as admitted both his mother and father are out there and wearing masks. Along these same lines, when Voldemort is addressing the Death Eaters during his rebirthing celebration he calls all, except Lucius, by their last names. There could be several reasons for this. Possibly he was closer to Lucius. The Detectives do not buy this theory, given Malfoy never went to find him and the fact Voldemort calls Lucius his "slippery friend," which is not exactly a compliment. Furthermore, Draco freaked out when Harry used the name, Voldemort. This suggests they are not mates, but have a boss/employee relationship. Another reason for using Lucius, as opposed to Malfoy could be Voldemort needed to clarify whom he was addressing. He was addressing Lucius, not Narcissa Malfoy. It would not be surprising that a married couple had joined the Death Eaters. Bellatrix and her husband joined. Why not her sister, Narcissa, and her husband? We know the Order of the Phoenix has many married couples in its ranks. Would it not make sense this paradigm would hold true within the organization of the Death Eaters as well?

Further evidence that Lucius is not the only Death Eater in the Malfoy family appears in the fifth book. Kreacher, the house elf, went to Narcissa, not Lucius or Bellatrix. He was serving two masters—Sirius and Narcissa. Kreacher gave Narcissa the necessary information on how to destroy Sirius Black and how to trap Harry. She told Kreacher to keep Sirius away from the fire in case Harry decided to check and see if he was at home. It is important to note Narcissa is playing this important active role of collecting and funneling information. She is not just sitting at home looking in the mirror, ignoring whatever it is that her husband and sister may be doing, she is planning and taking an active role. This clearly suggests to the Detectives Narcissa is a Death Eater, although she was not sent to Azkaban because she was not present in the Ministry. Narcissa's role will become more significant as her husband is in prison.

Mulciber

In Greek Mythology, there is some dispute over whether Mulciber is the son of Zeus and Hera, or Hera alone. Mulciber was ugly and lame. He was the God of Fire and worked closely with Athena[16]. He was also supposed to be a kind, peace-loving god, which makes this name a strange choice. Mulciber went to Azkaban after Voldemort's fall. Mulciber's name was one of the names Karkaroff gave to Crouch in order to get out of jail. Karkaroff also gave the important information that Mulciber specialized in the Imperius curse and forced countless people to do horrific things on his behalf. There is the possibility Karkaroff was lying, but if Mulciber was a spy, Dumbledore would have vouched for him, as well as, Snape. Unless, the Order needed one spy in Azkaban and one out so all Death Eaters groups were infiltrated. The Detectives are not positive and are extremely confused about Mulciber. Dumbledore did say they had several spies. Mulciber was a part of the raid at the Department of Mysteries, but was never seen attacking the children. When Malfoy split the group into pairs, he teamed up with Mulciber. This could be significant. The Detectives may want to watch out for Mulciber. In the end of Book 5, Mulciber was sent to Azkaban.

Nott

The word nott means to shear, to cut off or trim. So, what will Nott be trimming? The Detectives know very little about Nott. He has a son in the same year as Draco at Hogwarts, who is in Slytherin. Nott was cleared of being a Death Eater on round one. In the Hall of Prophecies, Nott was injured and did not participate in the major part of battle. He probably disapparated after he was injured. Lucky Nott, this enabled him to avoid Azkaban for a second time.

Peter Pettigrew or Wormtail

Peter Pettigrew or Wormtail, is a short, balding man. Several characters have stated Peter is a poor wizard, including McGonagall and Voldemort. The Detectives disagree. Perhaps it is the standard they are comparing him to that is the problem. Peter became an animagus in the fifth year, like James and Sirius. This is no small feat, even with help. In the graveyard, he conjures rope. Conjuring is highly advanced magic and not an easy thing to do. Next, Peter is able to brew the potion and restore Voldemort to his body. Again, that is advanced Dark Magic. He may have been following instructions, but he did the work. He was ordered to kill the spare, which means he used Voldemort's wand to kill Cedric. Again, this curse needs a great deal of power behind it. The Detectives believe McGonagall was comparing him to James, Sirius, and Remus and Voldemort compares him to Lucius and Severus. Of course, next to the best, even a skilled wizard looks poor.

Peter went to Hogwarts with James Potter, Sirius Black, and Remus Lupin and was in Gryffindor. Wormtail was also an original member of the Order of the Phoenix. Due to Lupin being a werewolf, Potter, Black, and Pettigrew decided to become animagus. They managed to become animagus in their fifth year at Hogwarts, which is an extremely difficult piece of magic. Of course, James, Sirius, and Peter never registered as is required by wizard law. Yet, they managed to do it after only five years of magical education. James transformed into a stag, Sirius into a dog, and Peter into a rat. It was their transformations that lead to the creations of their nicknames. Peter transformed into a rat, hence the name Wormtail. Pettigrew was the Potter's secret keeper and revealed their whereabouts to Voldemort. For a year prior to this time, Peter had been passing information to Voldemort. Betraying the Potters had been Peter's open declaration of where his loyalty lay. He sentenced one of his best friends to death. When Sirius cornered Peter intending to kill him, Peter blew up the entire street, cut off his finger and transformed. He escaped, but was presumed dead. Sirius went to jail and was thought to have murdered 13 people. Peter then found a wizard's home, so he could listen to the news and live a comfortable life, as a rat. This is how he came to be Ron's pet, named Scabbers. It was not until Ron's father won the Daily Prophet's Grand Prize and the whole family was pictured in the paper that there was a problem. Fudge gave Sirius his paper when visiting Azkaban and he saw the picture and recognized Peter. The article also said Ron would be returning to Hogwarts, which was where Harry was. This was enough to clear Sirius's mind and give him the strength to escape. Sirius cornered Peter. Lupin, Harry, Ron, and Hermione bore witness to the event and the truth was finally revealed. Harry stopped Sirius and Remus from killing Peter and encouraged them to turn him over to the Ministry of Magic instead. It appeared as though Sirius's name would finally be cleared. Unfortunately, Lupin transformed and Peter escaped again.

Just as Trelawney's prophecy foretold, the servant rejoined his master. Wormtail went to find Voldemort. He restored Voldemort to a feeble body, captured Bertha Jorkins, and enabled Voldemort to put his plans into action and rise to full strength and power again. But, Wormtail was careless and, like a rat, only kills when cornered. He did not want to kill Crouch, Sr. and allowed him to escape. Wormtail and Crouch, Jr. prepared the polyjuice potion. They subdued Moody and forced him into his magical trunk. Then Wormtail brewed the potion that restored Voldemort to his body. He also was the one who tied Harry up and took blood from his body. He, then, cut off his right hand for Voldemort's potion. It is interesting to note Peter Pettigrew has now denied the Potters three times, which is not unlike the Apostle Peter who denied Christ three times. The Detectives wonder if Pettigrew will turn his life around, like St. Peter, and become one of Harry's greatest followers.

Once the Death Eaters arrived Voldemort made a new hand for Wormtail. The Detectives are extremely suspicious of this new hand because it was a gift from Voldemort and could easily be jinxed. When Voldemort placed the new hand on Wormtail's arm he said, "May your loyalty never waver again, Wormtail[17]." The Detectives would not have put it past Voldemort to put something in the hand to make sure, if Wormtail's loyalty wavers he does not get to keep his nice powerful hand.

Wormtail was not seen in Book 5. This could be for several reasons. First, if the Ministry sees Wormtail alive, it would prove Sirius is innocent. Second, the Detectives believe Wormtail's job has not changed much since Voldemort has returned to his body. Voldemort does not think much of Wormtail's skill, but he did like the care Wormtail provided. The Detectives suspect Wormtail is Voldemort's personal servant or caretaker. This works out well in some ways because no one can hurt him. The "biggest bully on the playground" is on his side, so who can touch Wormtail? He has nothing to fear, right? This also puts him in a position where he hears a great deal, perhaps more than he would like given he owes his life to Harry Potter. The day will come when Wormtail will hear the plot of Harry's murder and the bond will click into place, just as it did for Snape. Wormtail will have to flee. He will go to Dumbledore in order to warn Harry and attempt to save his life. If he uses the hand to save Harry, the Detectives believe the hand will cause Wormtail's death.

Augustus Rookwood

Augustus Caesar is the most famous Augustus. He was the first Roman emperor, known for reform and reorganization of the army. Several of the Roman Emperors were named for Augustus. This is a powerful name. Also, august, in addition to being a month, means impressive and noble. A rook has two meanings. The first is a swindler or a cheat and the second is the name for the castle in chess. The rook occupies the two corner squares and can move both vertically and horizontally over any number of unoccupied squares. This is a powerful piece in chess. In fact, after the Queen, the rook is the most powerful piece on the chessboard. Remember in year one, Ron had Hermione take the place of one of the castles or rooks. Wood is either a thick growth of trees or a strong material used for building. Combined, they form a powerhouse. Augustus Rookwood is a very powerful name. The Detectives would advise watching him very carefully. He is powerful and will be dangerous if his name is any clue. Rookwood has a pockmarked face and greasy hair. He was convicted of leaking Ministry of Magic Secrets to Voldemort. He was the Head of the Department of Mysteries before his arrest. He was also a friend of Bagman's father and was using Ludo Bagman to pass information to Death Eaters. Rookwood was the one who told Voldemort, only those to whom the prophecies apply to can lift them from their shelves at the Department of Mysteries. It was giving Rookwood's name to Crouch that enabled Karkaroff to leave Azkaban. Rookwood is clearly, highly intelligent. He was the head of an intellectual department and was a spy, who did not get caught, until exposed by someone else. Rookwood will be a real asset to Voldemort. The Detectives will be keeping an eye on him. Rookwood, unsurprisingly, was on the mission in the Department of Mysteries, since it was his old stomping ground. He was caught with the rest and sent to Azkaban, but there is no doubt he will be seen again.

Severus Snape

See Hogwarts Professors

Travers

Travers is another word for traverse, which means to follow a zigzag course. Travers went to Azkaban and helped murder the McKinnons. Travers escaped from Azkaban during the mass breakout, but was not part of the Ministry of Magic raid. His role in future books in unclear at this point.

Dolores Jane Umbridge

See Hogwarts Professors

Chapter 10

Other Fully Qualified Witches and Wizards

Andromeda Black Tonks

Andromeda is also an interesting name. It literally means a shrub, but also comes from Greek Mythology. Andromeda was the unsurprising very beautiful daughter of Cepheus and Cassiopeia and wife of Persues, who rescued her from a sea monster[1]. Also, there is a constellation in the North Hemisphere named Andromeda, which contains a large spiral galaxy. Andromeda Tonks is a member of the Black family and the sister of Bellatrix and Narcissa. She was blasted off the family tree for marrying muggle born, Ted Tonks, who, apparently, is a slob. This explains where the Malfoy family got their impression all muggles live in filth. Andromeda and Ted have one daughter, Nymphadora. Both Nymphadora and Sirius are members of the Order. Thus, the Detectives wonder if Andromeda is a member of the Order as well. If not, does she know what her daughter and cousin are involved in? Jeepers, two sisters fighting on the Dark Side and your daughter and favorite cousin are fighting for the good guys. Sounds like the American Civil War to me. It will be interesting to see Andromeda's reaction to her sister, Bellatrix killing her favorite cousin and attacking her daughter. She is a very powerful witch given the skill of her family members and her daughter's statement, regarding the desire to master her mother's skill. The Detectives believe Andromeda will join the Order, if she is not already a member and take a more active role in the battles ahead.

Fleur Delacour

Fleur Delacour name is French for flower of the state meaning noblewoman. Fleur was tall, thin and had a sheet of long silver hair. She went to Beauxbaton, French for beautiful wand, and was their Triwizard Champion. Her wand is 9 ½ inches, rosewood, with a Veela hair[2]. Her grandmother was Veela. She has one sister, Gabrielle. During the second task of the Triwizard tournament, Harry saved her sister and the lake from the merpeople. The Detectives believe this earned Harry the respect and loyalty of both Fleur and her sister. In the fifth book, Fleur started dating Bill Weasley. The Detectives believe she will join the Order of the Phoenix and play a vital part.

Viktor Krum

Viktor Krum is surly and duck footed. He has dark hair and a hook-nose. He went to Durmstrang and was their Triwizard Champion. His wand is 10 ¼ inches with hornbeam and dragon heartstring[3]. During the tournament, Krum and Harry got to know each other. Krum also became friends with Diggory. The Detectives believe this will prove important, since Diggory was killed. He didn't like his headmaster. He was an excellent seeker for Bulgaria. In spite of the fact Krum went to a school devoted to the dark arts, which did not admit muggle born students, he dated Hermione. This did not please his headmaster, Karkaroff. Krum and Hermione are still keeping in touch and the Detectives believe she will persuade him to join the Order.

Mrs. Longbottom

Mrs. Longbottom is a tall, elderly witch, who always wears a green dress, a fox scarf, and a hat with a vulture on it and carries a red purse. She is the mother of Frank Longbottom and the grandmother of Neville.

She is extremely hard on Neville, frequently saying he does not have his father's talent. The Detectives believe Mrs. Longbottom simply does not want Neville to follow in his parents' footsteps. She has suffered a great deal in the loss of her son and daughter-in-law's sanity and cannot bear the thought of losing Neville as well. Thus, she has attempted to keep Neville downtrodden in order to protect him. She even provided Neville with his father's wand instead of buying him his own. This is insane! They have plenty of money and should know a wand does not function as well in the hand of another wizard. In addition, Mrs. Longbottom tells everyone who would encourage Neville to go down the same path as his parents, he is not talented enough to do so. This is the same irrational reasoning the Dursleys applied to squashing the magic out of Harry Potter. The Detectives believe once Mrs. Longbottom hears Neville fought the Death Eaters, particularly the Lestranges at the end of the fifth year, and survived, she will stop trying to prevent him from fulfilling his destiny and help him in every way she can. It is also important to note Mrs. Longbottom is a friend of Griselda Marchbanks, who is a friend of Dumbledore. The Longbottoms immediately believed Harry and Dumbledore when they said, Voldemort had returned. They also were willing to defend them when others scrutinized and called them liars.

Mr. Ollivander

Mr. Ollivander owns the wand shop in Diagon Alley. He is the Maker of Fine Wands and everyone who attends Hogwarts goes to him to buy their wand. He is an extremely old man with large pale eyes and very long fingers. He has a photographic memory and can remember every wand he has ever sold. This could be very beneficial in battle. Mr. Ollivander will know which wands are powerful, what they contain, and which ones are brothers. He will be able to share this knowledge with Dumbledore and the Order so they are forewarned. Mr. Ollivander made and sold both Voldemort and Harry their wands. These wands are brothers; both contain the feather of the same Phoenix. When Harry bought this wand Mr. Ollivander wrote to Dumbledore right away, which suggests he and Dumbledore are close friends or at least work together.

Mr. Ollivander was also the wand expert for the Triwizard Tournament. He examined the wand of each of the champions to be sure they were all in working order. It is significant, Mr. Ollivander did not share the information regarding Harry's wand with the entire room, during this examination. The Detectives expect to see Mr. Ollivander again, but are unsure what role he will play. He is an extremely powerful wizard, due to his long fingers and loyalty to Dumbledore, so he is expected to take part in the ensuing battle.

Madam Rosmerta

Rosmerta comes from the word rose. This is significant because in ancient times roses were used for medicinal purposes, in the same way alcohol was used. Roses also represent beauty and love, which is fitting because Madam Rosmerta is described as a pretty and curvy woman. She owns the Hogsmeade pub, called The Three Broomsticks. This pub has a broad clientele as she serves the townspeople as well as the Hogwarts professors and students. It is clear, based on her business, Madam Rosmerta meets many witches and wizards. She will also hear a great deal as a bartender, since people come to socialize and gossip.

Madam Rosmerta remembered James and Sirius from when they were in school. She stated, "I still have trouble believing it…of all the people to go over to the Dark Side, Sirius Black was the last I'd have thought[4]." This shows that Madam Rosmerta has a good sense of people and of what they are capable. In addition, she could be instrumental in detecting undiscovered Death Eaters.

Rita Skeeter

Rita Skeeter is 44 and a journalist, who delights in running stories, which will "puncture" the reputation of the highlighted person or persons. Rita has a heavy jawed face and three gold teeth. She wears her blond hair in elaborate rigid curls. Her hands are described as "mannish" and her fingers are thick with two-inch nails painted crimson. She wears jeweled spectacles and carries a crocodile skin handbag. The Detectives question whether Rita is really a witch or just pretending to be one? As a journalist Rita uses a Quick Quotes Quill, which is acid green. This enables her to talk to those she interviews and the quill makes up quotes in the many pauses throughout the conversation. The Detectives believe Rita is willing to attack anyone for a story. She was willing to put Harry in a good light or a bad light, it did not matter to her. She was only interested in what would further the interests of Rita Skeeter. In year four, she wrote nasty articles about Dumbledore, Hagrid, Harry, and Hermione. After she was banned from the grounds, she used her ability as an unregistered animagus to continue getting stories. She was able to turn into a beetle, sneak onto the grounds, and listen to private conversations as well. Hermione discovered this in Harry's hospital room and started blackmailing Rita. Part of the agreement was she not allowed to write for the Daily Prophet, for one year. What is really important about this is when Hermione discovered Rita. Had Rita published an article about the last conversation she heard, it would be deadly. Rita heard Dumbledore's orders to Snape. She saw Sirius. She saw the parting of the way between Dumbledore and Fudge. Even if Rita did not write an article, she could have let this information slip. This says a great deal about Rita Skeeter's integrity, she knew it was essential she keep quiet. If she had spoken, Snape and Sirius would have been killed and Dumbledore, Harry, Ron, and Hermione would have been arrested.

In the fifth year, Rita wrote the article telling Harry's story in *The Quibbler*. She was thrilled about the idea, but not about doing it for free, nonetheless she did it. Rita received no money for this story and her reputation was certainly punctured because of where she was being published. However, she was thrilled with the idea of exposing the "Death Eater still among us." She shows she is truly an equal opportunity poisonous author. The Detectives believe Rita may prove to be a useful tool. She cannot risk Hermione exposing her, which has already proven useful. Also, she has ticked off the Death Eaters and Voldemort by writing the story. She may need to ally herself with Dumbledore and Harry for her own protection. People typically are interested in saving their own skin. This, combined with the fact she kept her silence about Snape and Sirius, makes Rita a safe bet.

Stan Shunpike and Ernie Prang

The Knightbus is a violent purple triple-decker bus used as the emergency transport system for stranded witches and wizards. This bus can take the witch or wizard anywhere on land. Ernie Prang is the driver and Stan Shunpike is the conductor. Ernie is an elderly wizard with thick glasses, who seems to fear the Dementors. It is possible he spent some time in Azkaban. Stan is 18 or 19 and has pimples. The bus is full of mismatched chairs by day and beds by night. A ride on this bus is an adventure to say the least. It bangs when it starts and stops and the beds and chairs go flying inside the bus. Houses, cars, and anything else in its path jumps out of its way. This is not the bus to ride on if you get motion sickness. Possibly J.K. Rowling had the same triple-decker bus driver as the Head Detective had on her last trip to London. It would definitely explain this section.

Celestina Warbeck

Like so many names Celistina Warbeck is a clue to the character's importance. Celest means heavenly. Also, Pope Celestine was elected without his consent and abdicated. Perkin Warbeck led an uprising against Henry VII, who is remembered for restoring the rule of law [5]. With this name, the Detectives are not sure whether to place her on the side of good or evil. Celestina Warbeck is mentioned twice, first in Book 2 and then again in Quidditch through the Ages. Since her surname begins with war, the Detectives suspect she will become important during the war. Celestina Warbeck is a popular singing sorceress on a program called the Witching Hour. She also recorded the Puddlemore United team's anthem, "Beat Back Those Bludgers, Boys, Chuck That Quaffle Here[6]." She did this to raise money for St. Mungo's. So, is that her favorite charity? Watch out Oliver Wood! Dangerous! She and Lucius Malfoy share a favorite charity. Celestina Warbeck might be tied to the Death Eaters in the same way Frank Sinatra was tied to the mob. It was common procedure for the mob to help talented singers make it to the top so they owed their success to the mob and their debt was called in at a later time. She is not completely evil given she is still singing. The Detectives wonder what she will be asked to do, it is highly doubtful it will be limited to giving money to St. Mungo's. They are increasingly concerned about the well being of Oliver Wood given he was in Gryffindor House and knew Harry very well. She is in an excellent position to harm or put the Imperius Curse on him.

Chapter 11

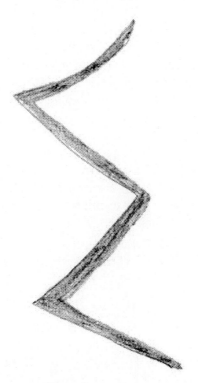

<u>Harry James Potter</u>

Harry Potter is the key to the entire series. Unfortunately, he knows less than our Detectives know about himself. Alas, he is but a boy and he will know in time. His name, like so many of the other characters is a Bludger to his role and importance to the series. Harry, according to Aunt Petunia, is a "nasty, common name[1]." Well, she did have a point, but more importantly, Harry means to assault or torment. This is precisely the story of Harry Potter's life. His middle name is James. The most famous James is King James, who united England and Scotland. Perhaps this is a Snitch-- Harry James Potter's destiny is to unite the wizarding world. Finally, a Potter's Field is where orphans, paupers, and unknown people are buried. Harry is an orphan! Until Harry discovered he was a wizard and his parents had left him a fortune, he thought he had no money and was completely unknown. Ironically, he is the most famous person in the wizarding world and everyone knows his name. Perhaps, the name Potter applying to the unknown is true for the Potter family, but not for Harry Potter himself.

Harry Potter is small and thin. He has knobby knees, black hair, and bright green eyes. In addition, he wears glasses. Mostly, he resembles his father, but everyone comments his eyes are clearly his mother's. His parents were James and Lily Potter, who Voldemort killed on Halloween, when Harry was just a year old. Since that time, Uncle Vernon and Aunt Petunia Dursley have raised Harry with his cousin, Dudley, who is the same age. The Dursleys are Muggles and do not like magic. They did not tell Harry he was a wizard. Uncle Vernon even took the family and hid on a rock out at sea in an attempt to prevent Harry from knowing the truth and attending Hogwarts. He was unsuccessful and Hagrid, the Hogwarts gamekeeper told Harry his story, and took him to buy his school supplies. Hagrid also bought Harry his snowy owl, Hedwig, who is the only one of her kind at Hogwarts. This is another interesting and appropriate name. Hedwig was patron saint of orphan children.

The Detectives have their work cut out for them when cracking the case of Harry Potter. His genealogy is a key question. Why did Voldemort want to kill him as a baby? Seems like a strange thing to do! Kill a baby? Unless the baby could grow to be more powerful than him. Furthermore, why didn't he want to kill Lily? Lily and James were among those fighting against him. Seems to the Detectives, the most evil wizard in the world would want to eliminate *both* of them. We have learned from information Dumbledore and Voldemort provided; he was unable to kill Harry, due to ancient magic. His mother, Lily, died to save Harry, giving him a lingering protection. In Book 5, we learned Voldemort attacked the Potters due to the prophecy Trelawney made before Harry's birth. It is also interesting to note, the prophecy could have applied to two boys born on July 31 of that year. Both boys had parents in the Order, who had narrowly escaped Voldemort three times—Harry Potter and Neville Longbottom. So, why did Voldemort choose Harry? Why the half-blood, instead of the pureblood? That goes against his creed. Well, it could be a simple explanation. Voldemort saw himself in Harry. There is however a more important question which neither Dumbledore nor Harry ask. The Detectives are on the trail. Why could the prophecy apply to two boys? What is it these two boys have in common, that other wizards do not have? What is it that would make them powerful enough to vanquish the Dark Lord, a power not even Dumbledore has? Is the answer perhaps in their bloodline? Do they share an ancestor that would make them the epitome of power? Who could defeat the heir of Slytherin? Possibly, the heir of the other houses, Gryffindor, Ravenclaw, and Hufflepuff? After all, Slytherin had to leave Hogwarts because the other three united against him. It would make sense, if the other three were joined in the blood of another wizard, the wizard could vanquish the heir of Slytherin. The Sorting Hat wanted to put Harry in three of the houses—Slytherin, Ravenclaw, and Gryffindor. There is plenty of evidence Harry is an heir of Slytherin, as well as, Voldemort. The Detectives believe Harry is a direct descendent of these three founders. Neville is loyal and true. He is also brave. In the battle with the Death Eaters it is important to note, Neville and Harry were the only two still standing at the end, not Hermione or Ron, like many would have predicted. Neville is a powerful wizard, who has not peaked yet. The Detectives believe he is a direct descendent of Gryffindor and Hufflepuff. Gryffindor is the link between Harry and Neville. Another equally important question is the second part of the prophecy, "he will have power the Dark Lord knows not[2]." Dumbledore says this power is love. Well, Dumbledore does not say it outright, but the Detectives believe it is clear Harry has the power of love. The better question is what can love do that can destroy Voldemort. As the cliché goes, "love conquers all." Possibly love is not supposed to destroy Voldemort, but it is Harry's love for others which will enable him to kill Voldemort and then rebuild the wizarding world.

Why do the Detectives say Harry is the heir of Slytherin?

The answer to this question is primarily in the Chamber of Secrets, but begins in the Sorcerer's Stone. The Sorting Hat wanted to put Harry in Slytherin and only chose Gryffindor because Harry was adamant that he did not want to be placed in Slytherin House. The next piece of evidence is in Professor Binns' lecture on the Chamber of Secrets. He states, "Slytherin, according to legend, sealed the Chamber of Secrets so that *none would be able to open it* until his own true heir arrived at the school. *The heir alone* would be able to unseal the Chamber of Secrets, unleash the horror within…[it] is believed to be some sort of monster, which *the heir of Slytherin alone can control[3]*." Well, there are two important points to note in this lecture. The first point is the heir alone would be able to open the chamber, not any parselmouth would be able to open it. Ginny was able to open the Chamber and control the Basilisk because Tom Riddle, the heir of Slytherin, was possessing her. So, why was Harry able to open the Chamber of Secrets? The logical conclusion is, he too, is an heir of Slytherin. The other important note worthy point is the *heir alone* can control the Basilisk. The Detectives have wondered for a long time why Harry never attempted to talk to the Basilisk. He knows he can talk to snakes. Possibly it was due to the fact he did not want to think he was in any way connected to Salazar Slytherin. In spite of the fact Harry does not try to talk to the Basilisk, there is a time the Detectives believe Harry did speak in parseltongue. "'Help me, help me,' Harry muttered wildly, someone-anyone- 'the snake's tail whipped across the floor again, Harry ducked. Something soft hit face. The basilisk had swept the sorting hat into Harry's arms[4].'" Hmmm, who answered Harry's cry for help? The Basilisk! Not Fawkes! In addition, Harry never knows when he is speaking parseltongue, Ron tells him. Harry is also talking too quietly for Tom Riddle to hear him and realize the snake is answering Harry. The important point is the snake answered Harry's call for help when it only obeys the heir of Slytherin. The Basilisk is obeying both Tom and Harry, which would logically mean they are both heirs of Slytherin. It is also important to note the snake does not attack Harry again until Tom Riddle orders it too. So, Harry again has all the markings of the heir of Slytherins.

In the interview with J.K. Rowling and the screenwriter, Steve Kloves states, he wanted to remove something from the Chamber of Secrets. J.K. Rowling told him it needed to be in the movie because it would become important in a later movie/book and she would not tell him why when he asked[5]. So, what is this mystery item? Well, the face of Slytherin with the Basilisk coming out of the mouth is where Tom Riddle got the idea for the Dark Mark, but that appeared in Book 4. So, clearly this was not the important item in the Chamber. The Detectives believe the item was the second entrance. It would have been easy to just show Harry entering one and to save some time delete the second entrance, but it is the second entrance that is extremely interesting. It is "a solid wall on which two entwined serpents were carved, their eyes set with great, glinting emeralds[6]." Wow! Harry has green or emerald eyes, which the Detectives believe are the key to an unknown power waiting to be unleashed, just like the monster in the Chamber of Secrets. In addition, Voldemort has red eyes, but the color of Tom Riddle's eyes has been conveniently omitted.

In order to prove Harry is an heir of Slytherin it is necessary to overcome Dumbledore's statement. He says, "Lord Voldemort—who *is* the last remaining ancestor [descendent] of Salazar Slytherin[7]." Well, did Voldemort have children, if so the line would have continued after Tom Riddle? Furthermore, did Tom's mother have any siblings? Dumbledore stated pages before "[Tom Riddle] disappeared after leaving school... traveled far and wide...sank so deeply into the Dark Arts...hardly anyone connected Lord Voldemort with the clever, handsome boy who was once Head Boy here[8]." Well, isn't it possible during this time period Tom Riddle may have had children? In the event he did, then Tom Riddle would not be the last heir of Slytherin. Likewise, if his mother had siblings, then he would again not be the last heir. The choice of the word *"is"* is interesting. The Chamber of Secrets was published in 1999, which was one year after Bill Clinton's infamous question during his impeachment, "what is the meaning of the word *is*?" The Detectives believe J.K. Rowling is using a play on words. Prior to that time this statement of Dumbledore's would have been considered absolute. Of course, one should never assume any character is all knowing. Dumbledore could have chosen not to share Harry's family tree with him. After all, the truth is both dangerous and powerful. Dumbledore says, it should "be treated with great caution[9]." Given Harry is already afraid he is like Tom Riddle, belongs in Slytherin, or could be evil, Dumbledore clearly would not want to tell Harry they were related and he was a descendent of Slytherin as well. No, that would have been too much for Harry to handle at this time. Another interesting point in this statement is the difference between the original and later editions. It originally said ancestor, but was later changed to descendent. Is it possible Voldemort or Slytherin is like Merlin and lives his life backwards?

Harry's Relationship with McGonagall

The relationship between Professor McGonagall and Harry Potter is especially captivating. There are three points the Detectives believe to be note worthy regarding this relationship and McGonagall's deep affection for Harry. These are the facts. She cannot discipline him, like the other students, she is highly emotional when Harry is being threatened or hurt, and heaven help anyone who attacks him in her presence. Another point that should be noted is each time McGonagall and Harry have a touching moment, they are interrupted and McGonagall or Harry is forced to leave the room immediately. Why? Clearly Dumbledore is afraid McGonagall is going to reveal the reason for her affection for Harry Potter.

At the very beginning of the series, Professor McGonagall was outside the Dursley's house and had been waiting there all day. She was extremely upset about the deaths of Lily and James and, unlike the rest of the wizarding world, she was not out celebrated the downfall and apparent death of Voldemort. Why not? Who would not be celebrating at this time? Well, only a very select group of people—The Death Eaters. McGonagall is clearly not in that group. We already know most of Lily and James' friends were celebrating because Diggle was out with the rest. But, what about their families and closest friends? We know Sirius was not celebrating. He was heartbroken, due to the night's events. Dumbledore, McGonagall, and Hagrid also had not joined in on the celebrations. It is clear why

Dumbledore and Hagrid had not joined in, but why not McGonagall? McGonagall is too old to fit in the category of best friend, since she was one of the Potter's professors at Hogwarts. So, is she family? It was also clear McGonagall did not want Harry to be left with the Dursleys regardless of the fact they were his aunt and uncle. The Detectives believe it is clear she wanted to raise him herself. McGonagall went so far as to cry when they left Harry on the Dursleys' front steps. Why does she care so much about this baby?

When Harry arrives at Hogwarts, the abnormalities with Professor McGonagall become more troubling. She is said to be a very stern woman, but appears to be an old softy when it come to Harry. In fact, she does not seem to be able to discipline him properly. Why? Harry never serves the detentions from Professor McGonagall with Professor McGonagall. She always finds someone else with whom he can spend his detentions from her. Is this normal? All of his other professors who give him detentions have him serve them with them personally. Why does she find other people to take Harry for her? In addition, these detentions do not seem to be as horrible as the other detentions Harry has received or other students have received from Professor McGonagall. Harry got to spend one detention with Hagrid and another answering Professor Lockhart's fan mail. I ask you, what kind of punishment is that? In addition, McGonagall is extremely easy on Harry when it comes to punishing him for his incessant rule breaking. For example, for flying a car to Hogwarts, Harry got one detention and a letter to the Dursleys. In contrast, when Neville lost the passwords to the common room he was given a detention, banned from all future Hogsmeade visits, not allowed to have the password to the common room, and a letter was sent to his grandmother[10]. Hmmm, can you detect a slight difference in the punishments? One was extremely light and the other was extremely harsh. Why the difference? Well, one rule breaker was Harry and the other put Harry in danger.

The next point is Professor McGonagall cannot handle Harry being hurt in any way. Regarding the matter of Harry's Hogsmeade Permission form, there was a remarkable interchange. When Harry asks if he can go to Hogsmeade, she looks down and shuffles papers as she repeats the rules. Why not look at him directly and give him a firm answer? Well, McGonagall cannot handle Harry's hurt expressions. Finally, Harry says, "'If you said I could go—' 'But I don't say so,' said Professor McGonagall…'the form clearly states that the parent or guardian must give permission.' She turned to look at him, with an odd expression on her face. Was it pity? 'I'm sorry, Potter, but that's my final word[11].'" There are several important points in this interchange. First, Harry believes Professor McGonagall can give him permission to visit the village. Teachers do not have this authority. Even, the Minister of Magic did not presume to have this authority. What is interesting about this is McGonagall does not point this out to Harry. She simply says she is unwilling to give him permission, which suggests she would have the authority. Why? Is she a relative? Another example of McGonagall's soft spot for Harry's hurt expressions is when McGonagall gave Harry a week's worth of detentions. She follows up with, "Do not look at me like that, Potter, you deserve it[12]!" Once again, the expression is causing McGonagall to feel guilty, but she will not waiver because she is convinced he deserves the punishment. Again, this seems so strange for such a stern woman. But when it comes to Harry, she is a soft touch.

Professor McGonagall consistently has a negative reaction when others verbally attack Harry. In the Chamber of Secrets, McGonagall was quiet until Snape wanted to punish Harry for the attack on Mrs. Norris. Then, McGonagall snaps at Snape and says "There is no evidence at all that Potter has done anything wrong[13]." Why did McGonagall snap at Snape? He had not accused her personally. He merely targeted a student in her House, who was found at the scene of the crime. McGonagall told him the suggested punishment was unreasonable because the attack had nothing to do with brooms or Quidditch. In the Prisoner of Azkaban, when Oliver Wood approaches her regarding the return of Harry's Firebolt. "[McGonagall] seemed to think [Wood] cared more about winning the Cup than I do about you staying alive. Just because I told her I didn't care if it threw you off…Honestly, the way she was yelling at me… you'd think I'd said something terrible[14]." This reaction seems a bit extreme for someone who is every bit as much a Quidditch fanatic as Wood. He did not say he did not care if Harry died, just that it did not matter if he got hurt. Well, as a Professor and Quidditch fan, McGonagall may very well have agreed with Wood, but as a relative, she was not as inclined to take an injury or the potential death of her family member so lightly. The last line of Wood's statement "the way she was yelling at me" implies he had not heard McGonagall yell at him or anyone else in that way before, which means clearly he hit a nerve[15]. This nerve seems to pulsate only when Harry is involved. Then in Goblet of Fire, McGonagall was letting Dumbledore handle the situation with Fudge, until he says, "'For heaven's sakes…his tales are getting taller…the boy can talk to snakes, Dumbledore, and you still think he's trustworthy?' 'You fool!' Professor McGonagall cried[16]." Again, McGonagall was allowing Dumbledore to handle the situation on his own, but the moment Harry was insulted and his integrity was questioned, McGonagall exploded. This time she went so far as to call the Minister of Magic a fool. This is a true statement, but it lacks tact and respect for the office. In the Order of the Phoenix, Umbridge states Harry will not achieve his dream in the McGonagall's presence. This causes all hell to break loose. In spite of McGonagall's insistence Harry should not lose his temper with Umbridge she does exactly this and vows she will assist Harry in achieving his dream, if it is the last thing she does. Even when Harry left the office, he could hear the shouting down the hall. The Detectives have to admire McGonagall's restraint with Umbridge, but it is interesting an attack on Harry triggered the explosion.

In addition to having a negative reaction to verbal attacks on Harry, she is very emotional when Harry is exposed to danger. When Harry's name came out of the Goblet of Fire, Professor McGonagall leapt to her feet to "whisper urgently to Professor Dumbledore, who bent his ear toward her frowning slightly[17]." It is unknown what McGonagall said to Dumbledore at this time, but the Detectives can guess. "You can't let him do it, Dumbledore. No way! How in the name of Merlin can this have happened?" The very fact McGonagall felt she had input on this matter is highly relevant. Then, in the room off the Great Hall, when everyone except Dumbledore accuses Harry of putting his name in the Goblet of Fire, McGonagall slips and calls him Harry, instead of Potter, in her defense of both Dumbledore and Harry. Remember McGonagall called him, Harry, when they were leaving him on the Dursley's front steps. So, she has two ways of referring to Harry, as she does for addressing Dumbledore? This would definitely build a case for a double life, of which, Harry is unaware. Before the First Task, McGonagall is worried sick. When she is walking Harry down to the task, she puts her arm around him and assures him everything will be fine and just do his best. Why did she escort him to the task? Also, this is the first time we see McGonagall show Harry affection. After the task, McGonagall is waiting for Harry with Hagrid and Moody and she has Madam Pomfrey attend to Harry's injury immediately. Then, after Voldemort's return, McGonagall has tears in her eyes and went to Harry immediately upon entering the room, whereas Dumbledore and Snape went to different parts of the room. She picked him up and was determined to take him to the hospital wing. This passage never says she let go of Harry. It was not until Dumbledore harshly stopped her that this ceased. She argued with Dumbledore insisting Harry was injured, and her voice cracked. Following this scene, Dumbledore had McGonagall leave the room immediately. Why? Would she have revealed something?

The Detectives believe this pattern of Minerva McGonagall's behavior, in regards to Harry's discipline, verbal attacks on Harry, and becoming emotional when he is faced with danger suggests a much deeper relationship than that of Professor and student. Based on the age difference and the fact she did not state that she was not his parent or guardian, the Detectives believe Minerva McGonagall is the grandmother or great aunt of Harry Potter. This theory has been developed over time. Arabella is her daughter and the name suggests she and James are first cousins. This would make McGonagall, Harry's great aunt. So, could McGonagall's maiden name be Potter. Based on the similarity in appearance, tall, thin, black hair. She looks like three people, Tom Riddle, James Potter, and Harry Potter. Thus, it is logical to assume they are all related. Tom Riddle's mother could have had siblings. Her name is deliberately omitted. Thus, his mother could have had a brother or sister, who also had children. Keep in mind, McGonagall wears green, which is the color of Slytherin, but she is Head of Gryffindor House. Also, remember two facts, it is our choices, which determine our future and all purebloods are related. Thus, James could be her deceased siblings' son and Harry her great nephew. In addition, McGonagall started teaching at Hogwarts the year James was born. This causes the Detectives to wonder if McGonagall needed to remain distant from her magical nephew in order to protect him from his cousin—Voldemort. Also, when Voldemort disappears, it appears the threat is gone, thus, she need not keep her distance from Harry. Dumbledore would certainly have cleared this issue up for her.

Why do the Detectives say Harry is the heir of Gryffindor?

In an interview with *The Sydney Morning Herald*, J.K. Rowling said, the name Hogwarts is a flower in the lily family[18]. Très intéressant! Hogwarts is part of the lily family, of which coincidentally is the name of Harry's mother. This implies Harry's mother could be the descendent of the Hogwarts' founders. But which founder is her ancestor? After the creation of Hogwarts, Slytherin divided the founders and they were only united under Godric Gryffindor. Thus, is it logical he named the school? Slytherin left the school and the Detectives believe Gryffindor became the Headmaster. This conclusion was reached for several reasons. The knocker on the door to Headmaster's office is a griffin. It would make sense that the first headmaster would have selected the décor for the office. Another clue about the Potter's is that they lived in Godric's Hollow, which is Gryffindor's first name.

The Detectives believe there are several clues to support the theory Albus Dumbledore is a descendent of Godric Gryffindor. First, Dumbledore was in Gryffindor House, when he attended Hogwarts. Second, his phoenix, Fawkes is scarlet and gold, which are the colors of Gryffindor

House.   One has to wonder where Dumbledore acquired this bird given Fawkes dies, but is reborn from his ashes. Also, Gryffindor was the most powerful wizard of his age, which is now a characterization applied to Dumbledore. Furthermore, Gryffindor united the other founders against Slytherin and Dumbledore united the wizarding world against Voldemort during his last reign of power. Now, Dumbledore is attempting to do this again, but the job may be passed on to Harry Potter. The final piece of evidence is Wulfric de Croxton was a descendant of Godric a Saxon[19]. Wow, Wulfric is one of Dumbledore's middle names. So, it is settled. Dumbledore is a descendant of Gryffindor.

The Detectives also believe the evidence suggests Harry is the great-great-grandson of Albus Dumbledore. First, Harry has Lily's eyes. This is a key feature. Everyone who knew the Potters, including Dumbledore remarks on Harry's eyes upon meeting him. Why? Clearly there was something very special about Lily's eyes. Dumbledore's eyes are also mentioned with some frequency. They twinkle behind his half moon spectacles when he is happy and blaze when he is angry. The Detectives believe both wizards have a great deal of power in their eyes. Most important is the way Dumbledore treats Harry. First, Dumbledore overruled Harry's parent's will. They had appointed Sirius Black, godfather and guardian of Harry, if anything should happen to the two of them. Who has the authority to overrule the deceased parents? The Headmaster of Hogwarts would not in the Head Detectives' opinion. As she is a godmother and an appointed guardian, she believes her opinion on this issue is sound. Very few people would have the legal right to take the guardian to court and have any chance of winning the case when the parents, prior to their death, arranged guardianship. The gall of Dumbledore is overwhelming in this situation. If he was not a member of the immediate family the case would have been thrown out of court, his being the most powerful wizard in the world is irrelevant. The fact, Sirius did not take the matter to court shows he knew he did not believe he could win the case. Remember the characters have more information than the Detectives, so what does Sirius know that we do not? Could it be Sirius knows Dumbledore is Harry's grandfather back a few generations, of course? Next, Dumbledore watches Harry continually. Why? He spies on the kid and has been doing so ever since he left him on the Dursley's doorstep. Well, he could be doing this because he is growing up to be a powerful wizard, but Harry's childhood with the Dursleys was not all that interesting and yet Dumbledore watched anyway. So, did grandpa just want to see Harry take his first steps, say his first words, and do his first bit of magic? Harry was frequently in trouble at the Dursleys and Dumbledore never stepped in to save him. Perhaps this was an agreement he and Aunt Petunia had made. Furthermore, Dumbledore treats Harry different from any of the other students at Hogwarts. He addresses Harry by his first name, when he addresses all the other students as Mr. and Miss. In addition, Dumbledore and Harry always have a private conversation sometime during the year. The battle between Dumbledore and Tom, or Voldemort, is quite revealing. The readers get a glimpse as to what frightens the great Dumbledore. "'Stay where you are, Harry!' For the first time Dumbledore sounded frightened[20]." It is clear Dumbledore fears losing Harry. Why? Harry's destiny is to save the wizarding world from evil, so does Dumbledore's fear of losing Harry represent a fear of losing the wizarding world to evil or does it suggest something deeper?

In the Order of the Phoenix, the conversation between Dumbledore and Harry is more revealing than ever before. When Harry is raging and throwing things, Dumbledore says, "If you are to attack me, as I know you are close to doing, I would like to have thoroughly earned it[21]." He would have allowed Harry to attack him, just like Sirius let Harry hit him. Why? Dumbledore does not seem the type to allow anyone to attack him and yet he allowed Harry to destroy his possessions. Based on his statement, he would have allowed Harry to strike him. Later Dumbledore again tells Harry, "You will have your chance to rage at me—to do whatever you like—when I have finished. I will not stop you[22]." This again suggests he would have allowed Harry to attack him. Sirius let Harry strike him several times before stopping him. The fact, Dumbledore would have allowed Harry to attack him suggests there is a relationship much deeper than that of Headmaster and student. Dumbledore acknowledges this fact "if [Voldemort] realized that our relationship was—or had ever been—closer than that of headmaster and pupil[23]." Well, this statement from Dumbledore is interesting. The Detectives have suspected a deeper relationship, but the confirmation one actually exists is quite exciting. So, what is this relationship? The only one we have confirmed is that of Headmaster and student. Was there one, which existed in the first year of Harry's life that he does not recall? It could possibly be that of great-grandfather and great-grandson. Harry is clearly Dumbledore's favorite student and Dumbledore took charge after the death of Harry's parents, so it was clear even before he came to Hogwarts and became famous there was something connecting Dumbledore and Harry.

Then, when Harry is exceptionally angry with Dumbledore and hurt over Sirius's death, "Dumbledore closed his eyes and buried his face in his long-fingered hands...this uncharacteristic sign of exhaustion, or sadness... did not soften [Harry][24]." Like McGonagall, Harry can bring out emotions in Dumbledore when no one else seems able to do. Harry is hurting and Dumbledore blames himself. The most intriguing statement came when Dumbledore was explaining why he had waited to tell Harry about the prophecy. "'I cared about you too much,' said Dumbledore simply. 'I cared more for your happiness than your knowing the truth, more for your peace of mind than my plans, more for your life than the lives that might be lost if the plan failed. In other words, I acted exactly as Voldemort expects we fools who love to act[25].'" Dumbledore loves Harry. He comes right out and says it here. Any question about the depth of the relationship is gone at this point. Headmasters do not love their students. There is something else here. Harry was gone for ten years and Dumbledore watched him the entire time. Also, why was he watching Harry when he was in a house where he was completely safe? Unless, Dumbledore just wanted to watch Harry grow. Dumbledore was extremely attached to this baby boy long before he placed him on the Dursley's front steps. Further evidence of this is Dumbledore's statement. "What did I care if numbers of nameless and faceless people and creatures were slaughtered in the vague future, if in the here and now you were alive and well, and happy[26]?" Again, this does not fit with Dumbledore's personality. He is putting Harry above the entire wizarding world. Dumbledore is the savior of the wizarding world and yet he does not care if it survives, as long as Harry does. Wow! This is out of character for Dumbledore and tells the Detectives his love for Harry is so strong, it is overriding his reason. Dumbledore tells Harry when he rose to the challenge in his first year, "I was...prouder of you than I can say[27]." This statement grabs the reader's attention. It is a comment a parent or grandparent would say to their child or grandchild.

Finally, when Dumbledore placed Harry on the Dursley's steps "the twinkling light that usually shone from Dumbledore's eyes seemed to have gone out[28]." Clearly, Dumbledore left Harry with the Dursleys out of necessity, not because it was what he wanted to do. Based on his reaction, it upset him greatly. Then, at the end of the Order of the Phoenix, after Dumbledore had told Harry about the prophecy and discussed the reality he would either have to be the murderer or the victim. "Harry looked up at him and saw a tear trickling down Dumbledore's face into his long silver beard[29]." Dumbledore cried! His heart was breaking because of the burden placed on Harry's shoulders.

Harry clearly has a special relationship with Dumbledore. The Detectives believe Harry is the great-great-grandson of Albus Dumbledore. If the Detectives are correct and Dumbledore is a direct descendent of Godric Gryffindor, then Harry is also a descendent of Gryffindor on his mother's side. First, the names Hogwarts and Lily suggest, she is a descendent of one of the founders. Additional evidence Lily is Dumbledore's great-granddaughter is her hair color, which is "thick, dark red hair that fell to her shoulders[30]." Dumbledore had "long sweeping auburn hair[31]." Wow, they both have red hair, the color of Gryffindor House and their eyes are routinely described. This would also explain why Petunia would be in contact with Dumbledore, as she is also a great-granddaughter. Furthermore, in the Chamber of Secrets, Harry pulled Godric Gryffindor's sword out of the Sorting Hat and Dumbledore tells him only a "true Gryffindor" would be able to do so. So, what exactly is the meaning of this statement? True, as in descendent, or true, as in placement in Gryffindor House?

Why do the Detectives say Harry Potter is the heir of Ravenclaw?

In order to have Harry and Neville be the descendants of all four of the founders, one of the two has to be a descendent of Ravenclaw. There is sufficient evidence to prove both Harry and Neville were descendants of Gryffindor. Also, that Harry is a descendent of Slytherin and Neville is a descendent of Hufflepuff. So, which one is a descendent of Ravenclaw? The Detectives believe Harry Potter is a descendent of Ravenclaw. The Sorting Hat considered three houses before placing him in Gryffindor. Three qualities are mentioned, courage, which is Gryffindor, the mind, which is Ravenclaw, and a thirst to prove himself, which is Slytherin. It is probable Harry is a descendent of all three of these founders.

Chapter 12

Voldemort

Early Life

Voldemort's given name was Tom Marvolo Riddle. The word riddle means perplexing mystery and to pierce with numerous holes. Riddle tells Harry he was named after his father, Tom and his grandfather, Marvolo. Tom Riddle's parents and paternal grandparents lived in a village, called Little Hangleton. His mother was a witch, but we are not told her name, and his father, a Muggle. His family were wealthy snobs, a great deal like the Dursleys. Tom Riddle, Sr. left his wife, after learning she was a witch because he did not like magic. This occurred before Tom, Jr. was born and his mother lived just long enough to name him. Thus, he was raised in a Muggle orphanage. Tom Riddle was tall, thin, and had jet-black hair. He already had the long fingers and high cold laugh for which Voldemort is known. Interestingly enough, the color of Riddle's eyes was left out of his description. The Detectives believe this piece of information is key to the plot. They also believe his eye color is green, based on the second entrance to the Chamber of Secrets. "On which two entwined serpents were carved, their eyes set with great, glinting emeralds[1]." There are two with emerald eyes, not one. Well, we know Harry has emerald eyes, thus, it logically follows Tom had the other set. The Detectives also wonder if Tom Riddle was born in mid-winter because of Professor Trelawney's comment to Harry. She thought, he was born under Saturn, due to his features, which are similar to those of Riddle, his mean stature, and the tragic losses early in life. Each of these statements could easily apply to Tom Riddle, as well as, Harry Potter. Trelawney incorrectly applied this to Harry, but like many of her visions what she sees is correct, just incorrectly interrupted. So, could she be seeing Riddle in Harry?

While at Hogwarts, Tom Riddle was both a Prefect and Head Boy. He received awards for Magical Merit and Special Services to the School. Interestingly enough, his special service was framing Hagrid for opening the Chamber of Secrets. Riddle, as the true heir of Slytherin, opened the Chamber of Secrets at the age of sixteen. It took him five years to find the entrance. After ordering the basilisk to kill Moaning Myrtle, he discovered he was going to be sent back to the Muggle orphanage and Hogwarts might close completely. Thus, he decided to frame Hagrid. Riddle knew Hagrid was keeping Aragog in the dungeons. The Detectives believe he may have even suggested it was a good place to hide the spider given the dialogue shown in the diary. First, they address each other as Rubeus and Tom, which suggests they were friends or, at least Hagrid thought Tom was his friend. Second, Riddle says, "I'm going to have to turn you in, Rubeus[2]." Again, this is as if this is not something he really wants to do. Tom Riddle reminds the Detectives of Anikan at this point, he is clearly turning to the dark side. Riddle's memory tells Harry, in the Chamber of Secrets, he was already using the name Voldemort with his most intimate friends at Hogwarts. One must question who these friends were and where are they now? They would all be around the age 70 given Voldemort's age. One would also expect them to be Death Eaters. Although, if Voldemort is like most dictators, they are dead because he has already risen to power once. If they survived the battles, most dictators kill those who put them in power shortly after the victory, so those who helped them rise cannot assassinate them. For example, Hitler killed the S.A. and Lenin killed Trotsky. The Detectives do believe Draco Malfoy's grandfather was one of these school friends, which would explain Hagrid's hatred for the entire Malfoy clan. It is likely he was killed in one of the battles given Lucius is a Death Eater.

Middle Life

After graduation from Hogwarts, Tom Riddle set out to accomplish his life mission of becoming the most powerful Dark Wizard in the world. He decided he should start his life of crime by killing the man who abandoned both him and his mother before his birth—his father, Tom Riddle, Sr. Well, he lived with his parents, so why not make it a triple homicide? Anakin clearly has moved a few steps closer to Darth

Vader, given he shows a complete lack of conscious. The Detectives also believe Tom and Minerva are related. They are same age and share a description, tall, thin, and black hair. Could they have kept in touch, but become estranged when he became so evil? Minerva McGonagall is highly reluctant to discuss anything regarding Tom Riddle or Voldemort. In fact, she remained completely silent during the discussion of him at the end of Book 2 and left the office immediately following the discussion. Is this normal behavior for Minerva? Hardly! She normally has something to say about every subject. So, why the silence? Is it because she and Tom are in some way connected or even related? Does she not want to discuss the black sheep in her family. The Detectives believe the answer is yes. This theory derives from the fact Tom's mother's name is conveniently omitted. Also, her family is not mentioned. Did she have siblings? The Detectives believe she had a brother, who was a wizard and a sister, who was a squib. As Slytherin's heir she undoubtedly was a pureblood and many pureblood families, do not approve of their children marrying Muggles. Thus, he was placed in an orphanage. Tom Riddle knew a great deal about his mother and his father's disappearance. Who would have told him these stories, when he lived in an orphanage? Could his mother's squib sister have shared them with him on several visits? She would have been very bitter about her sister's fate and blamed Tom Riddle, Sr. This is a plausible explanation. The wizard brother may have mentioned the child to his children, upon hearing the boy was attending Hogwarts. Thus, as a first cousin, Minerva would have wanted to befriend Tom Riddle. This would explain her silence and desire to keep her children and other family members from Voldemort's knowledge.

Dumbledore continued to give the room at large a glimpse of Voldemort's past. "He disappeared after leaving school...traveled far and wide...sank so deeply into the Dark Arts...underwent so many dangerous, magical transformations, that when he resurfaced...hardly anyone connected Lord Voldemort with the clever, handsome boy who was once Head Boy here[3]." These transformations were undoubtedly to make him immortal. Another point worthy of note is according to the timetable Tom Riddle graduated from Hogwarts in 1938, which was when fascism was on the rise in Europe. Also the end of WWII correlates with Dumbledore's defeat of the dark wizard Grindelwald. Thus, the Detectives believe it is feasible to think Tom Riddle may have become his apprentice, during his rise to power and terrorization of the wizarding people. Hence, Dumbledore's statement, he "consorted with the very worst of our kind[4]." Dumbledore would have seen Tom, and some of his transformations, when he battled Grindelwald and may have shunted him aside in much of the same way he did with Harry during the battle with Voldemort. After the defeat of Grindelwald, Dumbledore may have tried to encourage Tom to turn his life around now that his "master" is gone. The Detectives believe seeing Dumbledore defeat Grindelwald is the reason for Voldemort's deep fear of Dumbledore.

The Rise of Voldemort

The word Voldemort comes from French. Vol is flight de is of, and mort is death; so it literally means flight of death. This makes perfect sense given Voldemort thinks death is the ultimate evil. Thus, he is running away from his own death. This is really a bit nasty. He is so ready to bring death to others, but wants to be immortal himself. Interesting. Lord Voldemort is a tall, extremely thin man with long fingers. He has a snake-like face with "cat-like" slits for pupils and red eyes. (Did the detectives catch the cat reference? There are *four* other characters with something catlike about them. Minerva McGonagall, Argus Filch, Arabella Figg, and Harry Potter.)

Very few people call Voldemort by his proper name. The Detectives believe those who do, namely Dumbledore, Harry, Sirius, Lupin, and Hermione, think Voldemort is unworthy of fear and will ultimately be defeated. Voldemort's followers, the Death Eaters, refer to him as the Dark Lord, but address him as Master or My Lord. It should be noted, only two Death Eaters have been heard to call Voldemort "My Lord." They are Lucius and Wormtail. The Detectives believe these are the old and new deputies. Most of the wizarding community refers to him "you-know-who" or "He-who-must-not-be-named." These are both significant, both of these groups of people fear him, but on different levels. Those who call him you-know-who are the average wizards. Those who call him, "He-who-must-not-be-named" are calling him the evil one. The

Detectives have a theory as to why many people do not want to use his name and also why Dumbledore wants everyone to start using it. Sailors did not speak or sing about pirates when on the water for fear of bringing them down upon them. Perhaps this is the problem with the wizarding community. It is possible saying the name Voldemort in some way alerts him and Dumbledore wants everyone to use it so he is overloaded. (Of course, Dumbledore could also just want to knock Voldemort's ego down, which would definitely occur if everyone started using his name.) Another reason the Detectives believe using the name alerts Voldemort is the fact Snape, a former Death Eater, did not want Harry to use it in his presence. Snape would know things others would not know. Also, Harry's scar burned each time he said Voldemort's name. Again, this could be a special case, because the usual rules do not apply to Harry Potter.

During Voldemort's rise to power he steadily gained power and was taking over everywhere. He devised a creed saying he wanted to purify the wizard race. The parallel to Hitler is uncanny. Then, he recruited followers and called them Death Eaters. This was his elite organization. He burned the Dark Mark into each Death Eater's left forearm so they could distinguish each other and he could summon them to him. The Dark Mark was his sign, which was also shot into the air anytime the Death Eaters' killed. This was an interesting mark; it was a skull with a snake coming out of the mouth. Interesting choice! Clearly, Voldemort got the idea from the Chamber of Secrets, given the basilisk came out of the mouth of Slytherin. Voldemort operated in great secrecy and alone knew the names of all of his followers. This suggests he was extremely paranoid and feared one of them would try to overthrow him if they knew the names of their fellow Death Eaters. So, Voldemort continued to take power. Those who stood up to him were killed or put on the hit list. Interestingly, Hagrid tells Harry in Book 1, even at the height of Voldemort's power, he still feared Dumbledore and did not dare attempt to take over Hogwarts.

In June of 1980, a prophecy was made stating the one with the power to vanquish Voldemort approached and would be born on July 31 to those who had escaped him three times. Voldemort would mark him as his equal and one would kill the other. Voldemort, however, only received the first half of the prophecy because his spy was caught and thrown out of the Hogshead[5]. So, Voldemort had his choice, between Harry Potter and Neville Longbottom. He chose the half-blood like himself—Harry Potter. The Potters were aware Voldemort was after them because one of Dumbledore's spies informed them. The Detectives suspect Snape. So, they had a Secret Keeper, everyone was told or assumed this was their best friend, Sirius, who convinced them to use Wormtail as a bluff. This was a mistake because Wormtail was a spy for Voldemort and betrayed their whereabouts to him immediately. Thus, on Halloween in 1981 Voldemort murdered James and Lily Potter and attempted to kill Harry, only to have the curse rebound upon him, thus, breaking his power. So, why would an infamous murderer, who wants to kill a child and his father, not want to kill the mother? Well, there are three logical reasons, love, friendship, or family. Lily was too young to fit into the category of Voldemort's being in love with or friends with her. But it is possible they were related and Voldemort was aware of this relationship. The Detectives believe this ties into Tom Riddle's mother's family, which has been omitted from the series, thus far. Could Lily be the granddaughter of the squib aunt, who told Voldemort his family history? Does she resemble this woman? This would be a reasonable assumption as to why Voldemort did not want to kill Lily, unless it was absolutely necessary? It is curious, Voldemort even admits Lily outsmarted him. Surely, only a witch, who was related to him, would be able to outsmart Voldemort.

After Voldemort's attack on Harry, only one power still remained, the power to possess others. It is interesting the curse rebounded, but failed to kill Voldemort, as well as Harry. So, one may assume the magical transformations Voldemort underwent protected him from being killed by the Avada Kedavra curse. The Detectives are also curious if Voldemort went to the Potter's alone or if Wormtail/ Judas accompanied him. If he was alone, how is it he still has his wand? Perhaps Wormtail was there and accompanied Voldemort to the forest, but left saying he needed to frame Sirius. Wormtail was supposed to return following Sirius's imprisonment, but did not. This would explain why Voldemort does not want Wormtail to leave his sight anymore.

In Harry's first year at Hogwarts, Voldemort possessed Quirrell and attempted to steal the Sorcerer's Stone. Quirrell used Harry to get the stone out of the Mirror of Erised and tried to take it from him by force. Voldemort ordered him to kill Harry, but he could not touch Harry because of the protection Lily had left in his skin. This was Voldemort's second failed attempt to kill Harry Potter.

Voldemort's Rebirth

After Sirius escaped from Azkaban and cornered Wormtail, he was left with no choice, but to return to his master, Voldemort, or be killed by Sirius and Remus. This made Professor Trelawney's second prophecy a reality. Wormtail became Voldemort's nurse. His tasks included, milking Voldemort's snake, Nagini, so that he could feed Voldemort a potion of snake venom and unicorn blood, in order, to give him strength. He also performed the Dark Magic necessary to give him a crude body, which would be suitable until he could be returned to his old body. On the way to find Voldemort, Wormtail met Bertha Jorkins, overpowered her, and brought her to Voldemort, which proved to be key in developing the plans for his return to full strength and power. Voldemort and Wormtail went to the Crouch home and freed Barty Crouch, Jr. and then assigned him to the task of becoming Moody's double and guiding Harry Potter through the Triwizard Tournament. When Harry won the tournament, the Triwizard Cup had been made into a porkey and he was transported directly to Voldemort. Unfortunately, Cedric Diggory and Harry took the porkey together. Diggory was killed immediately and Harry was tied up on Tom Riddle, Sr. grave. Wormtail, then, began the process.

The potion used to return Voldemort had a base of unicorn blood and snake venom. Before anything is added to the potion the surface is described, as diamond encrusted. Diamonds are several colors so the color of the potion is not definite at this point, but the Detectives suspect it is silver and white given unicorn blood is silver and the most common color of diamond is white. Wormtail added three additional ingredients while saying the spell. When the bones of the father are added the potion turns a "vivid, poisonous-looking blue[6]." Next, Wormtail cuts off his right hand to supply Voldemort with the flesh of the servant, which turned the potion a "burning red[7]." The Detectives wonder if this puts Voldemort in Wormtail's debt, from this point forward Voldemort owes his life to Wormtail, although it is in a completely different sense than that which Wormtail owes his life to Harry. Also, he made the statement in chapter one, "I could never have formed our plan, and for that, you will have your *reward*, Wormtail. I will *allow you* to perform an *essential* task one that many of my followers would give their right hands to perform[8]." Well, Voldemort definitely has a twisted sense of humor. Cutting off one's hand would not sound like a reward under normal circumstances, so why would this be a coveted job? Unless of course, this *essential task* makes Wormtail, Voldemort's right-hand man literally or, as Dumbledore put it, Wormtail is now Voldemort's deputy. Also, why would Voldemort *allow* Wormtail to do it if he thinks he is so brainless and not his faithful servant? Well, Wormtail will never be a threat to his power. Also, if this puts him in Wormtail's debt, all he really has to do is protect Wormtail, so he has to kill the same people he already wants to kill and tell his Death Eaters to leave his caregiver alone, so he can do his job properly. This will work out fine, right? Wrong! What happens when Voldemort's debt and Wormtail's debt conflict? The final part of the potion was the "Blood of the enemy...forcibly taken...you will...resurrect your foe[9]." When Harry's blood was added to the cauldron it turned the potion "instantly, a blinding white[10]." Harry's blood is full of the very thing Voldemort despises—love. Ironically, now it is coursing through his veins. The cauldron turns white when Harry's blood is added because of the purity and humanity being added to the potion. It should also be noted, when Voldemort rises he comes from "a surge of white steam[11]." So, it seems the core or strongest ingredient was Harry's blood. Perhaps, Voldemort should have heeded Wormtail's insistence that this process could be done without Harry Potter. The Detectives believe Voldemort has sealed his own demise with this choice. Voldemort wanted Harry's protection so he would have the power to destroy him. Well unfortunately this also makes you human again, Tom.

After Voldemort had risen again, he examined his body, which suggests a love of his body. Next, Voldemort recalled his Death Eaters. His plan was to reward Wormtail in front of all of them and them kill Harry publicly. Oh, "the best laid plans of mice and men[12]." Needless to say he made a fool of himself, but the Death Eaters are still too afraid of him to tell him so. While waiting for the Death Eaters to arrive Voldemort does something quite intriguing. He tells Harry his family history, about his parents, being raised in a Muggle orphanage, and vowing revenge on his father. This speech is cut off due to the arrival of the Death Eaters before he reached the part about his time at Hogwarts. Interesting stopping point, the Detectives wonder if Voldemort would have told Harry and Wormtail too much. Voldemort realizes this speech is not "normal" behavior for him. "Listen to me, reliving family history...why, I am growing quite sentimental...But look Harry! My *true* family returns[13]." Harry's blood is so full of love it is like a poison in Voldemort's veins, which is already affecting him. The Detective's believe this will ultimately destroy Voldemort. He prides himself on being pure evil, killing without thought, and now he has love coursing through his body. This will only grow stronger. It is foreign to him and not something he understands. Further evidence, Harry's blood is affecting Voldemort is seen in the fact he does not torture the treacherous Death Eaters. Clearly this does not fit Voldemort's past profile. Crouch, Jr. tells Harry, "I expected him to punish them. I expected him to torture them. Tell me he hurt them[14]." This would explain why the same Death Eaters ran from the Dark Mark at the Quidditch World Cup. They clearly feared his return because they had betrayed him and yet Voldemort only tortures one—Avery.

After Voldemort's speech to the Death Eaters, he instructed Wormtail to give Harry back his wand and proceeded to duel with him. Voldemort hit Harry with the Cruciatus Curse. When Harry would not ask him not to do it again, he put the Imperius Curse on Harry in order to force the desired answer. Harry fought this curse and dodged Voldemort's next attempt to hit him with the Cruciatus Curse. Finally, Harry decided to attempt to disarm Voldemort as he used the killing curse on Harry. The spells hit in midair and the wands connected. The reason for this is Voldemort and Harry have brother wands. They share the core of a Phoenix feather, which belonged to Fawkes, Dumbledore's Phoenix. It should be noted Fawkes loves Harry. Also, the phoenix song instills hope and courage in the pure of heart, but fear in those who are not pure of heart[15]. So, these very powerful wands may be a blessing to one wizard and a curse to the other. Brother wands will not battle properly against one another. If their owners force them to do battle then one wand will force the other to regurgitate the spells that it has performed. This is called priori incantatem[16]. When the wands connected with a golden thread, Voldemort and Harry were raised into the air and moved out of the graveyard. Then the golden thread splintered and formed a golden web, which was filled with the phoenix song and the beads of light. Harry pushed one of the beads of light onto the end of Voldemort's wand and it started to regurgitate spells. Echoes of people Voldemort killed came out of the wand, including Cedric Diggory, Frank Bryce, Bertha Jorkins, Lily Potter, and James Potter. These echoes circled Harry and Voldemort and encouraged Harry and hissed things to Voldemort. There is an interesting description of Voldemort in this passage, "his face now livid with fear as his victims prowled around him[17]." This is extremely interesting and important. Voldemort has a fear, more than one actually, but he fears his dead victims. He believes death is the worst thing in the world, hence his name, but he has already killed these people and they are back and there is nothing more he can do to them. The echoes helped Harry to escape. Upon Harry's return, he immediately alerted Dumbledore to Voldemort's return and the Order of the Phoenix was recalled.

As a result of the miraculous escape of Harry Potter, Voldemort wants to hear the prophecy in its entirety. The prophecy was made in the Hogshead and the eavesdropper was caught a short way into it. During the gathering of the Death Eaters, Avery asked for forgiveness and was tortured for his request. Voldemort stated he does not forgive or forget, but the question remains why was Avery tortured and not the others? They all abandoned Voldemort. Does he blame Avery for his downfall? Whoever failed to get the entire prophecy could not warn Voldemort an attack on either child risked the loss of power, thus Voldemort would clearly resent the messenger. The Detectives believe it was Avery who was caught a short way through the prophecy and consequently Avery is blamed for Voldemort's fall from power. Avery has been trying to repair this blunder by attempting to steal the prophecy from the Department of Mysteries, but is only digging himself in deeper. Voldemort finally learns from the former Head of the Department of Mysteries, Rookwood, he would either have to take the prophecy or have Harry Potter take it for him. Thus, he chose to have Harry lured to the Department, in order, to get him to lift the prophecy from its shelf. Unfortunately for Voldemort, his Death Eaters failed again, the prophecy smashed during the battle and because of the noise, no one heard what it said.

During this battle, Bellatrix killed Sirius, and as a result, Harry chased her into the atrium intending to kill her. She still believed him to have the prophecy and was still trying to get it from him. Harry taunted her with the fact it shattered, which alerted the connection between himself and Voldemort and, as a result, he too appeared in the atrium. When Voldemort attempted to kill Harry, Dumbledore arrived and waved his wand at the Fountain of Magical Brethren, which removed Harry and Bellatrix from the fight and cleared the way for Voldemort and Dumbledore to duel. This definitely was not what Voldemort had in mind, but again he would not heed the warning of one of his Death Eaters. Bellatrix tried to tell him Dumbledore was below and they should just get out of there. During the duel Voldemort tries, but fails to kill Dumbledore six times. Gee, no wonder he fears this man or is it Dumbledore simply controls the mind game over Voldemort? Fascinatingly, Dumbledore did not attempt to kill Voldemort even once. Why? This probably did more to scare Voldemort, than anything else Dumbledore did. Or did it make him suspicious? After all, his eyes narrowed and he asked probing questions. Clearly, he wanted to know why Dumbledore was not shooting to kill. The Detectives believe Voldemort had a very good point here. The first curse Dumbledore aimed at Voldemort "the force of the spell that emanated …was such that Harry, through shielded…felt his hair stand on end…[it] caused no visible damage to the shield, though a deep, gonglike note reverberated from it, an oddly chilling sound[18]." So, what was this spell? Was it music, humanity, or love? In response to Voldemort's probing questions about why Dumbledore is not seeking to kill him, he states, "we both know that there are other ways of destroying a man, Tom[19]." So, clearly this is part of Dumbledore's plan to destroy Voldemort. So, what would completely destroy Voldemort? He wants power and immortality more than anything, so it would make sense to make it impossible for him to have either. Perhaps Dumbledore wants to humiliate him by not allowing him to be killed by a great wizard whom he fears, but rather to allow a child, for whom he has no respect, Harry Potter, kill him. It is meaningful Dumbledore does not give Voldemort the curtsy or respect of addressing him as Voldemort instead, he calls him by his given name, Tom. This is significant. Dumbledore is reminding him in a small way, he is still human, which is the one thing Voldemort does not want to be. It is in this sequence, we learn Voldemort believes death is the worst thing in the world and Dumbledore informs him "your failure to understand that there are things much worse than death had always been your greatest weakness[20]." Awfully nice of Dumbledore to continue to try to teach Tom, while dueling with him, don't you think? Telling someone their weakness gives them the opportunity to work on it and change it before it destroys them, but Voldemort is far too arrogant to take into account anything Dumbledore tells him. So, it is not likely, he will heed this warning. Finally, Voldemort attempts to possess Harry to defeat Dumbledore. At last, he has found Dumbledore's weakness and greatest fear, but again Harry defeated him. Harry wanted to die; he wanted to be with Sirius. This was something Voldemort could not understand—love. When Harry's heart filled with love Voldemort was forced to leave his body because he could not stand to share a space filled with the very thing he despises. This love affected him, again. Before leaving the atrium, Voldemort grabbed Bellatrix. He did not just save his own skin, which would have fit his profile and that of Slytherins. In the words of Phineas Nigellus, "We Slytherins are brave, yes, but not stupid. For instance, given the choice, we will always choose to save our own necks[21]." Well, Voldemort did not just save himself, but he also saved Bella. This exposed him to the Minister of Magic and the aurors. In addition, Dumbledore could have aimed another curse at him. This action fits more with the profile of what Harry would have done than with what Voldemort would normally have done. So it appears in his attempt to possess Harry more humanity leaked into Voldemort's body. Boy, oh boy, he keeps slitting his own throat! As a side note, the Detectives think it is ironic Voldemort calls Bellatrix, Bella given his presumed niece's name is Arabella, which could be shortened to Bella.

The Detectives believe Voldemort has three fears. First, he fears his own death, above anything else. This is why he is chasing immortality. Clearly, he fears assassination, which anyone who has killed as many people as Voldemort has certainly should. Also, if you recruit mass murderers and people who enjoy torturing others, clearly you should distrust them. The only reason they do not attack him is due to fear. His second fear is of those he has killed coming back. This was clear when the wands connected and the echoes were encircling Voldemort and Harry. Voldemort feared his victims, they were already dead and in his mind there was nothing worse he could do to them. Could he be afraid that they intended to take his life? Voldemort's final fear is Dumbledore, who is the only wizard Voldemort believes is more powerful than himself. Ironically, Dumbledore does not believe he is more powerful than Voldemort, but can exercise mind control over him and win. It is clear if one plays on a fear it will consume the individual. Dumbledore knows Voldemort fears him and takes advantage of this weakness.

Voldemort's downfall is already in the works. The Detectives have a theory on how it will happen based on the clues. Voldemort did the first part to himself, he insisted on having Harry's blood, which is full of love. This will not work well for the most evil wizard in the world. Next, Dumbledore's goal is to humanize him. Voldemort could not be killed in his old body given the curse did not succeed in killing either Harry or Voldemort. Dumbledore's attempt to humanize Voldemort is already happening due the use of Harry's blood, which is coursing through his veins like a poison or maybe it would be more appropriate to call it an antidote. There are many examples showing this transition, including reliving family history in the graveyard and not punishing the Death Eaters who betrayed him. Although, Dumbledore was unable to hit him with a spell to humanize him, Voldemort possessed Harry. Again, Harry oozed love into him and, as a result, Voldemort took Bellatrix with him when he fled the Ministry. The Detectives believe Dumbledore will use McGonagall as a last resort and as his trump card. Until this year, a Death Eater has never harmed McGonagall. It will be interesting to see if Umbridge dies under mysterious circumstances for her attack on McGonagall. If the detectives have ever watched Charmed they know the Source does not like his family to be attacked and typically kills the offender quietly. A demon, who hurt Phoebe, could be sure of a one way ticket to the Demonic Wasteland at Cole's hand, even if they did not know the individual is off limits. The humanization of Voldemort will be completed before the final battle so that Harry will be able to kill him.

Chapter 13

Themes

There are many themes and motifs found in the Harry Potter series. J.K. Rowling uses both themes and motifs to teach children right from wrong in a very clever way. She has the characters, who are portrayed in a positive light, primarily make good choices and the characters, who are portrayed in a negative light, make bad choices. Therefore, the children reading the series are not likely to emulate the actions of the characters they already dislike. One can only hope when adults read the series, they may also consider their own actions and to which characters their actions correlate.

Abuse

Abuse is one of the more depressing themes in the series. There are many kinds of abuse, physical, mental, emotional, and neglect. The most blatant case is the treatment of House-elves. Dobby and Kreacher were both treated poorly if not abused by their masters and as a result they betrayed the one abusing or neglecting them. Dumbledore says, "wizards have mistreated and abused our fellows for too long, and we are now reaping our reward[1]." Thus, as a result of abuse, loyalty is lost and those who may have protected the wizard can cause a great deal of damage.

Ambition versus Obsession

There is a key difference between ambition and obsession. Ambition is when one has the desire and drive to do something well in order to achieve an end result. Obsession is when that desire consumes the individual. Dumbledore has reached the highest point of power, but has never allowed the power to consume him. In contrast, Voldemort became obsessed with his quest for power. Another example of an obsession is Mr. Crouch's quest to become the Minister of Magic. Mr. Crouch cast everything and everyone aside when they interfered with his goal. As a result of neglect or indifference, his son joined the Death Eaters and considered it is personal mission to return Voldemort to power. Thus, when Crouch allowed himself to become obsessed, he lost everything. Percy was Crouch's assistant and shares the dream of becoming Minister of Magic. He is very ambitious and is willing to cut off contact with is his family in order to reach his goal. Thus, Percy is headed towards obsession. If he's not careful he will lose everything just as his mentor did.

Cleanliness

The issue of cleanliness is approached in both the muggle and wizard world. The Malfoys believe all muggles are filthy. They base this belief on their brother-in-law, Ted Tonks, who is a slob. "Cleanliness is next to godliness" and both the Malfoys and Dursleys believe it is of the utmost importance. Likewise, they share many suppositions of the others' world. Ironically, the character of Aunt Petunia, who is a muggle, is a cleaning fanatic, and the pureblood House of Black was filthy.

Corruption

Corruption is a major theme in Harry Potter. It is seen in both the government and organizations. Both the Death Eaters and the Order of the Phoenix are infiltrating the government and both sides are trying to persuade the leader to side with them. The Minister of Magic, Fudge, and several others inside are willing to be bought and sold. There are several reasons for this. Fudge has become corrupted due to his love of power and his desire to be in power, regardless of the consequences. The Head of the Department of Magical Games and Sports has become corrupted due to his gambling problem.

The two major organizations, the Death Eaters and the Order of the Phoenix, have also been corrupted. The majority of the Death Eaters fear Voldemort too much to cross him, yet Dumbledore had "a number of useful spies[2]." Among them is Snape, who is corrupting the Death Eater organization by feeding information to the Order of the Phoenix. The Order had this same problem the last time when Wormtail became a double agent and ultimately caused the death of the Potters. Recently, Kreacher was able to corrupt the organization and cause the death of Sirius.

Corruption is a key theme in the series. J.K. Rowling uses corruption to show the damage that can be caused by a corrupt individual. She craftily shows how it can eat away at an organization or even a government.

Death

The theme of Death began in the first chapter of Book 1. Harry's parents were killed and he was taken from his old life and put in a new life. Thus, it was the death of one life and the birth of a new life. In subsequent books, each one ends with a murder or attempted murder. Then, Book 5 ends with the death of Sirius Black. After Black's death Harry is told about his destiny, which again symbolizes death and rebirth. The theme of death is used to teach children about the value of life. This is a crucial lesson and much easier for children to learn in a book than in their own lives.

Enslavement

The enslavement of House-elves has become a major issue as the series has progressed. Wizards have enslaved House-elves for centuries. The elves are bound to serve one family until they die or are set free. Most of the elves are so brainwashed they do not realize they are enslaved, but Dobby, the first elf the readers met, wanted to be free. As Dobby warned Harry continually of the danger at Hogwarts in the second year, Harry learned how severely abused and brainwashed Dobby was and that he was enslaved until his master freed him. The next House-elf the readers meet is Winky. The Detectives believe Winky was treated more like an equal in the Crouch household than a slave given that she seemed to make decisions with Crouch, Sr. and not just take orders. Also, she does not seem to work at Hogwarts, instead she allows the other elves to do the work for her. If the Hogwarts House-elves are representative of the majority of the populous, freedom is regarded as something dangerous and undesirable. When Winky was freed she cried continually and became an alcoholic. Dobby, on the other hand, loves freedom and enjoys wearing clothes and being paid for his work. The Hogwarts House-elves believe both Winky and Dobby are a disgrace to their kind. Interestingly enough, Kreacher, the House-elf of the Black family, was threatened with clothes and had the opportunity to be rid of Sirius. This was an excellent idea, but he could not keep his mouth shut. So, did Kreacher want to be freed or did he deliberately anger Sirius? The Detectives believe Kreacher, like many elves, did not want freedom. As much as he hated Sirius, life with him was too easy and he would not be able to find a life that easy anywhere else. If he went to serve the Malfoy family full time, he would find he would be treated just as Dobby had been treated—abused and forced to work continually. So, instead he had Sirius killed. We shall see what happens to Kreacher in Book 6. The Detectives doubt he will be living his comfortable life alone with his mistress's portrait again. The message portrayed here is, when those on the top mistreat or neglect those on the bottom, often times the result is catastrophic. The Malfoys abused Dobby and have now given Harry a loyal friend, one who will go to any length to save him and also have the freedom to disclose a great deal of private information about the family to both Harry and Dumbledore. According to Dumbledore, Sirius neglected Kreacher and this is why he had Sirius killed. The Detectives believe it was also due to the fact the Sirius allowed

Kreacher to get away with way too much. In contrast, Winky loved the Crouch family and would not betray them even after she had been freed.

Good versus Evil

The most prominent theme in the Harry Potter series is that of Good v. Evil. It is the basis of the entire series. This timeless theme surfaces in every book. The two sides battle in each book, with good winning the battle, but there are losses. The battle is never ending. The series begins with the news that the main character has lost both of his parents and at the end of Book 5, he loses his godfather, the closest thing to a parent he has ever known. Other characters have suffered at the hands of evil as well. Neville's parents were tortured into insanity and many others have lost family and friends. The important point is that in spite of the losses, the battle rages on. Good is still fighting evil and still coming out ahead with the hope of ultimately winning the battle. "You can't eat [hope] but it sustains you[3]."

Family

What is family? Harry's parents were murdered when he was one year old. He then went to live with his relatives, but they do not treat him like family. The Detectives believe Aunt Petunia really loves Harry. She is risking her own life and that of her family in order to protect him with her blood. Later, Harry discovers another life where he is loved and his friends become his family. The Weasleys treat Harry as another son and Sirius wants to play the role of father.

Freedom

"Live free or die!" This is the New Hampshire state motto and it expresses the attitude toward freedom in the Harry Potter series. When Harry entered the wizarding world, he was born again into a new freedom— the freedom to be himself. Likewise, Dobby's freedom from enslavement to the Malfoys is a central point in the series. Dobby is so grateful to the boy who freed him he is willing to risk his own future to save Harry time and time again. Dobby subscribes to the spirit of Patrick Henry, "Give me liberty or give me death." The desire for freedom is a hunger, which exists in all people. Thus, it is not surprising it is a central theme in Harry Potter.

Friends

The importance of friendship is key in the Harry Potter series. This unique bond between people has enabled Harry's survival. The pooling of his friends' talents and their willingness to fight and sacrifice themselves in order to save each other is one of the most persistent themes in Harry Potter. As Hermione said, "Books! And cleverness! There are more important things—*friendship* and bravery[4]." J. K. Rowling also shows her readers the pain caused by broken friendships. When Slytherin betrayed his friends, there was hatred and fighting. He ultimately left a curse, which killed someone in a later generation. Also, when Peter, or Wormtail, betrayed his friends, it cost Lily and James their lives. In contrast, when Ron meets Sirius and thinks he is a mass murderer who's after Harry. Ron tells Sirius, he will have to kill all three of them in order to kill Harry. This theme shows the readers the importance and value of a good friend.

Love

"Love conquers all!" This theme is one that is very important in Harry Potter. It was Lily's love for her son that prevented Voldemort from killing Harry when he was just a baby. This love provided a protection, which still runs through Harry's veins today. Lily's love has enabled Harry to escape Voldemort three times. Another example is Molly and Arthur Weasley's love not only for their children, but also for the boy who has no parents. The Weasleys are willing to take in both Harry and Hermione and act as their parents for the entire summer and Christmas holidays, in spite of the fact two extra children are quite expensive and they are very poor. Dumbledore is another character whose love has been used to protect Harry. It is Dumbledore's love for the child, which prevented him from telling Harry about the prophecy. Harry's happiness and safety meant more to him. Finally, there is the mutual love between Harry and Sirius. "Greater *love* hath none than that which will lay down his life for a friend[5]." Sirius loves his godson, so much, he was willing to die for him. This again saves Harry from Voldemort because Harry's love and grief from the loss of Sirius prevents Voldemort from consuming him. Harry will use the power of love to defeat Voldemort because it is the one power evil cannot understand.

Loyalty

Loyalty is very important in the Harry Potter books. Harry's loyalty to Dumbledore calls Fawkes to him in a time of great danger, which ultimately saves Harry's life. It is important to note enslavement does not equal loyalty. Two prominent examples of this are Dobby and Kreacher. Both betrayed the masters to whom they were enslaved because they felt no sense of loyalty. In contrast, Dobby was extremely loyal to Harry even before he set Dobby free. Embracing his freedom, Dobby is now willing to go to any length to save Harry. He stole from Snape so Harry could perform the second task in the Triwizard Tournament. He warned Harry when Umbridge was on her way to catch them in the act of holding secret meetings. The lack of loyalty is also important. Kreacher betrayed the Black family, which caused Sirius' death. Likewise, when Wormtail betrayed his friends, it cost them their lives and led him to a life of enslavement to Voldemort.

Money

Money has been consistent theme since the very first book. Some families have a great deal of money and others have very little. At first sight one is tempted to believe J.K. Rowling is participating in class warfare. The Malfoys are extremely wealthy, snobbish, and evil & Lupin and the Weasleys are extremely poor, kind, and good. Like everything else in Harry Potter, appearances are deceiving and it is the choices, which are made, not the money itself. The Potters were also wealthy, and so was Sirius, yet they are good. The difference is they did not allow money to control or consume them, like the Malfoys. So, as the cliché says, "Money doesn't buy happiness."

Power

Power! This theme is strung throughout the entire series. It ties into the theme of ambition versus obsession. There are many powerful witches and wizards in the series, but a select few outshine the others. Voldemort was born a very powerful wizard, but he has been consumed by the power he seeks. In contrast, Dumbledore is extremely powerful and uses his power to protect the innocent and prepare them for what lies ahead. "Size is no guarantee of power[6]." This statement referred to Ginny, who is a powerful little witch, but it can also applied to Harry, who even before he was born was given the destiny to defeat Voldemort.

Prejudice

There is a great deal of prejudice in the series. This theme is demonstrated primarily in three issues, Mudbloods, half-breeding, and

Money. There are some wizards who believe they are superior to others because they are pureblood and call anyone of muggle parentage, a mudblood and those who are mixed, half-bloods. This is the wizarding world's version of racism. The basis for this is these wizards regard muggles as inferior to wizards. This is an extremely clever way for J.K. Rowling to teach children to be tolerant of others' backgrounds. The people who use the term mudbloods and half-bloods are the Malfoys, Voldemort, Death Eaters, and other characters are put in a very negative light. Ironically, Voldemort is a half-blood himself. This compares with Adolf Hitler who had Jewish blood; yet he targeted and murdered Jews while terrorizing Europe. Viewed in a positive light are those who treat everyone the same, regardless of their background, are Dumbledore, the Weasleys, Harry, and other wizards. The reverse of this is the Dursley's prejudice against wizards. Vernon's view of wizards correlates with the Malfoy's view of muggles. The prejudice regarding half-breeds is another issue. There are several half-breeds the readers have encountered so far, including half-giants, werewolves, merpeople, and centaurs. All of these people are nice and coexist peacefully with wizards when they are treated with kindness and respect. Some wizards believe they are superior to these half-breeds, as well as muggle borns. The battle lines are drawn exactly the same in the case of the "mudbloods" and "half-bloods." The final prejudice is money. Some of the characters, particularly the Malfoys, believe because they are wealthy, they are superior to those who are not so blessed. Again, the characters, which hold these beliefs to be true, are put in a negative light so it is not likely that children will want to emulate their beliefs or actions. Other characters are equally wealthy, but do not put on airs and attempt to help the less fortunate. For example, Harry, who has a vault full of gold, gives his Triwizard winnings to the Weasley twins in order to help them realize their dream of opening a joke shop. Again, showing it is a matter of choice.

Motifs

Eyes

Very few characters' eyes are mentioned when you consider the series as a whole. The Detectives believe this is because some characters have power in their eyes while others do not. Everyone who meets Harry and also knew his parents notes he has his mother's eyes. Likewise, Dumbledore's eyes are defined as twinkling when he is content, but this twinkle is non-existent when it is time for battle. He also seems to have the power to see through invisibility cloaks, which suggests a kind of xray vision. Similarly, Moody has a magical eye that is capable of seeing through anything, including the back of his head. Another example of the power in the eyes is Voldemort's red, snakelike eyes. Voldemort has the power to detect a lie through a process called Legilimency, where eye contact is often essential. Another interesting example of eyes is the snake eyes at the entrance to the Chamber of Secrets. There were two snakes with emerald eyes. This make the Detectives wonder what color were Tom Riddle's eyes? Were they green like Lily's and Harry's? In the Chamber of Secrets, the basilisk kills by looking people in the eye. This shows eyes do have a special power in the wizarding world. Other eyes mentioned include Ginny's, Firenze, McGonagall, Snape, Hagrid, Ollivander, and Aunt Petunia.

Fingers

The description of fingers is highly significant in the Harry Potter series. The fingers of very few characters have been described. Dumbledore, Voldemort, Mr. Ollivander, Snape, and Dobby are all described as having very long fingers. The Detectives believe long fingers represent great power. Interestingly, Umbridge is described as having short, stubby fingers, which is appropriate because she is a poor witch. Likewise, the Detectives believe short fingers represent weakness and a lack of power.

Music

Music has been a consistent motif since the first book. In the words of Dumbledore, "Ah, music...a magic beyond all we do here[7]!" The Detectives believe music is a sign of humanity or a sign that a person isn't completely evil yet. Dumbledore enjoys chamber music and Flammel is an opera lover. Thus, in spite of their power, neither has forgotten to enjoy the simple things in life. In contrast, Voldemort and the Death Eaters are never heard singing or listening to music because they are consumed with seeking power. Thus, it can be interpreted the Slytherin kids and Dudley's gang are not completely evil because there are still singing. This means there is still hope for them.

Noses

J.K. Rowling describes almost every character's nose. One can assume, in her world the nose is a clue to the character. For example, Snape has "a hooked nose[8]." This is appropriate given he is a spy and is trying to fish for information from the Death Eaters. Dumbledore's nose is "very long and crooked, as though it had been broken at least twice[9]." Again, this is fitting because Dumbledore has seen his share of battles, yet is still fighting for what is right. Finally, Voldemort "has slits for nostrils[10]." He also claimed he could smell the guilt of his Death Eaters, which again is representative of a poisonous snake or an animal hunting its prey. Thus, the description of a person's nose is a clue to his character.

Serpents

The serpent motif is probably the most wide spread motif in the Harry Potter series. Just like in the Book of Genesis, where the devil disguised himself as a snake in order to trick Eve, J.K. Rowling uses the serpent to represent Dark Magic or evil. The snake or the hissing sound is often a clue to alert the reader of evil in disguise. The students in the Slytherin house are portrayed as mean and the house itself is famous for turning out the most dark wizards. Slytherin sounds like slither, which is how a snake moves. In addition, the symbol of Slytherin House is a snake because Salazar Slytherin was a parseltongue, which means he could talk to snakes. He was probably also a snake when disguised as an animagus. In fact, when he left the school he put a basilisk in the Chamber of Secrets in order to kill the students he did not deem fit to study at Hogwarts. Likewise, Voldemort, the most evil wizard to ever live, uses a potion from a snake named Nagini in order to stay alive. Harry, the hero of the series is often seen communicating with serpents showing evil can be rejected. In fact, before Harry knew he was a wizard he talked to a Boa Constrictor. Thus, he has the ability to use the serpent, but has not turned evil. This proves to the readers that Dumbledore is right and "it is our choices…that show what we truly are, far more than our abilities[11]."

Socks

Socks are the most frequently mentioned piece of clothing in the series. They represent freedom. Dobby tells Harry, "the family is careful not to pass a *sock[12]*." After Dobby is free he gives socks to Harry as a gift, illustrating, the greatest gift of all is freedom. Moody's attention is drawn to Harry's socks from Dobby, at Christmas. Another reference to socks is in the Mirror of Erised. Dumbledore sees himself "holding a pair of thick, woolen *socks[13]*." The Detectives believe this shows Dumbledore's greatest desire is freedom from the burden of protecting the entire wizarding world.

Wind

Harry frequently feels a breeze or the wind in times of trouble. The Detectives believe this is a motif representing his parents' continued presence. James and Lily Potter are not ghosts, so they cannot walk and talk in the wizarding world, but their presence is felt when Harry is in danger or frightened. Thus, they are helping to protect Harry from the afterlife. This is a crafty way of letting the readers know Harry is not alone.

4s

The use of the number 4 has been persistent since the very beginning of the series. The story begins at Number 4 Privet Drive. There are more 4's throughout the books; far more than is normal or even probable using the rules of probability for the frequency each number will appear, in the normal course of events. So, is the constant use of the number 4 a coincidence? Check the guidelines! Number 4 clearly states that there are no coincidences. There are several more significant fours in the series. There were *four* founders of Hogwarts, but one betrayed the others. When James Potter was in school, there were *four* friends and again one betrayed the other three. Also, if a house needs four walls to stand and one keeps falling, the house is going to be lopsided and in danger of falling if not repaired. Currently attending Hogwarts, there are *four* friends, Harry, Ron, Hermione, and Neville. Will one of them betray the other three? Will History repeat itself again? Does the wizarding world have the chance to overcome evil again once and for all? If these *four* pillars stand strong, good will succeed. The Detectives believe they will do just that. Voldemort has affected them all. Harry lost his parents and his godfather. Neville, also for all intents and purposes, lost his parents. Hermione was attacked and is muggle born, thus a prime target and Ron's father was nearly killed. The Detectives believe they are the chosen *four*. Other significant fours to consider: Harry lives in a number *four* house in which *four* people (Aunt Petunia, Uncle Vernon, Dudley, & Harry) reside, at Hogwarts he sleeps in a *four*-poster bed. When Harry was left at Privet Drive, there were four people present, Dumbledore, McGonagall, Hagrid, and Harry.

10s

Ten is yet another number which probability suggests appears more than normal. The Detectives believe 10 is Dumbledore's number or the number of good. Dumbledore enjoys 10-pin bowling, which ties the number to him. Also, Harry lived with the Dursleys for 10 years. In the Death Chamber, 10 Death Eaters surround Harry immediately before the Order comes to rescue him. On the Defense Against the Dark Arts O.W.L. for Harry's father's generation, question 10 asks about werewolves. The only werewolf the readers have met is Lupin, a member of the Order. Thus, it is clear the number 10 is used to represent the good guys.

11s

Eleven is another number that appears more often than probable. The Detectives believe 11 is Harry's number. It is on Harry's 11th birthday, he discovers he is a wizard. When Harry is choosing a wand, he like his father, James, selected a wand 11 inches in length. In addition, Harry stays in room 11 at the Leaky Caldron. This could represent Harry is the savior of future wizarding generations, as they all start their magical learning at age 11. The constant reference to the number 11 as it applies to Harry later becomes a way the reader can detect when the odds shift to Harry's favor.

12s

The number 12 also appears far more than is probable. The Detectives believe 12 is Voldemort's number. The mountain troll, Harry and Ron knock out, is 12 feet tall. Voldemort's servant Wormtail was chained for 12 years before he returned to his master. There are a dozen Death Eaters in the Department of Mysteries from whom Harry and the others must escape. The frequency of this number as it applies to Voldemort is a key motif in the series, as it warns when evil is present.

Chapter 14

Names which have been mentioned and should be noted

(But the Detectives know very little or nothing about them yet)

Ali Bashir—is an Arab name. He sells flying carpets and wants to import to England. The Detectives are weary of him because they believe he will side with anyone who promises him they will give him the opportunity to make more money.

Agnes—is a patient in the closed ward whose face is covered with fur and barks loudly. It appears to be a polyjuice potion gone wrong because dog hair was used. So, why hasn't this woman been cured? Again, is there some reason she is being prevented from getting well? Her son was visiting that evening. Who is her son? Is he important?

Archie—Was wearing a muggle dress at the World Cup and would not change into trousers. He was wearing muggle clothes and adamant he was doing exactly what he was instructed.

Augustus Pye—is the Trainee Healer in the Dai Llewellyn Ward for Serious Bites. He works under Hippocrates Smthwyck. Pye is a young wizard who was willing and interested in trying a muggle remedy—stitches. This makes him similar to both Mr. Weasley and Dumbledore. First, he is interested and fascinated, in the muggle ways. Second, he realizes just because something comes from a different world doesn't make it bad or mean it will not work.

Bozo—He was mentioned in Book 4 and was Rita Skeeter's photographer. His name implies he is an idiot.

Bulgarian Quidditch Team—Dimitrov, Ivanova, Zograf, Levski, Vulchanov, Volkov, and Krum. Other than Krum, nothing is known about these characters except they play Quidditch and they know Krum. Possibly Krum was able to alert them of the return of Voldemort and they will be able to fight on the side of good.

Colonel Fubster—He is a friend of Aunt Marge, who is willing to drown dogs, which are too small. Although, the Detectives are aware this is common practice among breeders, they believe it cruel and believe the puppy could be given away instead of killed. It would not cost anything. Another important point to make is Aunt Marge said she had a glass shatter in her hand when she was talking to Colonel Fubster the other day. Really? The Detectives question if he is a wizard? Or if an animagus was present? His name was mentioned twice, which typically means he will play a role.

Doris Crockford—Is the witch who kept coming back to shake Harry's hand in the Leaky Cauldron. Her name is mentioned three times in two pages, therefore the Detectives really want to know why she is important.

Florean Fortescue—Owns an Ice Cream Parlor in Diagon Alley. He gave Harry free sundaes and helped him with his History of Magic homework. In addition, he is probably related to one of the former Headmasters of Hogwarts, which would suggest Dumbledore had arranged for him to keep an eye on Harry.

Gladys Gudgeon—is mentioned in Books 2 and 5, but the only thing the readers know about her is that she writes Gilderoy Lockhart weekly. Since she has been mentioned twice the Detectives expect her to play a role in the ensuing battle, but have not determined on which side of the battle she will fight.

Gordon—is one of Dudley's gang

Jim McGuffin—the weatherman on the evening news program the Dursley's watch.

Mark Evans—is a 10 year old boy, who Dudley and his gang beat up. The Detectives wonder if Harry will meet him in year 6 at Hogwarts. Also, are he and Harry related? Evans was Lily's maiden name.

Hassan Mostafa—was the referee for the World Cup. He is the Chair Wizard of the International Association of Quidditch. Mostafa is from Egypt and is small, skinny, and completely bald, but has a mustache.

Healer Miriam Strout—is a Healer in the Closed Ward at St. Mungo's. She was the Healer who encouraged Bode to care for the Devil's Snare and thus, enabled Malfoy to murder him. She is also fond of Lockhart, which makes her all the more untrustworthy. Healer Strout is responsible for the Longbottom's care and seems to be a bit loose lipped in the hallway about the condition of the patients in the Closed Ward. For example, she told Harry, Ron, Hermione, and Ginny, without having a clue who they were, that they were seeing a real improvement in Bode, but he was not yet speaking a language they could understand. Was someone else listening? Or had she already told someone else? Strout was suspended after the death of Bode. So, will the Longbottoms start to improve? Has she been actively keeping them from improving? Is she perhaps a Death Eater? Or are Malfoy and his money simply controlling her?

Hippocrates Smethuyck—is the Healer-in-Charge of the Dai Llewellyn Ward for Serious Bites. He eventually found an antidote for whatever was in the snake's venom that attacked Arthur Weasley. Hippocrates Smthuyck is named for the Greek physician, Hippocrates, the father of medicine and the oath all doctors take is named for him.

Irish Quidditch Team—Connolly, Ryan, Troy, Mullet, Moran, Quigley, and Lynch. Again, nothing is known about these characters, other than, they are very good Quidditch players.

Kevin—was a small boy playing with his father's wand at the World Cup.

Madam Malkin—A witch who owns the robe shop in Diagon Alley. Ironically, her name means a woman who dresses in an untidy way.

Madam Marsh—A witch, who was on the Knightbus and had motion sickness both times she and Harry rode the bus. Is this her primary mode of transportation? This seems strange for someone who gets such severe motion sickness each time she rides. The Detectives don't trust Madam Marsh and want to know what she is up too and why she is on the bus every time Harry takes it. She is let off before him each time.

Malcolm—is one of Dudley's gang.

Mr. & Mrs. Mason—are a rich builder and his wife. This is appropriate given a mason is a builder. They were the people Uncle Vernon was trying to sell drills to the night Dobby smashed the pudding. This was going to be the biggest deal of his life, but due to Dobby's magic and the owl, which arrived afterward, the evening was a disaster.

Mortlake— means dead lake. In Book 2, his home was raided and he was questioned regarding odd ferrets. Watch out Draco! Maybe Mortlake is another Death Eater, but there is not enough information to convict. It is interesting his home was raided though, given Fletcher's home was also raided and he is in the Order, clearly one does not have to be a Death Eater to be paid a visit by the Ministry of Magic, just a criminal.

Mr. Oblansk or Obalonsk—is the Bulgarian Minister of Magic.

Mr. Payne—was the other campsite manger, presumably another muggle.

Poliakoff—was a Durmstrang student Karkaroff was not very nice to. It is important to note he was the only student mentioned by name, other than Krum. Poliakoff spilled food on his robes and recognized Harry's scar immediately. He heard Dumbledore's speech announcing the return of Voldemort. Thus, the Detectives believe he may be useful in the ensuing battle.

Piers Polkiss—Dudley's best friend and a member of the gang. He was cruel to Harry before he went to Hogwarts. His mother Mrs. Polkiss is also mentioned.

Mr. Prentice—He is mentioned in Book 5 and lives in Harry's neighborhood. Mrs. Figg did not seem concerned he had seen the two of them and Harry with his wand out. Could he be someone else protecting Harry? Could he be another Squib or a wizard? Or could he be Perkins? Clearly, this was not one of the average neighbors because Harry having his wand out would not be acceptable in that "normal" subdivision. Also, the only muggle see magic done that night was Dudley.

Mr. Roberts—Owner of the Campground at the World Cup. The Death Eaters levitated his family of four and were spinning them around in the air. They are all muggles and their memories were modified.

Ted—The news anchor on the evening news which the Dursley's watch

Tom—is the old bartender, in the Leaky Cauldron. He is bald and toothless. He seems to be trusted quite a bit given Harry stayed in one of his rooms for two weeks and it was his responsibility to look after him. If Dumbledore did not trust Tom, Harry would have been taken to Hogwarts early. Also, as the bartender in the Leaky Cauldron he is in a position where he will hear a great deal. The Detectives would not be surprised if he was a member of the Order. He was talking to Diggle in Book 1.

Yvonne—Aunt Petunia's friend, who Uncle Vernon suggested they ask to watch Harry.

Chapter 15

Prophecies

Mary C. Baumann

O.W.L. Predictions for Harry

Test	Score
Astronomy	A
Care of Magical Creatures	O
Charms	E
Defense Against the Dark Arts	O
Divination	P
Herbology	A
History of Magic	D
Potions	O
Transfiguration	E
Total O.W.L.s	7

O.W.L. Predictions for Neville

Test	Score
Astronomy	A
Care of Magical Creatures	O
Charms	E
Defense Against the Dark Arts	O
Divination	A
Herbology	O
History of Magic	A
Potions	O
Transfiguration	E
Total O.W.L.s	9

O.W.L. Predictions for Ron

Test	Score
Astronomy	A
Care of Magical Creatures	O
Charms	E
Defense Against the Dark Arts	O
Divination	P
Herbology	A
History of Magic	P
Potions	A
Transfiguration	E
Total O.W.L.s	7

O.W.L. Predictions for Hermione

Test	Score
Ancient Runes	E
Arithmancy	O
Astronomy	A
Care of Magical Creatures	O
Charms	O
Defense Against the Dark Arts	O
Herbology	O
History of Magic	E
Potions	O
Transfiguration	O
Total O.W.L.s	11

The Final Battle

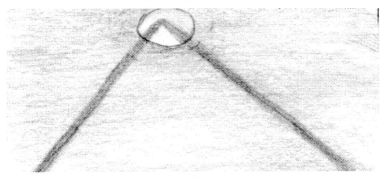

The Detectives' prophecy regarding the final battle is based on the clues and the Head Detective's twisted mind. The final battle between Harry and Voldemort will take place in the Chamber of Secrets. The reason for this is only two people can enter the Chamber. Once, after they have entered, it will seal itself and only one will leave the Chamber alive.

There will be two battles occurring simultaneously. The first is the human battle between Voldemort and Harry. (Fawkes will be present to heal Harry's injuries.) The second, a snake battle between Nagini, the Boa Constrictor, and the new Basilisk. The Boa Constrictor owes his freedom to Harry and will fight the two poisonous snake. The new Basilisk will be confused as to whom it should obey given both Harry and Voldemort are heirs of Slytherin. Nagini, as an older and wiser snake, will know her master and fight on his behalf.

As for the wands neither is any use because brother wands will not duel against each other. Instead, there will be a sword fight and Harry will ultimately kill Voldemort with Gryffindor's sword.

Why with Gryffindor's sword? Two reasons, first it will be symbolic. The heir of Gryffindor defeats the true heir of Slytherin. Second, when Dumbledore tells Harry about his prophecy, his office is described.

"The sun had risen fully now…The glass case in which the sword of Godric Gryffindor resided gleamed white and opaque, the fragments of the instruments Harry had thrown to the floor glistened like raindrops…baby Fawkes made soft chirruping noises in his nest of ashes[1]."

The Detectives believe this symbolizes a new day has come and shows the tools Harry will use to defeat Voldemort.

A Detective's Analysis of Harry Potter and the Mysteries Within

The Whole Twisted Web
In a Nutshell

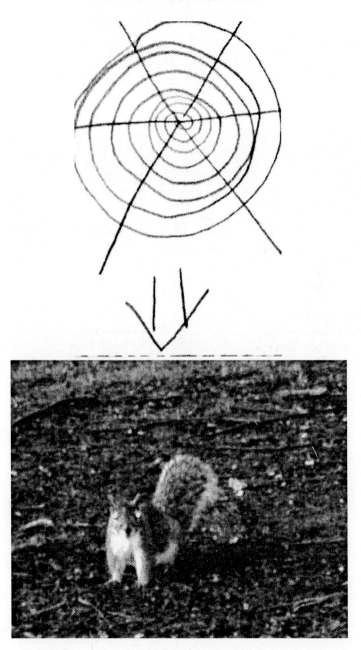

For the sake of keeping the numbers as close to accurate as possible, the Detectives will use the 500th Death Day of Nearly Headless Nick, October 31, 1992, as the basis for all calculations comprised in this section.

Descendants of Godric Gryffindor

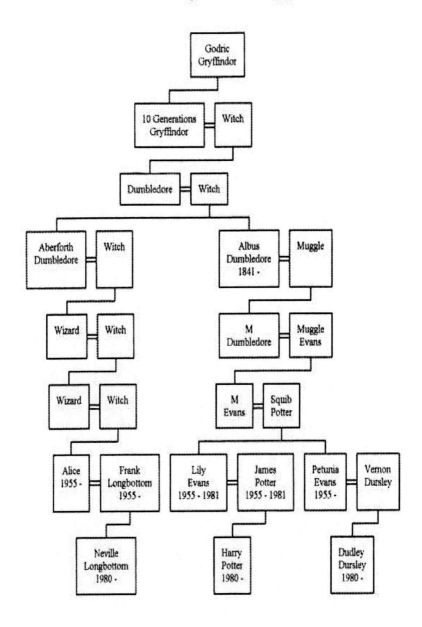

Descendants of Helga Hufflepuff

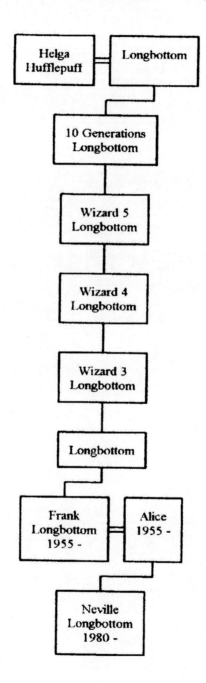

Descendants of Salazar Slytherin

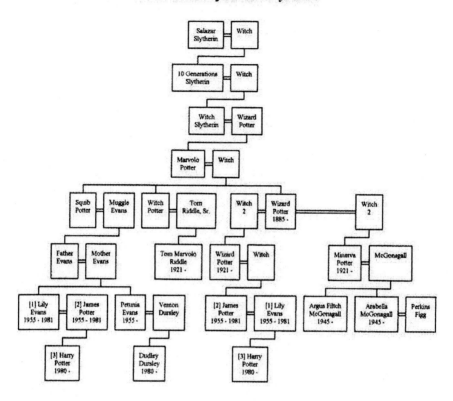

Descendants of Rowena Ravenclaw

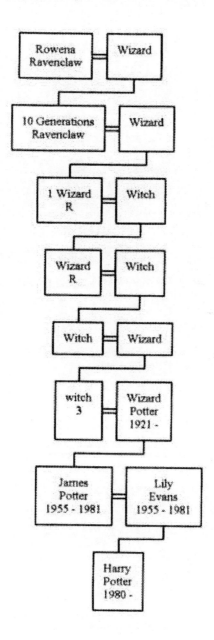

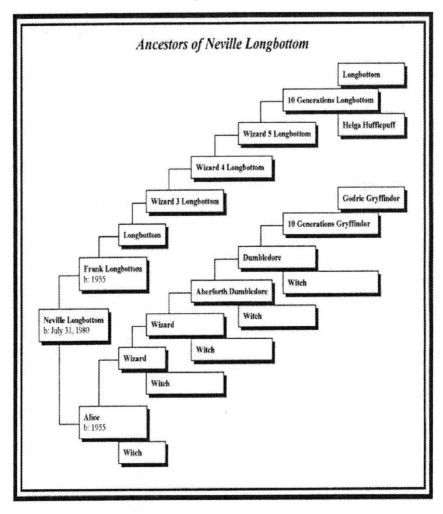

Ancestors of Neville Longbottom

Ancestors of Harry Potter

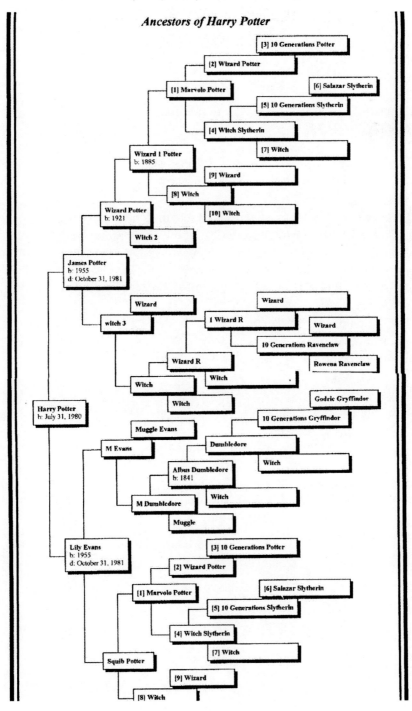

Hogwarts Friendships and Foes

1852 Year 1 at Hogwarts
Albus Dumbledore (G)
Alastor Moody? (G)
Dedalus Diggle?
The Detectives believe Dumbledore was Head Boy.
Graduated in 1858.

1932 Year 1 at Hogwarts, Armando Dippet, Headmaster
Tom Riddle (S) (Perfect)
Minerva McGonagall (G)
Graduated in 1938. Tom was Head boy and the Detectives believe Minerva was indeed Head Girl. So, who were Tom Riddle's close friends with whom he was already using the name Voldemort? Possibly they were members of the Black, Malfoy and Snape families, but too young to be the parents. So, it could possibly be the grandparents of these individuals.

1934 Year 1 at Hogwarts
Rubeus Hagrid (G)
Moaning Myrtle (?)
Olive Hornby (?)

1945 Dumbledore defeats dark wizard, Grindelwald

1955 (December) Minerva McGonagall started teaching at Hogwarts

1957 Year 1 at Hogwarts
Broderick Bode (Could have attended in 1956 depending on whether he was born in January or a later month)
Graduated in 1963

1958 Year 1 at Hogwarts
Rita Skeeter (R?)
Graduated in 1964

1960 Year 1 at Hogwarts?
Molly Weasley (G) (Prefect) (Head Girl?)
Graduated in 1966

1961 Year 1 at Hogwarts
Lucius Malfoy (S)
Narcissa Black (S)
Crabbe (S)
Goyle (S)
Arthur Weasley (G) (Prefect)
All graduated in June of 1967. The Detectives wonder whether Lucius or Arthur was Head Boy and whether or not Narcissa was Head Girl. We vote for Lucius.

1964 Year 1 at Hogwarts
Andromeda Black (G or R)
Ted Tonks (G or R or H)
Graduated in June of 1970.

1966 Year 1 at Hogwarts
James Potter (G) (Seeker) (Head Boy)
Sirius Black (G)
Remus Lupin (G) (prefect)
Peter Pettigrew (G)
Kingsley Shacklebolt (?)
Lily Evans (G or R) (Head Girl)
Severus Snape (S)
Avery (S)
Bellatrix Black (S)
Rodolphus Lestrange (S)
Rosier (S)
Wilkes (S)
Graduated in June of 1972.

1971 Voldemort takes hold of wizarding society

Approximately 1973 Year 1 at Hogwarts
Barty Crouch Jr. (R?)
Graduated in 1979

1980 Sybill Trelawney started teaching at Hogwarts
Harry Potter was born (7/31/1980)
October 31, 1981 Voldemort falls from power

1982 Professor Snape started teaching at Hogwarts
1982 Year 1 at Hogwarts
Bill Weasley (G) (Prefect) (Head Boy)
Graduated in 1988

1983 Year 1 at Hogwarts
Nymphadora Tonks (G or R)
Graduated in 1989.
1984 Year 1 at Hogwarts
Charlie Weasley (G)(Quidditch Captain & Seeker)
Graduated in 1990

1986 Year 1 at Hogwarts
Marcus Flint (S) (Quidditch Captain & Chaser)
Terence Higgs (S) (Seeker)
Graduated in 1992. Flint graduated a year late in 1993 because he was a dunce.

1987 Year 1 at Hogwarts
Percy Weasley (G) (Prefect) (Head Boy)
Penelope Clearwater (R) (Prefect)
Oliver Wood (G) (Quidditch Captain & Keeper)
Graduated in June of 1993.

1988 Year 1 at Hogwarts   1988 Year at Durmstrang/ Beauxbaton
Derrick (S) (Beaters)   Vikor Krum & Fleur Delacour
Bole (S) (Beaters)
Graduated in June of 1994.   Graduated in June of 1994.

1989 Year 1 at Hogwarts
Fred Weasley (G) (Beater) (DOB 4/78)
George Weasley (G) (Beater) (DOB 4/78)
Lee Jordan (G)
Angelina Johnson (G) (Quidditch Captain & Chaser) (10/77)
Alicia Spinnet (G) (Chaser)
Patricia Stimpson (?)
Kenneth Towler (G)
Adrian Pucey (S) (Chaser)
Bletchley (S) (Keeper)
Eddie Carmichael (R)

Most graduated in June of 1995. Fred and George dropped out in the spring of the seventh year.

1990 Year 1 at Hogwarts
Cedric Diggory (H) (Prefect) (Quidditch Captain & Seeker)
Cho Chang (R) (Seeker)
Marietta Edgecombe (R)
Katie Bell (G) (Chaser)
Harold Dingle

1991 Year 1 at Hogwarts
Harry Potter (G) (Seeker) (7/31/80)
Ron Weasley (G) (Prefect) (Keeper) (3/80)
Hermione Granger (G) (Prefect) (9/19/80)
Neville Longbottom (G) (7/31/80)
Dean Thomas (G)
Seamus Finnigan (G)
Lavender Brown (G)
Pavarti Patil (G)
Draco Malfoy (S) (Prefect) (Seeker)
Vincent Crabbe (S) (Beater)
Gregory Goyle (S) (Beater)
Pansy Parkinson (S) (Prefect)
Millicent Bulstrode (S)
Theodore Nott (S)
Blaise Zabini (S)
Hannah Abbott (H) (Prefect)
Susan Bones (H)
Justin Finch-Fletchley (H)
Ernie Macmillan (H) (Prefect)
Terry Boot (R)
Mandy Brocklehurst (R)
Padma Patil (R) (Prefect)
Lisa Turpin (R)
Anthony Goldstein (R) (Prefect)
Daphne Greengrass (?)

1992 Year 1 at Hogwarts
Ginny Weasley (G) (Seeker)
Colin Creevey (G)
Luna Lovegood (R)

1993 Year 1 at Hogwarts
Dennis Creevey (G)
Natalie McDonald (G)
Stewart Ackerley (R)
Orla Quirke (R)
Malcolm Baddock (S)
Graham Pritchard (S)
Eleanor Branstone (H)
Owen Cauldwell (H)
Laura Madley (H)
Kevin Whitby (H)
Emma Dobbs (?)

June 1994 Voldemort is returned to his body

1994 Year 1 at Hogwarts
Euan Abercrombie (G)
Rose Zeller (H)

Other students the Detectives are unsure which year they belong
Roger Davies (R) (Quidditch Captain) (Chaser)
Bradley (R) (Quidditch team)
Sloper (G) (Beater)
Kirke (G) (Beater)
Michael Corner (R)
Fawcett (R)
Zacharias Smith (H) (Chaser)
Summerby (H) (Seeker)
Stebbins (H)
Vicky Frobisher (G)
Geoffrey Hooper (G)

Burning Questions

*Did McGonagall buy Harry's Nimbus 2000 in Year one? If not, who did? If so, this would have Dumbledore, Hagrid, and McGonagall, the three who dropped Harry off at the Dursley's each giving Harry a very nice gift in his first year.

*Why didn't Voldemort want to kill Lily Potter?

* Can ghosts ever choose to move on into the after life?

* Why is the Bloody Baron covered in blood? Who did he kill and when?

* Which professors are married, other than McGonagall and Dumbledore? Is Snape married? If not, he and Tonks would make an amusing pair. Then, when he dies, Charlie Weasley can comfort her.

* What happened to the old Order of the Phoenix headquarters and where was it?

* Is James and Lily Potter's house still standing? If so, where is it?

* Where did the Potters work before they were killed? Were they Aurors?

* What happened to Sirius's motorbike? The Detectives have three theories. It could be at the Potter's house. (Note: Hagrid just said the house was ruined. The shrieking shack is a ruined house, but it is still standing.) Second, it could be at the old headquarters for the Order. Third, it could be wild in the Forbidden Forest.

* Did Voldemort go to the Potter's alone or did Wormtail Judas accompany him? If he was alone, how is it he still has his wand?

Message for Concerned Parents and Sanctimonious Christians

This is, as the heading suggests, a message for all concerned parents and sanctimonious Christians who are concerned or believe the Harry Potter series is the work of the devil or promoting witchcraft. THIS IS A FARCE! Technically this is not what my book is about, but as these statements irritate me to such a level I feel compelled to defend J.K. Rowling on this issue. I receive emails telling parents they need to protect their children from these "dangerous" books of the "occult" and my blood boils. Furthermore, I have had several friends ask me if I thought they should allow their children to read the books or see the movies because of the references to witchcraft and magic. My own aunt was appalled I was a fan and told me it was not harmless fantasy, but witchcraft and Satanism. My response was, "And what was *Snow White* or any other Disney movie for that matter?" But then I remembered my aunt is crazy and would not allow us to watch *Bednobs and Broomsticks* at her house when we were kids because it was satanic too. Anyway the point is Harry Potter, like the Disney movies, is a creative way children can learn life's lessons and have the fringe benefit of enjoying reading in the process. If sanctimonious Christians, like my aunt, would stop and think for about a half a minute they would praise J.K. Rowling for the Harry Potter series, just like C.S. Lewis and the *Chronicles of Narnia.*

Notice, for example, Harry is always fighting evil, whether it is Voldemort, his Death Eaters, or an internal struggle. Also, good comes out ahead at the end of each book. Yes there are losses, but good is winning the battle. Next, Harry is learning life's lessons. Harry and his friends are learning about prejudice, abuse, oppression, corruption, and power all the hard way. Harry, Ron, and Hermione have several people to teach them moral lessons along the way, including Harry's godfather, Sirius Black, Professor Lupin, Mr. & Mrs. Weasley, and the Headmaster Dumbledore. There is a great deal of wisdom in the words of Dumbledore. For example, the readers are still learning from the wisdom of his words, at the end of Goblet of Fire. He tells the entire school "Remember Cedric. Remember if the time should come when you have to make a choice between what is right and what is easy[1]." The readers see the different children make their choice, some choosing what is easy and others choosing what is right. Of course, Harry and his best friends choose what is right. The importance of this lesson is key. The damage done from taking the easy road costs others their jobs and lives. Children learn from these action-packed stories in a way they would never learn from a speech or a sermon. Likewise, children dislike Draco Malfoy because he is mean and they see him and his friends lie, cheat, and steal, thus, they do not want to be like him.

I will not preach a sermon, but I ask that people read the books and give them some thought before judging them to be "satanic" or "corrupting our children." It is my opinion these statements are ludicrous and the majority of Christians can tell the difference between fantasy and the occult. Magic has always been a part of fantasy, Disney uses it, and even C.S. Lewis, one of the most famous Christian authors, used magic in his children's books. Thus, it is my belief children can learn a great deal from the Harry Potter series, just as I did as a child reading the *Chronicles of Narnia*. So, if you are a parent there is no cause for concern. If you are a Sanctimonious Christian don't worry about Harry Potter corrupting the morals of children. There are far more dangerous things than fantasy, possibly in your own family or church, which could damage your children's morals.

Acknowledgments

Special thanks to my dear friend, Christiane Hassel and my sister, Lisa Baumann, without whom I would never have read the Harry Potter series. Also, to my dad, who enjoyed analyzing and theorizing with me, for hours at a time. He is my Watson! Also, thanks to my mother and sister for editing my manuscript. Your work is greatly appreciated!

Works Cited

Ash, Mary Kay. <u>Mary Kay You Can Have It All: Lifetime Wisdom from America's Foremost Woman Entrepreneur</u>. Prima Publishing. 1995. Rocklin, CA.

Brady, Bernadette. <u>Brady's book of Fixed Stars.</u> Samuel Weiser, INC. 1998. York Beach, Maine.

Euripides. <u>Medea</u>

Hamilton, Edith. <u>Mythology: Timeless Tales of Gods and Heroes</u>. Penguin Group. 1940. NY, NY.

Kingsley, Charles. <u>Alton Locke, Tailor and Poet. An Autobiography.</u> MacMillan & Co. 1884. London, UK.

Marquez, Gabriel Gracia. <u>No One Writes to the Colonel</u>. Harper & Row Publishers, 1968. NY, NY

<u>New Webster's Dictionary and thesaurus of the English Language</u>. Lexicon Publishing, INC. 1993 Danbury, CT.

Robson, Vivian E. <u>The Fixed Stars and Constellations in Astrology</u>. Samuel Weiser, INC., 1973. NY, NY

Rowling, J.K.. <u>Harry Potter and the Sorcerer's Stone.</u> Scholastic, INC., 1998. NY, NY

Rowling, J.K.. <u>Harry Potter and the Chamber of Secrets</u>. Scholastic, INC., 1999. NY, NY

Rowling, J.K.. <u>Harry Potter and the Prisoner of Azkaban.</u> Scholastic, INC., 1999. NY, NY

Rowling, J.K.. <u>Harry Potter and the Goblet of Fire</u>. Scholastic, INC., 2000. NY, NY.

Rowling, J.K.. <u>Harry Potter and the Order of the Phoenix.</u> Arthur A. Levine Books, 2003. NY, NY.

Rowling, J.K. under alias Newt Scamander. Fantastic Beasts & Where to Find Them. Arthur A. Levine Books, 2001. NY, NY

Rowling, J.K. under alias Kennilworthy Whisp. Quidditch Through the Ages. Arthur A. Levine Books, 2001. NY, NY.

Webster's New World Dictionary of the American Language, College Edition. The World Publishing Company. 1957. Cleveland, OH.

Chats & Interviews with J.K. Rowling
The Connection, October 12, 1999
SouthWestNews.com Interview, July 8, 2000
Scholastic.com interview, October 16, 2000
Barnes and Noble.com Chat, October 20,2000
BBC Online Chat, March 12, 2001
With Steve Kloves on Chamber of Secrets DVD, 2002

The Sydney Morning Herald, October 28, 2001
World Book Day Chat, March 4, 2004

Arabella Stuart, British and Irish History Biographies. AllRefer.com Reference. http://reference.allrefer.com/encyclopedia/S/StuartAr.html

Benario, Herbert W. De Imperatoribus Romanis. Emory University. An Online Encyclopedia of Roman Emperors: Alexander Severus (A.D. 222-235). http://www.roman-emperors.org/alexsev.htm

http://www.artmaick.com/artists/cowper.aspx

http://www.catholic.org/saints/print_news.php?saint_id=2053

http://www.weddingvendors.com/babynames

http://www.hyw.com/Books/WargamesHandbook/5-histor.htm

Women of Achievement and Herstory. Women's Military History. http://www.undelete.org/military/spies.htm

Endnotes

Guidelines

---

[1] Doyle, Sir Arthur Conan Sherlock Holmes
[2] Rowling, J.K.. <u>Harry Potter and the Goblet of Fire</u>. Scholastic, INC., 2000. NY, NY.

Chapter 1
[1] Rowling, J.K.. <u>Harry Potter and the Sorcerer's Stone.</u> Scholastic INC., 1998. NY, NY. p.7
[2] Rowling, J.K.. <u>Harry Potter and the Order of the Phoenix.</u> Arthur A. Levine Books, 2003. NY, NY. p.31
[3] Ibid p.31
[4] Ibid p.32
[5] Ibid p.32
[6] Ibid p.40
[7] Ibid p.38
[8] Rowling, J.K.. <u>Harry Potter and the Sorcerer's Stone.</u> Scholastic INC., 1998. NY, NY. p.5
[9] Barnes and Noble.com Chat with J.K. Rowling, October 20,2000
[10] Rowling, J.K.. <u>Harry Potter and the Goblet of Fire</u>. Scholastic, INC., 2000. NY, NY. p.488

Chapter 2
[1] SouthWestNews.com Interview with J.K. Rowling, July 8, 2000
[2] BBC Online Chat with J.K. Rowling, March 12, 2001
[3] Rowling, J.K.. <u>Harry Potter and the Order of the Phoenix.</u> Arthur A. Levine Books, 2003. NY, NY p.846
[4] http://www.catholic.org/saints/print_news.php?saint_id=2053
[5] http://www.weddingvendors.com/babynames/
[6] Fraser, Lindsey. <u>Conversations with J.K. Rowling</u>. Scholastic, INC, 2001. NY,NY. p.55
[7] Ash, Mary Kay. Mary Kay You Can Have It All: Lifetime Wisdom from America's Foremost Woman Entrepreneur. Prima Publishing. 1995. Rocklin, CA. p.202
[8] Ibid. p.202
[9] Scholastic.com interview with J.K. Rowling, October 16, 2000
[10] http://goldstraw.net/godric/pafg02.htm

[11] Rowling, J.K.. Harry Potter and the Goblet of Fire. Scholastic, INC., 2000. NY, NY. p.679

[12] Hamilton, Edith. Mythology: Timeless Tales of Gods and Heroes. Penguin Group, 1940. NY, NY. p.29

[13] Ibid. p.30

[14] Ibid. p.29

[15] Scholastic.com interview with J.K. Rowling, October 16, 2000

[16] Dictionary.com http://dictionary.reference.com/search?q=Severus

[17] Benario, Herbert W. De Imperatoribus Romanis. Emory University. An Online Encyclopedia of Roman Emperors: Alexander Severus (A.D. 222-235). http://www.roman-emperors.org/alexsev.htm

[18] New Webster's Dictionary and thesaurus of the English Language. Lexicon Publishing, INC. 1993 Danbury, CT. p.22

[19] BBC Online Chat with J.K. Rowling, March 12, 2001 Rowling stated, Snape was either 35 or36.

[20] Rowling, J.K.. Harry Potter and the Goblet of Fire. Scholastic, INC., 2000. NY, NY. p.651

[21] Women of Achievement and Herstory. Women's Military History. http://www.undelete.org/military/spies.html

[22] World Book Day Chat with J.K. Rowling, March 4, 2004

[23] Rowling, J.K.. Harry Potter and the Prisoner of Azkaban. Scholastic INC., 1999. NY, NY. p.285

[24] Rowling, J.K.. Harry Potter and the Sorcerer's Stone. Scholastic INC., 1998. NY, NY. p.288

[25] Rowling, J.K.. Harry Potter and the Goblet of Fire. Scholastic, INC., 2000. NY, NY. p.566

[26] Rowling, J.K.. Harry Potter and the Prisoner of Azkaban. Scholastic INC., 1999. NY, NY. p.429

[27] Fraser, Lindsey. Conversations with J.K. Rowling. Scholastic, INC, 2001. NY,NY.p.40

[28] J.K. Rowling on The Connection October 12, 1999

[29] Webster's New World Dictionary of the American Language, College Edition. The World Publishing Company. 1957. Cleveland, OH. p.651

[30] Barnes and Noble.com Chat with J.K. Rowling, October 20,2000

[31] Rowling, J.K.. Harry Potter and the Sorcerer's Stone. Scholastic INC., 1998. NY, NY. p.14

[32] World Book Day Chat with J.K. Rowling, March 4, 2004

[33] Hamilton, Edith. Mythology: Timeless Tales of Gods and Heroes. Penguin Group, 1940. NY, NY. p.226

[34] Rowling, J.K.. Harry Potter and the Sorcerer's Stone. Scholastic INC., 1998. NY, NY. p.257

[35] Hamilton, Edith. Mythology: Timeless Tales of Gods and Heroes. Penguin Group, 1940. NY, NY. p.291

[36] Rowling, J.K.. Harry Potter and the Sorcerer's Stone. Scholastic INC., 1998. NY, NY. p.253

[37] Rowling, J.K.. Harry Potter and the Order of the Phoenix. Arthur A. Levine Books, 2003. NY, NY p.656

[38] Hamilton, Edith. Mythology: Timeless Tales of Gods and Heroes. Penguin Group, 1940. NY, NY p.79

[39] Rowling, J.K.. Harry Potter and the Sorcerer's Stone. Scholastic INC., 1998. NY, NY. p. 289

[40] Fraser, Lindsey. Conversations with J.K. Rowling. Scholastic, INC, 2001. NY,NY. p.39

[41] Ibid p.39

[42] Rowling, J.K.. Harry Potter and the Order of the Phoenix. Arthur A. Levine Books, 2003. NY, NY p.511

[43] Rowling, J.K.. Harry Potter and the Goblet of Fire. Scholastic, INC., 2000. NY, NY p.206

[44] Rowling, J.K.. Harry Potter and the Order of the Phoenix. Arthur A. Levine Books, 2003. NY, NY p.212

[45] Ibid. p.746

[46] Ibid. p.364

[47] Ibid. p.302

[48] Webster's New World Dictionary of the American Language, College Edition. The World Publishing Company, 1957. Cleveland, OH. p.698

[49] New Webster's Dictionary and thesaurus of the English Language. Lexicon Publishing, INC., 1993. Danbury, CT. p.1090

Chapter 3

[1] Webster's New World Dictionary of the American Language, College Edition. The World Publishing Company, 1957. Cleveland, OH. p.503

[2] Rowling, J.K.. Harry Potter and the Order of the Phoenix. Arthur A. Levine Books, 2003. NY, NY p.113

[3] http://www.artmaick.com/artists/cowper.aspx

Chapter 4

[1] Rowling, J.K.. Harry Potter and the Order of the Phoenix. Arthur A. Levine Books, 2003. NY, NY p.675

[2] Scamander, Newt. Fantastic Beasts & Where to Find Them. Arthur A. Levine Books, 2001. NY, NY p.1

[3] Ibid. p.1

[4] Rowling, J.K.. Harry Potter and the Sorcerer's Stone. Scholastic INC., 1998. NY, NY p.254

[5] Ibid. p.253

[6] Webster's New World Dictionary of the American Language, College Edition. The World Publishing Company, 1957. Cleveland, OH. p.76

[7] Part IV of CBC News Interview with J.K. Rowling, July 2000

[8] Scamander, Newt. Fantastic Beasts & Where to Find Them. Arthur A. Levine Books, 2001. NY, NY p.viii

[9] Rowling, J.K.. Harry Potter and the Order of the Phoenix. Arthur A. Levine Books, 2003. NY, NY.
p.86

Chapter 5

[1] Rowling, J.K.. Harry Potter and the Sorcerer's Stone. Scholastic INC., 1998. NY, NY p.118

[2] World Book Day Chat with J.K. Rowling, March 4, 2004

[3] Rowling, J.K.. Harry Potter and the Order of the Phoenix. Arthur A. Levine Books, 2003. NY, NY.
p.187

[4] Rowling, J.K.. Harry Potter and the Sorcerer's Stone. Scholastic INC., 1998. NY, NY. p.84

[5] Dictionary.com

[6] Rowling, J.K.. Harry Potter and the Sorcerer's Stone. Scholastic INC., 1998. NY, NY p.147

[7] Rowling, J.K.. Harry Potter and the Goblet of Fire. Scholastic, INC., 2000. NY, NY p.650

[8] World Book Day Chat with J.K. Rowling, March 4, 2004

[9] Ibid.

[10] http://www.hyw.com/Books/WargamesHandbook/5-histor.htm[11] Rowling, J.K.. Harry Potter and the Sorcerer's Stone. Scholastic INC., 1998. NY, NY p.118

[12] Rowling, J.K.. Harry Potter and the Order of the Phoenix. Arthur A. Levine Books, 2003. NY, NY p.262

[13] Ibid. p.864

[14] Rowling, J.K.. Harry Potter and the Sorcerer's Stone. Scholastic INC., 1998. NY, NY p.118

[15] Hamilton, Edith. Mythology: Timeless Tales of Gods and Heroes. Penguin Group, 1940. NY, NY. p.203

[16] Rowling, J.K.. Harry Potter and the Order of the Phoenix. Arthur A. Levine Books, 2003. NY, NY p.612

[17] Webster's New World Dictionary of the American Language, College Edition. The World Publishing Company, 1957. Cleveland, OH. p.872

[18] Rowling, J.K.. Harry Potter and the Sorcerer's Stone. Scholastic INC., 1998. NY, NY p.118

Chapter 6

[1] Rowling, J.K.. Harry Potter and the Goblet of Fire. Scholastic, INC., 2000. NY, NY p.702

[2] Rowling, J.K.. Harry Potter and the Sorcerer's Stone. Scholastic INC., 1998. NY, NY p.65

[3] Rowling, J.K.. Harry Potter and the Goblet of Fire. Scholastic, INC., 2000. NY, NY. p.709

[4] Ibid. p.710

[5] Rowling, J.K.. Harry Potter and the Chamber of Secrets. Scholastic, INC., 1999. NY, NY p.58

[6] Hamilton, Edith. Mythology: Timeless Tales of Gods and Heroes. Penguin Group, 1940. NY, NY. p.33

[7] Rowling, J.K.. Harry Potter and the Goblet of Fire. Scholastic, INC., 2000. NY, NY p.504-5

[8] Rowling, J.K.. Harry Potter and the Order of the Phoenix. Arthur A. Levine Books, 2003. NY, NY p.297

[9] Ibid. p.177

[10] Rowling, J.K.. Harry Potter and the Goblet of Fire. Scholastic, INC., 2000. NY, NY p.603

[11] Ibid. p.451

[12] Ibid. p.450

[13] Ibid. p.382

[14] Ibid. p.127

[15] Ibid. p.132

[16] Rowling, J.K.. Harry Potter and the Order of the Phoenix. Arthur A. Levine Books, 2003. NY, NY p.610

[17] Ibid. p.610

[18] Ibid. p.721

[19] Shakespeare, William. Hamlet. Act 1, Scene 4, Marcellus

[20] Rowling, J.K.. Harry Potter and the Order of the Phoenix. Arthur A. Levine Books, 2003. NY, NY p.817

[21] Ibid. p.129

[22] New Webster's Dictionary and Thesaurus of the English Language. Lexicon Publishing, INC., 1993. Danbury, CT p.1126

[23] Rowling, J.K.. Harry Potter and the Order of the Phoenix. Arthur A. Levine Books, 2003. NY, NY p.612

[24] New Webster's Dictionary and Thesaurus of the English Language. Lexicon Publishing, INC., 1993. Danbury, CT p.81

[25] Ibid. p.81

[26] Rowling, J.K.. Harry Potter and the Goblet of Fire. Scholastic, INC., 2000. NY, NY p.91

[27] Ibid. p.89

[28] Ibid. p.527

[29] Ibid. p.525

[30] Ibid. p.527

[31] Ibid. p.527

[32] Ibid. p.137

[33] Ibid. p.529

Chapter 7

[1] Brady, Bernadette. Brady's book of Fixed Stars. Samuel Weiser, INC., 1998. York Beach, Maine. p.338

[2] Rowling, J.K.. Harry Potter and the Order of the Phoenix. Arthur A. Levine Books, 2003. NY, NY p.610

[3] Rowling, J.K.. Harry Potter and the Sorcerer's Stone. Scholastic INC., 1998. NY, NY p.106

[4] Rowling, J.K.. Harry Potter and the Order of the Phoenix. Arthur A. Levine Books, 2003. NY, NY p.111

[5] Ibid. p.113

[6] Ibid. p.114

[7] Brady, Bernadette. Brady's book of Fixed Stars. Samuel Weiser, INC., 1998. York Beach, Maine. p.30

[8] New Webster's Dictionary and Thesaurus of the English Language. Lexicon Publishing, INC., 1993. Danbury, CT p.840

[9] Rowling, J.K.. Harry Potter and the Order of the Phoenix. Arthur A. Levine Books, 2003. NY, NY p.112

[10] Hamilton, Edith. Mythology: Timeless Tales of Gods and Heroes. Penguin Group, 1940. NY, NY. p.139

[11] Rowling, J.K.. Harry Potter and the Sorcerer's Stone. Scholastic INC., 1998. NY, NY p.5

[12] Rowling, J.K.. Harry Potter and the Order of the Phoenix. Arthur A. Levine Books, 2003. NY, NY p.174

[13] Ibid. p.454

[14] Ibid. p.336

[15] http://reference.allrefer.com/encyclopedia/S/StuartAr.html

[16] Rowling, J.K.. Harry Potter and the Sorcerer's Stone. Scholastic INC., 1998. NY, NY p.2

[17] Rowling, J.K.. <u>Harry Potter and the Order of the Phoenix.</u> Arthur A. Levine Books, 2003. NY, NY p.19

[18] Ibid. p.21

[19] Ibid. p.145

[20] World Book Day Chat with J.K. Rowling, March 4, 2004

[21] Ibid.

[22] Hamilton, Edith. <u>Mythology: Timeless Tales of Gods and Heroes.</u> Penguin Group, 1940. NY, NY. p.35

[23] New Webster's Dictionary and Thesaurus of the English Language. Lexicon Publishing, INC., 1993. Danbury, CT p.618

[24] Dictionary.com

[25] Rowling, J.K.. <u>Harry Potter and the Order of the Phoenix.</u> Arthur A. Levine Books, 2003. NY, NY p.298

[26] Kingsley, Charles. <u>Alton Locke, Tailor and Poet. An Autobiography.</u> MacMillan & Co.,1884. London, UK. p.x

[27] Ibid. p.388

[28] Euripides. <u>Medea</u>

[29] Rowling, J.K.. <u>Harry Potter and the Order of the Phoenix.</u> Arthur A. Levine Books, 2003. NY, NY p.652

[30] Ibid. p.665

[31] Ibid. p.177

Chapter 8

[1] Rowling, J.K.. <u>Harry Potter and the Order of the Phoenix.</u> Arthur A. Levine Books, 2003. NY, NY p.111

[2] Rowling, J.K.. <u>Harry Potter and the Goblet of Fire.</u> Scholastic, INC., 2000. NY, NY p.379

Chapter 9

[1] The Bible, Revelations 3:16

[2] Rowling, J.K.. <u>Harry Potter and the Chamber of Secrets.</u> Scholastic, INC., 1999. NY, NY p.51

[3] Ibid. p.53

[4] Rowling, J.K.. <u>Harry Potter and the Goblet of Fire.</u> Scholastic, INC., 2000. NY, NY p.651

[5] Robson, Vivian E. <u>The Fixed Stars and Constellations in Astrology.</u> Samuel Weiser, INC., 1973. NY, NY. p.145

[6] Ibid. p.145

[7] Ibid. p.146

[8] Ibid. p.146

[9] Rowling, J.K.. <u>Harry Potter and the Order of the Phoenix.</u> Arthur A. Levine Books, 2003. NY, NY p.114

[10] Ibid. p.112

[11] Robson, Vivian E. <u>The Fixed Stars and Constellations in Astrology.</u> Samuel Weiser, INC., 1973. NY, NY.p.146

[12] Rowling, J.K.. <u>Harry Potter and the Prisoner of Azkaban.</u> Scholastic INC., 1999. NY, NY. p.17

[13] Hamilton, Edith. <u>Mythology: Timeless Tales of Gods and Heroes.</u> Penguin Group, 1940. NY, NY.p.88

[14] Ibid. p.86

[15] Rowling, J.K.. <u>Harry Potter and the Goblet of Fire.</u> Scholastic, INC., 2000. NY, NY p.122

[16] Hamilton, Edith. <u>Mythology: Timeless Tales of Gods and Heroes.</u> Penguin Group, 1940. NY, NY.p.34,35

[17] Rowling, J.K.. <u>Harry Potter and the Goblet of Fire.</u> Scholastic, INC., 2000. NY, NY p.650

Chapter 10

[1] Hamilton, Edith. <u>Mythology: Timeless Tales of Gods and Heroes.</u> Penguin Group, 1940. NY, NY.p.146

[2] Rowling, J.K.. <u>Harry Potter and the Goblet of Fire.</u> Scholastic, INC., 2000. NY, NY p.308

[3] Ibid. p.308

[4] Rowling, J.K.. <u>Harry Potter and the Prisoner of Azkaban.</u> Scholastic INC., 1999. NY, NY. p.203

[5] New Webster's Dictionary and Thesaurus of the English Language. Lexicon Publishing, INC., 1993. Danbury, CT p.1109

[6] Whisp, Kennilworthy. <u>Quidditch Through the Ages.</u> Arthur A. Levine Books, 2001. NY, NY. p.36

Chapter 11

[1] Rowling, J.K.. <u>Harry Potter and the Sorcerer's Stone.</u> Scholastic INC., 1998. NY, NY p.7

[2] Rowling, J.K.. <u>Harry Potter and the Order of the Phoenix.</u> Arthur A. Levine Books, 2003. NY, NY p.841

[3] Rowling, J.K.. <u>Harry Potter and the Chamber of Secrets.</u> Scholastic, INC., 1999. NY, NY p.151

[4] Ibid. p.319

[5] J.K. Rowling & Steve Kloves Interview on Chamber of Secrets DVD, 2002

[6] Rowling, J.K.. <u>Harry Potter and the Chamber of Secrets</u>. Scholastic, INC., 1999. NY, NY p.304

[7] Ibid. p.332,333

[8] Ibid. p.329

[9] Rowling, J.K.. <u>Harry Potter and the Sorcerer's Stone.</u> Scholastic INC., 1998. NY, NY p.298

[10] Rowling, J.K.. <u>Harry Potter and the Prisoner of Azkaban.</u> Scholastic INC., 1999. NY, NY p.271

[11] Ibid. p.110

[12] Rowling, J.K.. <u>Harry Potter and the Order of the Phoenix.</u> Arthur A. Levine Books, 2003. NY, NY p.144

[13] Rowling, J.K.. <u>Harry Potter and the Chamber of Secrets</u>. Scholastic, INC., 1999. NY, NY p.144

[14] Rowling, J.K.. <u>Harry Potter and the Prisoner of Azkaban.</u> Scholastic INC., 1999. NY, NY p.244-5

[15] Ibid. p.245

[16] Rowling, J.K.. <u>Harry Potter and the Goblet of Fire</u>. Scholastic, INC., 2000. NY, NY p.706

[17] Ibid. p.272

[18] *The Sydney Morning Herald*, J.K. Rowling interview October 28, 2001

[19] http://goldstraw.net/godric/pafg02.htm

[20] Rowling, J.K.. <u>Harry Potter and the Order of the Phoenix.</u> Arthur A. Levine Books, 2003. NY, NY p.815

[21] Ibid. p.825

[22] Ibid. p.834-5

[23] Ibid. p.828

[24] Ibid. p.834

[25] Ibid. p.838

[26] Ibid. p.839

[27] Ibid. p.837

[28] Rowling, J.K.. <u>Harry Potter and the Sorcerer's Stone.</u> Scholastic INC., 1998. NY, NY p.16

[29] Rowling, J.K.. <u>Harry Potter and the Order of the Phoenix.</u> Arthur A. Levine Books, 2003. NY, NY p.844

[30] Ibid. p.647

[31] Rowling, J.K.. <u>Harry Potter and the Chamber of Secrets</u>. Scholastic, INC., 1999. NY, NY p.245

Chapter 12

[1] Rowling, J.K.. <u>Harry Potter and the Chamber of Secrets</u>. Scholastic, INC., 1999. NY, NY p.304

[2] Ibid. p.246

[3] Ibid. p.329

[4] Ibid. p.329

[5] Rowling, J.K.. Harry Potter and the Order of the Phoenix. Arthur A. Levine Books, 2003. NY, NY p.843

[6] Rowling, J.K.. Harry Potter and the Goblet of Fire. Scholastic, INC., 2000. NY, NY p.641

[7] Ibid. p.642

[8] Ibid. p.11

[9] Ibid. p.642

[10] Ibid. p.642

[11] Ibid. p.643

[12] Burns, Robert. Poem *To a Mouse*

[13] Rowling, J.K.. Harry Potter and the Goblet of Fire. Scholastic, INC., 2000. NY, NY p.646

[14] Ibid. p.676-7

[15] Scamander, Newt. Fantastic Beasts & Where to Find Them. Arthur A. Levine Books, 2001. NY, NY p.32

[16] Rowling, J.K.. Harry Potter and the Goblet of Fire. Scholastic, INC., 2000. NY, NY. p.697

[17] Rowling, J.K.. Harry Potter and the Goblet of Fire. Scholastic, INC., 2000. NY, NY p. 667

[18] Rowling, J.K.. Harry Potter and the Order of the Phoenix. Arthur A. Levine Books, 2003. NY, NY p.815

[19] Ibid. p.815

[20] Ibid. p.815

[21] Ibid. p.495

Chapter 13

[1] Rowling, J.K.. Harry Potter and the Order of the Phoenix. Arthur A. Levine Books, 2003. NY, NY p.834

[2] Rowling, J.K.. Harry Potter and the Prisoner of Azkaban. Scholastic INC., 1999. NY, NY p.204

[3] Marquez, Gabriel Gracia. No One Writes to the Colonel. Harper & Row Publishers, 1968. p.39

[4] Rowling, J.K.. Harry Potter and the Sorcerer's Stone. Scholastic INC., 1998. NY, NY p.287

[5] The Bible John 15:13

[6] Rowling, J.K.. Harry Potter and the Order of the Phoenix. Arthur A. Levine Books, 2003. NY, NY p.100

[7] Rowling, J.K.. <u>Harry Potter and the Sorcerer's Stone.</u> Scholastic INC., 1998. NY, NY p.128
[8] Ibid. p.127
[9] Ibid. p.8
[10] Ibid. p.293
[11] Rowling, J.K.. <u>Harry Potter and the Chamber of Secrets</u>. Scholastic, INC., 1999. NY, NY p.333
[12] Ibid. p.177
[13] Rowling, J.K.. <u>Harry Potter and the Sorcerer's Stone.</u> Scholastic INC., 1998. NY, NY p.214

Chapter 14
[1] Rowling, J.K.. <u>Harry Potter and the Order of the Phoenix.</u> Arthur A. Levine Books, 2003. NY, NY p.840

Message for Concerned Parents and Sanctimonious Christians
[1] Rowling, J.K.. <u>Harry Potter and the Goblet of Fire</u>. Scholastic, INC., 2000. NY, NY p724

About the Author

Mary Baumann was born and raised an Ohio State Buckeye fan. Despite her family history, she selected Indiana University (another Big Ten Conference school). Mary graduated with a B.A. in political science and a history minor. She has traveled extensively throughout the United States of America and backpacked through Europe. Mary recently earned a TEFL (teaching English as a foreign lan-guage) certificate from the Boston Language Institute. Currently, Mary resides in the greater Cincinnati area.

Printed in the United States
66588LVS00005B/192